Being Adolescent

BEING
ADOLESCENT

Conflict and Growth in the Teenage Years

Mihaly Csikszentmihalyi

AND

Reed Larson

A Member of The Perseus Books Group

Library of Congress Cataloging in Publication Data

Csikszentmihalyi, Mihaly.
  Being adolescent.

  References: p. 314
  Includes index.
  1. Adolescence. 2. Adolescent psychology. 3. Youth
—United States—Case studies. 4. Maturation
(Psychology) I. Larson, Reed, 1950–   . II. Title.
HQ796.C89   1984   305.2′35   83–45253
ISBN   0–465–00646–9 (cloth)
ISBN   0–465–00645–0 (paper)

To the seventy-five students

who shared their experience

with us

Contents

LIST OF FIGURES   ix

LIST OF TABLES   xi

PREFACE   xiii

PART I
PERSPECTIVES

Chapter 1
Paths to Adulthood   3

Chapter 2
The Age of Choice: Opportunities and Obstacles
in Adolescence   11

Chapter 3
Charting Adolescent Life   30

PART II
ENVIRONMENTS

Chapter 4
The External Landscape: What the Teenagers' World
Looks Like   57

Chapter 5
The Internal Landscape: What the Teenagers' World
Feels Like   84

CONTENTS

Chapter 6
Peaks and Valleys: Variability in Daily Experience 108

PART III
INTERACTIONS

Chapter 7
Familiar Aggravations: Relations with Parents
and Siblings 129

Chapter 8
The Companionship of Friends 155

Chapter 9
The Self in Solitude: Perils and Possibilities 176

Chapter 10
Coping with Classes 198

PART IV
TRANSFORMATIONS

Chapter 11
Conflict and Chaos in Daily Life 221

Chapter 12
Converting Challenges to Enjoyment: The Flow
Experience 239

Chapter 13
The Growth of Complexity: Shaping Meaningful Lives 261

APPENDICES 285

REFERENCES 314

INDEX 323

List of Figures

FIGURE
NUMBER

3.1 Profile of Rob Miranda's Daily Experience   38
3.2 A Self-Report of an Angry Moment   52

4.1 Where Adolescents Spend Their Time   59
4.2 What Adolescents Spend Their Time Doing   63
4.3 Whom Adolescents Spend Their Time With   71
4.4 Shifts in Companionship across the Weekday   77

5.1 The Relationship of Intrinsic Motivation to Location   90
5.2 The Relationship of Intrinsic Motivation to Type of Activity   92
5.3 The Subjective Landscape of Adolescents' Activities   97
5.4 The Relationship of Intrinsic Motivation to Companionship   100
5.5 Intensity of Intrinsic Motivation in Different Activities and with Different Companions   104
5.6 Intensity of Concentration in Different Activities and with Different Companions   105

6.1 The Week of Gregory Stone   111
6.2 The Week of Katherine Tennison   117
6.3 The Rate of Decay for Extreme Moods   122

LIST OF FIGURES

7.1	What Teenagers Do with Their Families	135
7.2	Quality of Experience with Family	137
8.1	What Teenagers Do with Their Friends	158
8.2	Quality of Experience with Friends	159
8.3	The Shift from Same-Sex to Opposite-Sex Friends	160
8.4	The Week of Lorraine Monawski	163
8.5	Losing Control on Weekend Nights	169
9.1	What Teenagers Do Alone	184
9.2	Quality of Experience Alone	185
9.3	Changes in Alertness when Entering and Leaving Solitude	192
9.4	The Relationship of Average Affect to Amount of Solitude	195
10.1	What Teenagers Do in Class	203
10.2	Quality of Experience in Class	204
10.3	A Profile of Activation Levels in Four History Classes	209
10.4	Excitement and Boredom during the School Day	212
11.1	The Week of Jerzy Madigan	232
13.1	Model of the Flow Experience	265
13.2	Alternative Paths for Returning to the Flow Channel When Playing the Piano	268

List of Tables

TABLE
NUMBER

3.1   Rob Miranda's Week   36
12.1 Survey of Most Enjoyable Activities   242
12.2 Students' Rankings of Favorite Activities and
      Classes   254

Preface

Of all stages of life, adolescence is the most difficult to describe. Any generalization about teenagers immediately calls forth an opposite one. Teenagers are maddeningly self-centered, yet capable of impressive feats of altruism. Their attention wanders like a butterfly, yet they can spend hours concentrating on seemingly pointless involvements. They are often lazy and rude, yet, when you least expect it, they can be loving and helpful.

This unpredictability, this shifting from black to white and from hot to cold is what adolescence is all about. The years from twelve to nineteen are special because they offer a developing person the opportunity to experiment with contrasting life styles, with different selves. Without this period of trials and errors, the adult would grow up to be just a larger copy of the child it had been earlier. During adolescence all bets are off: The shy, obedient child has a chance to be a show-off or a bully; the friendly extrovert might become a recluse. If human life is such an exciting mystery, it is to a large extent due to the choices that biology and culture open up during the teenage years.

The fluidity of adolescence allows freedom to alter the course of life, but it does make the job of social scientists a great deal harder. Psychologists like to be able to explain what people have done and to predict what they will be doing. Confronted with the provocative contradictions of this age, they are likely to be frustrated.

One way out of this dilemma is for the social scientist to focus on the "hard facts" of adolescence; to tabulate the number of friendships teenagers have or to survey the percentage of adolescents who use drugs or are sexually active. One can document the improvements in cognitive performance, the strides in social, economic, or mathematical understanding that prepare a teenager to fulfill the abstract requirements of adult roles. Such accounts are true to the outside reality of adolescence, to the changes that an observer can detect in their behavior. What they leave out is the subjective reality: what it is like to be a teenager, what teenagers do and think, and how they feel about themselves and their changing lives.

It would be safer to avoid this subjective dimension altogether. How can scientific rigor be applied to something so ephemeral? Yet it is our belief that no description of human beings is complete without an account of subjective experience. How happy a person feels, how happiness is affected by what he or she does, how intentions and goals evolve to channel a person's time and energy—these are issues that are at least as important to understand as the more factual, more tangible aspects of life.

Therefore, in this book we have tried to describe what it is to be an adolescent from the inside, by letting teenagers tell us what they do, feel, and hope for as they go about their daily rounds, from breakfast to school, from French class to lunch period, from the afternoon spent watching television to the wild parties on Friday night.

Naturally our picture of what it is like to be a teenager will not be an accurate representation of every adolescent. We all know—or perhaps we have once been—an adolescent who does not fit any description one can make up, no matter how unusual. We cannot even pretend that our book will provide an accurate picture of the average American adolescent or a representative sampling of different types of teenagers in proportion to their frequency in the population—so many jocks, so many greasers, a sprinkling of serious students, and a dash of delinquents.

What we have tried to do in this book is something less and something more than provide a scale model of adolescence "as it really is." From the complex pattern of experiences reported by teenagers, we have tried to extract what we thought to be some of the central themes, the major problems, and the most powerful opportunities of this stage of life. These themes go beyond what *is*, and evoke what *could be*. If one boy out of a hundred finds a way to get along splendidly with his parents, this is something that hardly warrants mention in a statistical description of what teenagers are like. But this one-in-one-hundred finding can become the most important fact if we wish to understand what adolescence could be like. So as we go about our systematic descriptions we are not only concerned with proportions and averages; perhaps the most telling insight on this age of transition comes from persons and events that show how, despite widespread confusion or boredom, it is possible to create enjoyment and meaning.

The research that made this book possible was funded by the Spencer Foundation, whose support of basic research in education and development has become legendary in the last decade. We wish in particular to thank H. Thomas James, President of the Foundation, for his critical yet sympathetic support over the years.

The original impetus for the study came when our colleague Patrick Mayers first envisioned the idea of applying the Experience Sampling Method developed by the senior author to a comprehensive study of high-school experience. It was his energy that got the research going and his unique rapport with young people that accounts for much of the richness in the data. Readers are encouraged to look at his dissertation for early findings from the study.

We also feel an enormous debt to the faculty and administration of Belmont High (a pseudonym), without whom the study could not have been done. If the task of describing adolescent experience is difficult, the task of weathering its storms on a day-to-day basis is doubly hard; yet this special group of people appears to do so with unfailing grace, charm, and warmth. They not only put up with our sometimes disruptive presence, but they also taught us much about listening and doing research with young people. While we would like to thank many of them by name, we must keep the identity of the school disguised to insure the anonymity of individual students.

Among our friends and colleagues we wish to acknowledge the encouragement of Daniel Offer, a foremost leader in adolescent research and Director of the Psychiatric and Psychosomatic Institute at Michael Reese Medical Center, as well as that of Bertram Cohler, Professor of Human Development at the University of Chicago. We both also owe important intellectual debts to our teachers Bernice Neugarten and Robert Havighurst who opened up the study of lives to us.

Other colleagues played important collaborative roles in one way or another: Ronald Graef, Mark Freeman, Larry Chalip, Jean Hamilton, Jane McCormack, Olga Emory Beattie, Ed Donner, Suzanne Prescott, and Susan Gianinno, among others. We are thankful for the typing of Judith Hochberg, Linda White, and Babette McNairy. We also wish to give a special thanks to our wives, Isabella Csikszentmihalyi and Sharon Irish, not only for their patience and daily support, but for their critical assistance in reading drafts, providing reactions, and telling us when we were wrong.

To all of these people and some we may have missed we extend our warmest thanks. These friends and associates deserve much of the credit for the assets of the book; if there are faults, the responsibility lies with us.

Finally, we reserve our greatest appreciation for the seventy-five teenagers—now adults—around whom this book revolves. We hope that their adolescent experiences have blossomed into lives of enjoyment and richness.

PART I

PERSPECTIVES

Chapter 1

Paths to Adulthood

HOW do children, usually so full of promise and vitality, turn into adults who are either confident and productive, or disillusioned and bitter? What accounts for the difference? To a large extent, the answer lies in events that take place between the ages of twelve and nineteen, the stage of the life cycle called adolescence.

In the past these were called the "formative years" because people believed that adult character was shaped during this period. Younger children were thought to be too malleable to retain any lasting impression, so what happened to them made no difference in the long run. They could not reason, they had no conscience, so little could yet be expected from them. Responsibility for one's action began only after the child was mature enough to be initiated into adult society, with appropriate ceremonies like the Christian Confirmation or the Jewish Bar Mitzvah. These usually took place in early adolescence and signaled that the young person was ready to begin the serious task of becoming an adult.

Nowadays, of course, we know that the first dozen years of life are much more important than they previously had been thought to be. In fact, some psychologists claim that early child-

3

hood experiences determine the shape of a person's future life, once and for all.

While childhood is certainly important in shaping future growth, adolescence provides opportunities for fresh starts, for new directions that are not predictable from the events of childhood. There are so many people whose early years were full of trauma and pathological symptoms—one thinks of examples like Thomas Edison, Eleanor Roosevelt, Albert Einstein, Antonio Gramsci—yet who forged in adolescence a sturdy enough self to overcome their handicaps and lead full, productive lives. Opposite examples also are abundant: children from "normal," even happy backgrounds who fail to develop a strong sense of self in adolescence, and thus enter adulthood ill-prepared for its responsibilities.[1]

The simplest task of adolescence is to learn the patterns of action required for participation in society. Teenagers must acquire habits to live by. They must learn that there are times for sleeping and eating, for working and studying, for relaxing and playing. If they do not learn to concentrate on these tasks at the prescribed times in the prescribed ways, they will not be able to function as adults. Hence much of the conflict between parents and their adolescent children revolves around simple issues such as getting up in the morning, cleaning their rooms, and going to bed at night, as well as more central issues such as how much to study and how much time to spend with friends. Learning to allocate attention to various activities in a manner acceptable to adults is the first task of adolescence.

But this is only half of the story. The other is that as self-discipline increases, the young must feel that their actions are worthwhile, that the goals society presents make sense. Otherwise adolescents will grow up to be well-socialized but confused and discontented adults. When we think of outstanding individuals, what strikes us most often is the energy and enthusiasm

1. The open-ended, life-span view of human development which contrasts with the view that personality is determined by the early years has recently been reviewed by Baltes (1978); Brim and Kagan (1980); and Lerner (1982). Among the earlier proponents of this perspective are Bühler (1930); Erikson (1950); Havighurst (1953); and Neugarten (1969).

they bring to their lives. Teenagers have to learn how to enjoy what they are doing, and they must learn how to give meaning to the events unfolding in their lives, by relating them to freely accepted goals.

The difference between confident and productive adults and disillusioned ones is to be found in how they experience their day-to-day activities. The hidden curriculum of growing up lies in how a person learns to respond to daily situations: in mastering interactions with parents, achieving harmony with friends, learning to handle the pressures of school, and developing means to transcend everyday conflicts.

By looking closely at the daily experience of adolescents we can begin to understand the special significance of the teenage years. Let us consider what some of the youngsters about whom this book is written were doing on a typical weekend in May. What they felt, how they acted, what they thought reveal the kind of shape their lives are beginning to take.

The big weekend event for Warren Stillman[2] was a high-school graduation party on Saturday night. He provided a narrative description of the events, which begins as he is about to leave home:

> I was still getting dressed at about six when Bo came. He and my mom helped me finish dressing. Then I said good-bye to my parents and grandfather, and he gave me some money.
> Bo was driving, and we picked up my girlfriend Leah and his girlfriend Sissy. Then we went to Red's brother's house for a before-the-dance cocktail party. He made a whole barrel of punch. I had a few glasses, and I then started to go to my usual self; I took off my coat and tie and cracked a six pack of beers.

At this point Warren reports feeling great; he is happy, excited, and energetic. As the night goes on he experiences many ups and downs:

> Leah got me dressed up again, and I took one more glass of punch, and we all headed for the cars. So we went to the dance. It

2. Names have been changed throughout this volume to protect the privacy of respondents.

was very nice and decorated better than the others, but somehow it still seemed like any other formal.

The dance went fine until there was a fight in the bathroom. Ron punched out Jim. Mr. Sullivan, my track coach, told me to help Jim clean himself up, and I did.

We then went down to eat at the Como Inn; we had a party of twenty-four at our table. While waiting to eat, Dennis, Bob, and I hit the bar for more beers. Dennis bought the rounds. Then he ordered a bottle of wine with the food. I was drunker than all hell, and it was a good thing Bo was driving. Good too so that I could get down in the back seat all night.

Warren's experiences show one side of adolescence: the frenetic search for "good times." In his case this search is helped out by alcohol, which alters his consciousness and helps him escape from the regimented discipline of school and the adult-controlled world. Warren enjoyed himself, and he relished relating the events to us the next week. The pleasure he experienced reinforced this pattern of behavior, a pattern he had rehearsed many times before and may well continue into his adult life. But this pattern of enjoyment did not order his experience with respect to long-term life goals. While it might provide a reprieve from the pressures of school, it does not contribute to the fund of personal skills he will need later in life.

Lilly Moss, a classmate of Warren's, passed the weekend in a very different way. She spent her time primarily at home, helping her mother clean closets and listening to Barbra Streisand records. She also spent part of Saturday at her job as a clerk at Walgreen's drug store. Overall, it was a dull weekend for her. The high point was buying a camisole top and a garter belt during her noon break at work, an event which temporarily relieved the boredom she found in waiting on listless, uninteresting customers.

In contrast to Warren's weekend, Lilly's shows her growing up in an adult mold. She complies with her mother's wishes and devotes her spare time to earning money for college. Even her purchases reflects conformity to adult standards of dress. What is missing is any true relish in her experiences; she has allowed her life to be filled with the narrow preoccupations of adult roles. It lacks any of the spontaneous enjoyment that Warren experienced so freely.

Another student, Andy Gridwell, spent his weekend making a movie for film class. The project took him all over the neighborhood, including down into manholes and up into trees. Throughout the weekend he deliberates with collaborators as they splice film clips, listen to sound tracks, film scenes, and joke about putting obscenities into the script. From Friday to Sunday he is completely absorbed, feeling more challenged and motivated than he has been in a long time. His involvement causes a fight with his mother which he quickly forgets, dismissing her as an "incompetent bitch."

Is Andy Gridwell's weekend the model of optimal growth? Certainly not. He violates many norms of adult behavior, and he demonstrates little control over his actions, staying up all night and creating havoc around him. If this pattern of life were to continue, he could grow up to become a disruptive adult, a nuisance to the community, and perhaps also a victim of heart problems and drug abuse as a result of his disregard for his body. Nonetheless, there are sparks of enthusiasm in Andy's weekend that set him apart from Warren Stillman and Lilly Moss. He is finding enjoyment in doing something constructive, something that with a little discipline might develop into a meaningful adult goal.

It was a weekend like many others for these students at Belmont High School near the city of Chicago. None was injured in a car accident, no one ran away to New York to become a teenage prostitute, nobody crashed from a bad drug trip—the ghosts that haunt their parents' nightmares were resting. Some Belmont students even went to church on Sunday. One practiced the clarinet, another spent most of Saturday rehearsing steps at a ballet school; Steve plowed through 200 pages of *John Brown's Body*. Brian fixed an old car, and Sarah made preparations for her sister's Bath Mitzvah.

All the while, these Belmont students, like teenagers everywhere, were growing up. Would Warren's drinking turn the hopes of a good job and marriage into a nightmare of disappointments? Would Lilly come out of her rut and blossom into a lively adult? Would Andy become a successful filmmaker, translating the realities of suburbia into meaningful statements about American life? Experimenting with different ways of being, these teenagers were establishing paths into adulthood. Buffeted by contradictory impulses and injunctions, opportunities and prohibitions, each was searching for the answer to one central question: What kind of person am I turning out to be?

During the adolescent years, young people go through great emotional, cognitive, and social transformations. Out of these changes emerges a pattern of thought and volition that defines the self. Erik Erikson (1950) has called it ego identity; when successfully achieved it is a stable feeling of confidence that one knows who one is. In a constantly changing and diversified society such as ours, it is not easy to attain a consistent, comfortable interpretation of oneself. Yet without a cohesive sense of self, life passes by without pattern or purpose, a welter of unrelated actions and impulses; and one might suddenly wake up in middle age to the realization that life no longer makes sense.

This book is about the obstacles, and above all, the opportunities that confront adolescents on their way to forging an adult identity. It is about how it feels to be a teenager, as gleaned from thousands of reports and numerous interviews with seventy-five high-school students, from a suburb of a large metropolis. The book is not like the usual psychological study. It does not restrict itself to a particular set of questions, or try to test a specific hypothesis. Instead we provide a systematic account of adolescent *experience*, of the subjective reality that unfolds in the consciousness of teenagers—with their friends, with their families, alone, and in school. We emphasize experience rather than behavior because we believe that the most important events in life are internal ones. Adolescents' joys and pains, excitements and frustrations, hopes and disillusions matter more than objective external events. We deal comprehensively with what teenagers do—with their behavior—but the focus of the inquiry is always on how their activities are related to internal feelings, thoughts, and motives.

The data that provide the basis for this account are of a novel form. They consist of numerous self-reports made by teenagers at random times during their lives. All the subjects in our study carried electronic pagers for one week, and a transmitter sent them signals to fill out reports on their experience from early morning to late at night. This method gave us several thousand "samples" of what typical adolescents do and feel—the where, what, why, and how of their daily lives. Combined with long and repeated interviews, this series of self-report snapshots provides an excitingly vivid record of what it is like to be a teenager.

The rest of Part I presents the background of the study. Chapter 2 reviews the cultural and historical setting in which adolescents find themselves, and develops a theoretical perspective from which to view their current state. In Chapter 3 we describe the adolescents who participated in the study, the community from which they came, and the methods used to measure dimensions of experience in their lives.

In Part II we begin to describe our research findings. Our purpose here is to provide a systematic account of what adolescents do all day long and how they feel. In the fourth chapter we examine the external contexts: where adolescents spend their time, doing what, and with whom. To understand what it means to be a teenager, one must first know the patterns of their lives: their daily environment with its constraints and opportunities. But the most important question is how this environment relates to experience. This is the issue of Chapter 5, which details how adolescents feel in the different contexts of daily life. As they move from one setting to another, the moods and thoughts of teenagers swing drastically between extremes. These patterns of variability are explored in Chapter 6.

Part III of the book focuses in more depth on the four major contexts of adolescent life—family, school, friends, and solitude—each one of which takes up approximately one fourth of their waking time. Chapter 7 describes teenagers' interactions with their families, and how they experience these interactions.

Chapter 8 describes their encounters with friends. The characteristics of their solitude (time spent alone) are explored in Chapter 9, and Chapter 10 discusses the impact of school on teenagers' experience.

Part IV takes a long-term perspective on adolescent development. In Chapter 11 we discuss the inevitability of conflict and frustration in daily experience, and pose the simple question: How can teenagers grow into mature adults without losing the enthusiasm that is the best feature of youth? In Chapter 12 we approach this question by looking at the most enjoyable occasions in adolescents' lives, to see what is common to them, what makes them happen, how they can be made compatible with adult goals. Finally, in the last chapter, we examine how adolescents create order and meaning out of all the complexity of their daily lives.

Chapter 2

The Age of Choice: Opportunities and Obstacles in Adolescence

THE more a species depends on learning for its survival, the more it must find ways to transmit learning from one generation to the next. Most birds, for instance, need not worry about passing on to their young any knowledge beyond that contained in their genes. After a few weeks of care, the fledgling is ready to face life on its own, armed with the unchanging wisdom of the species. Almost as smooth a transition occurs in isolated, traditional human groups where adult roles are undifferentiated and stable: the young simply grow up to take their elders' places without being aware of alternatives (Redfield 1953).

In our culture, however, youth cannot rely either on the instructions contained in their genes or on unchanging adult models as guides for living. They cannot just relax and wait for the passage of time to turn them into adults. Maturation is not a preprogrammed process that unfolds automatically; a young person has to learn habits of thought, action, and feeling that are often difficult and unnatural. This is a process which, not surprisingly, is cause for much tension and conflict.

Young people in our society face a bewildering variety of potential life goals, life styles, and values. Should one become a merchant? A doctor? A soldier? A computer programmer? Each choice entails the learning of skills that are not natural and that are meaningful only within the limits and conventions of the chosen role. To make matters more difficult, the ladder one must climb to achieve competence in each role keeps getting longer and longer. The years of schooling and training stretch even further, postponing the feeling of control that a young person derives from mastery of a craft or profession.

These conditions are producing increasing amounts of stress on young people. The universal tensions of adolescence become greatly exacerbated when adult responsibilities are so diverse, abstract, and diffuse that young persons cannot imagine what they will be doing when they grow up, and why. The prospect of being a "research accountant," a "systems analyst," or a "media consultant" is unlikely to inspire dreams, and without dreams there can be little continuity between present and future. A relatively unproblematic adolescence can then turn into a long struggle to determine who one is and who one should become. Despite all its technological progress and material affluence, our culture produces many young people who have no desire to participate in it. Adolescence is fast becoming a weak link in the transmission of a way of life between generations.

In order to understand how our species, and our society in particular, attempts to pass its learning on from one generation to the next, we must consider the general requirements of cultural transmission, first from the point of view of society and then from that of the adolescent. Socialization must be a process of compromise; the question is how the two parties, the individual and the society, can meet each other halfway. When we have considered this question, we can then ask how this process is played out in daily experience. How is socialization resolved in day-to-day interactions with family and friends, at school and at home? The purpose of this chapter is to determine what kind of evidence we should look for to evaluate whether transmission between generations is taking place.

Restructuring Consciousness

If teenagers are to progress through the complex stages of growth, their consciousness must be changed until it resembles that of adults. Their emotions, goals, actions, and thoughts must fit the tasks confronting adult members of the community. How does this occur? How do impulsive kids become responsible adults who will carry the human form of life one generation further?

This transformation, if it is to occur at all, must involve adolescents' *attention*, that is, their conscious experience. Attention has two important defining properties. First, every conscious human act requires its use. Thinking a thought, experiencing a feeling, reaching for a pen or a cup of coffee, whatever we do requires that we attend, that we devote some fraction of our consciousness to the action. Therefore, the way adolescents' attention is allocated—what they attend to, how intensely, and for how long—delimits their potential for growth and the range of their life accomplishments (compare James 1890). He cannot become a plumber, or a nurse, or a poet, unless he pays considerable attention to the skills required for plumbing, nursing, or writing poetry.

The second important property of attention is that it is finite. We cannot attend to more than a few thoughts, feelings, or actions at the same time, and the total amount of attention at our disposal is limited. If we devote attention to one goal we do so at the exclusion of many others. Hence the information a person can process is severely constrained (Hamilton 1981; Kahneman

1973). If you are going to be a plumber, you can't also become a baker, a policeman, and a rock star. The opportunities for growth have finite bounds, and adolescents must choose which pattern to actualize by investing their attention into it.

It takes attention to process information, to make things happen, to bring order into our inner lives and overt behavior. Attention is needed to deal with an emotion, to plan a goal, to solve a problem; it is necessary for reading a book, holding a conversation, driving a car to work. In effect, attention might be viewed as *psychic energy*, because without it the work of responding adaptively to the environment cannot be accomplished. If this energy were inexhaustible, life would have few problems. We could attend to each task in turn, knowing that eventually everything would be accomplished. Studying would not detract from being with friends, the ball game would not interfere with being with family. But because of its scarcity we are always forced to make choices and skip desirable experiences that we just do not have energy to attend to (Csikszentmihalyi 1978a, 1982b).

Thus the transition to adulthood involves restructuring the psychic energy of youth. In childhood, boys and girls pay attention to whatever is spontaneously enjoyable; they concentrate on playful activities that are fun and immediately pleasurable. However, to be adults they must learn to concentrate also on tasks that may not be rewarding right away, but are necessary to getting along later on. This, in essence, is what socialization means: the transformation from one type of consciousness to another. Success depends on how adolescents use their limited supply of psychic energy. If their attention is directed to goals that extend their skills while strengthening the self, it is being used effectively. But when it is squandered on boredom, rebellion, or amusements, socialization fails because valuable psychic energy is wasted.

Violence, drugs, and sex are the three problems usually associated with adolescents. They represent deviance, because they involve patterns of attention that differ from, or are destructive of, the norms of society. The normal patterns are those that past experience has shown to work tolerably well, and that are spelled out in the laws and traditions of the culture. A community composed of violent, spaced-out sexual adventurers would be unworkable; neither individuals nor the society would survive for long.

In our culture we expect men and women to live together in serial monogamy; to restrict their attention to only one member of the opposite sex at a time. This norm limits the investment of psychic energy in sexual goals: Those who follow it generally have more attention left for other concerns. Adolescents who "play the field" waste their own energy and perhaps that of others, because so much of this attention gets tied up in intrigues, disappointments, and redundant pleasures.

Society also proscribes the use of substances that alter conscious processes. Drugs interfere with the normal patterns of attention, therefore with socialization. A person who is drunk or high does not use psychic energy in the ways expected of responsible adults. Yet close to 10 percent of American high-school seniors report using drugs every day (Johnston, Bachman, and O'Malley 1981). Again, from the point of view of the social system, such a patterning of energy is wasteful.

In order for a community to function, its members must respect one another's body and property. Murder, rape, vandalism, or robbery undermine society by wasting psychic energy. They destroy the fruits of previous investments of psychic energy, and perhaps most seriously, they undermine the trust which makes communal life possible. When people are afraid—that is, when their attention is invested in worrying about violence or expecting it to happen—social, economic, and political life cannot flourish.

While a majority of teenagers apparently still lead untroubled lives (Offer, Ostrov, and Howard 1981), there is evidence that deviance keeps increasing. According to reliable estimates, teenage suicide has gone up by almost 300 percent in the last three decades—much more than among any other age group (U.S. Department of Commerce 1981). Most of these losses are among the privileged cohorts of white, middle class, male adolescents.

15

Poverty and deprivation can be ruled out as causes. Other indices of disruption—crime, homicide, illegitimate pregnancies, drug use, venereal disease, even psychosomatic complaints—show the same pattern (Wynne 1978; Yankelovich 1981). It is as if, faced with the task of taking on adult responsibilities, youth were saying, "Stop the world, I want to get off."

Of course, disillusionment with adult society is not unique to a diversified, technological society such as ours. Youth in ancient Greece often railed against the world of their elders, and adolescents have often been perceived as an irksome and troublesome lot (Fox 1977). After reviewing biographical accounts of adolescence as old as fifteen centuries and as far away as India, China, and Africa, Kiell concludes that "the great internal turmoil and external disorder of adolescence are universal and only moderately affected by cultural determinants" (Kiell 1969, p. 9). Regardless of the society, physiological changes at puberty transform the former child into a youth armed with new powers of strength and sexuality. These upheavals, both social and physical, can never be entirely smooth. Every culture must find ways to prevent them from disrupting its continuity. In effect, every culture must find ways of engaging its youth in the responsibilities of being adults. Stated simply, the issue is: How can we help adolescents to like the world into which they are born?

The Adolescent's Point of View

We have stressed the importance of restructuring teenagers' consciousness for the sake of the social system, as if the welfare of the society were all that mattered. Communities have to hold and enforce this principle if they wish to survive. However, it is quite natural for adolescents to see their interests as different from those that safeguard the efficient running of the social system. Going out with friends is often more important than studying. The latest Stones album may seem more attractive than

Shakespeare. And washing dishes, straightening out one's room, or doing yardwork may not seem important at all. The final decision as to whose goals will take precedence, the adolescent's or society's, is arrived at through a gradual process in which conflicting forces, struggling for control over psychic energy, reach equilibrium.

Where the teenager's attention will go at any given moment, depends on the interaction of three broad principles of organization: instincts, habits, and values. Instincts are the result of thousands of years of selective pressures. They make us pay attention to information that matters for survival, and they make us invest our limited attention in tasks that enhance selective fitness. When we are hungry, our psychic energy is attracted to the task of seeking out food. Our attention is attracted to persons of the opposite sex, because if it were not, the species would have long ago ceased to exist. Instinctive patterns of attention help us to notice and withdraw from things that are dangerous, and to be interested in things that in the past have helped the survival of our bodies and the genes they carry.

While instincts develop during the history of the species, habits are acquired during a person's life. In the course of growing up we learn to ignore certain things and to attend to others, depending on whether past encounters with them were on the whole painful or pleasurable. For example, some teenagers develop the habit of never being alone, because they find solitude intolerable. Others begin to use time by themselves to practice music or sports, to study science—or to develop patterns of delinquent behavior—because when they structure their attention in one of these habitual patterns they feel most satisfied.

Instincts and habits shape attention from behind, as it were, by channeling and structuring psychic energy in terms of past experience. Values, on the other hand, shape attention in terms of future expectations. Of all living organisms, humans appear to have the exceptional ability to do things not only because it is their nature to do so (that is, because of genetically patterned instincts), nor because they benefit from the action at the present time (as habits would suggest), but because they want to achieve

17

some future valued state. A celibate monk, fasting in the monastery, uses his attention to enact patterns of prayer, meditation, and song. He does so not because of genetic instructions, nor because it makes him feel better, but because he believes that investing psychic energy this way will bring him closer to God. Likewise the young executive who postpones marriage and drives himself to exhaustion in order to advance in his firm lets values determine the pattern of his attention.

At any given time, instincts, habits, and values all are involved in shaping attention. Sometimes, instinct might predominate; at others, values are more effective. Instincts and values are in some respects at opposite ends of a continuum, and they often set conflicting goals for attention to follow. Consciousness, which directs where attention is to be paid, must mediate between two competing principles: Should I listen to this music, as instincts and habit suggest, or should I prepare for that exam, as my values require?

It might seem that instincts represent the person's *real* interests, while values are nothing more than societal requirements smuggled into consciousness, regardless of whether they benefit the person or not. Values might even be seen as detrimental to the individual, since they compete with instincts for the allocation of limited psychic energy.

However, this simple assumption, which underlies much of the Freudian model of the psyche, can be misleading. From an evolutionary point of view, instincts serve individual advantage only insofar as they promote transmission of a person's genes. "A chicken is only an egg's way of making another egg," say the geneticists, and the sociobiologist Richard Dawkins entitled his book *The Selfish Gene* to highlight the fact that it is not individual happiness, or even welfare, that genetic instructions evolve to provide, but only the survival of their own pattern.

Thus, a young woman aroused by sexual desire is not necessarily listening to her own essential, unique, individual needs when she decides to follow the bent of her instincts. She is actually doing what she was made to do as a member of a biological species, serving the needs of the genes that have programmed her behavior for their own ends. It is true that she would be experiencing pleasure if she satisfied her desire; but then pleasure is simply the bait that evolution has devised to entice her to reproduce. And, of course, if she gives full rein to her sexual interests, she could create a great deal of trouble for herself in the future.

On the other hand, if the young woman decides to curb her desire in order to finish a physics assignment or to work on a fund-raising drive, it could again be said that she is not serving her own interest, but obeying the interests of the social system that she has internalized in the form of values. It seems, then, that whether she acts on her instincts or not, she ends up being manipulated by outside interests—either genetic or social.

The only way out of this double trap is through consciousness itself. Although adolescents cannot prevent genes, society, or accidental events from directing their attention, they can reflect on this predicament and choose to go along with either one or the other force that seeks to determine how they will expend their psychic energy. They can decide to ignore instinctual desires or to develop them for constructive ends. They can give weight to voices of friends or family, and select among values the ones they want for themselves. Decisions will never be entirely free, but as long as we are conscious of making them, they will not be entirely determined either. This is a limited freedom, a far cry from the "free will" contemplated by philosophers, but enough to preserve an unalienable integrity for those who take the trouble to exercise it.

Adolescents' real interests, therefore, lie neither in instincts nor in values, but in the course they are able to thread between them.

Entropy: Disorder in Consciousness

The tension between adolescents and the rest of society usually takes the form of a conflict between goals structured by instincts and by values. On the one hand, a young person develops goals

19

based on sexual desires, the need for dominance, for a social territory, for acceptance by peers. These urges are experienced as coming from the body, and therefore many adolescents accept them as their own, even though, as we have seen, this belief is based on an illusion, because instincts are geared to help the survival of the genes and not necessarily the welfare of the person carrying them.

On the other hand, young persons simultaneously face pressures to shape their attention around goals established by society—to attend school, do chores, and conform to accepted behavioral norms. Parents, teachers, even peers use reinforcements and threats to get them to follow societal values, even though these may conflict with the personal needs of the adolescent.

This rivalry between competing forces is one of the major factors that lead to a conflict in consciousness, disrupting the process of socialization, or setting it off course. As they attempt to follow both instincts and social directives, adolescents find themselves in a labyrinth of difficult and confusing choices. Just when the path seems clear, they run into another wall.

One form that disorder in consciousness takes is what we call a bad mood; sadness, loneliness, anger, and irritability emerge when goals are frustrated or in conflict with each other. A boy in our study described feeling so terrible after he let his family down that for a whole day he was immobilized by guilt and depression. Students sometimes mentioned being so enraged by a teacher's unfairness that they refused to do an assignment. A girl reported becoming upset after another girl whom she thought a friend accused her of stealing her boyfriend. Such experiences temporarily disrupt the ability to relate effectively to the environment. Consciousness is no longer in control of its psychic energy. If prolonged over an extended period of time, negative feelings reduce one's freedom to use attention for growing into adulthood.

Another form in which disorder in consciousness occurs is when the adolescent becomes tired. Overwhelmed by events, impulses, pressures, and choices, he falls into a state of weak passivity. After Andy Gridwell stayed up all weekend long making his film, he was so drained that he vegetated for the entire following week. A number of students reported feeling so meek in the presence of a forceful parent that they were unable to carry on a dialogue. Sheer boredom—with friends, with school, with life—also fits into this category. When people feel exhausted, weak, or bored, they have trouble mustering enough psychic energy to cope with the environment, let alone pursue goals that will increase their skills.

Both negative feelings and passivity relate to a third process that can block the efficient use of attention: loss of motivation. When something stands in the way of a person's goals, when goals become confused, or when external goals are imposed by adults, adolescents become disinterested and have a hard time investing psychic energy in their pursuits. This is a state in which thoughts and actions are in conflict. One girl whose friends went out of town for a weekend, fell into this state, as did a boy forced to polish silverware when he really wanted to be biking with his girl. Both these teenagers wished to be doing something else, and used their attention to daydream instead of concentrating on what they were doing. When a person is not motivated, less psychic energy is available for the task at hand.

A last form of disorder relates to the quality of attention itself. It is the inability to focus or use attention constructively. For example, a girl could not concentrate on school work because she was madly in love; although she *wanted* to do homework, her thoughts kept returning to the fellow she loved and the assignment never got written. "This is not like me," she said, perplexed. A boy was literally unable to hear what his parents were saying because he was "messed up" on drugs; and a girl missed the chance to write a lead story in the school newspaper because she was so overwhelmed by a fear of failing that it kept her from thinking straight. It is through concentration that we are able to use psychic energy effectively. When thoughts get clouded, both socialization and pursuit of personal goals become impaired.

Bad moods, passivity, lack of motivation, and unfocused attention are the four dimensions of experience we are calling *psychic entropy*. They are ways in which effective use of attention

21

for growth is disrupted. Entropy is a concept borrowed from physics and information theory. In physics it denotes disorder in physical systems, which results in loss of energy. In information theory it denotes disorder in the pattern in which stimuli are transmitted or received, which results in the loss of meaning. Psychic entropy refers to conflicting information in consciousness which reduces the person's capacity to do work and produces unpleasant experiences.

Psychic entropy, while it lasts, is experienced as frustration, anxiety, alienation, guilt, or boredom, and feels terrible, but it is not necessarily disruptive in its long-range effects. It can force attention inward to restore order among the unreconciled goals. Like pearls formed by the oyster to protect itself from painful grains of sand, many of the outstanding accomplishments of humankind were in part reactions against psychic entropy. Attention turned in on itself does work in consciousness that could not have been done without the pain caused by emotional disorder. Even normal cognitive development seems to require the experience of internal conflict for a person to give up the no-longer-adequate stage of reasoning and to move up to the next. And sometimes this struggle for order and meaning may produce a creative accomplishment as a side effect: a work of art, a philosophical system, a religious insight.

However, repeated or prolonged psychic entropy—enduring states of depression, confusion, or aimlessness—may be permanently damaging to a person's participation in life. Perpetual unhappiness eventually leads to despair; constant fear prevents the learning of new skills (Suomi and Harlow 1976); repeated frustration creates helplessness (Seligman 1975); and boredom eventually destroys interest in living. Human development is ideally a process of expansion and growth, but entropic experiences can slowly extinguish the fire of dreams that give life direction and purpose.

Entropic experiences are a necessary part of adolescence. There is no way to grow up without occasionally feeling sad, confused, or hopeless. But a consistent pattern of entropy in consciousness means that a teenager is developing attentional habits that might interfere with his ability to function well as an adult. If a teenager is *always* bored in school and nowhere learns habits of mental discipline, it is unlikely that he later will be able to tackle complex tasks requiring the use of thought. A young person who is always angry or distressed with his parents is not likely to become a loving parent when his turn comes.

In the round of daily life, order and disorder alternate in consciousness. Like the shadows of clouds passing over the prairie that are followed by sunshine, the sadness and anger of adolescence are replaced by serenity and joy. We shall now consider these positive experiences.

Negentropy: Order in Consciousness

Some early psychologists believed that when a person is in a good mood, his body becomes lighter in weight, making his movement more buoyant (Lange 1922). Although objectively farfetched, this belief has a kernel of subjective truth to it. For a number of years we have been studying what makes experiences enjoyable and satisfying. We interviewed rock climbers, chess players, dancers, artists, and others to find out how it feels when they are at their best (Csikszentmihalyi 1975, 1976, 1978b). Regardless of the specific activities, people mentioned a set of consistent elements that are related to optimal experience. They described profound involvement with their activity, which combined a loss of self-consciousness with deep concentration. The experience was subjectively pleasing—compelling enough to inspire rock climbers to risk their lives—and at the same time required highly complex use of mental or physical skills. Many respondents used the word "flow" to describe the effortless buoyancy of the experience.

This state of consciousness we will call *psychic negentropy,* literally "negative psychic entropy." It is a condition in which one feels whole and acts with clarity, commitment, and enthusiasm.

In physics and information theory negentropy refers to an ordered state of energy or knowledge, a state in which work can be carried out with the least waste and effort. A negentropic system, whether physical, informational, or mental, is one in which the parts function together in synergy, with minimal friction or disorder.

The elements of this state are opposite from those identified with psychic entropy. First, psychic negentropy includes positive feelings toward self and others: happiness, friendliness, and good cheer. This is a common part of adolescent experience, set off by a wink from a girlfriend, a good shot on the basketball court, or just the taste of spring in the air. Often, however, a positive feeling for teenagers is but a short-lived burst of emotion that does not develop into a sustained negentropic experience. The rock climbers, chess players, artists, and others we studied often became so absorbed in their activity that they went on doing it for hours and even days at a time, without awareness of hunger or fatigue.

A second characteristic of psychic negentropy is psychological activation. This happens when action follows action without need for thought or hesitation, and the person experiences a sense of energy and competence. For example, a boy in our study who enjoyed baking elaborate cakes found that each little step led effortlessly to the next and provided him with a sense of excitement and confidence. This is a common experience in sports, in games, in work one enjoys doing.

Third, psychic negentropy includes intrinsic motivation: spontaneous involvement with whatever is going on. Intrinsic motivation means a person identifies with the goal of the activity. As with the other elements, this one can exist independently of the others—a girl might wish very much to go out with her boyfriend even though he makes her miserable—but generally, positive feelings and activation accompany intrinsic motivation.

The last dimension of psychic negentropy is effective concentration: A person is absorbed in what he is doing and is able to think about it clearly. A rather extreme example of this was given by a group of boys who sometimes hung from the trestles of a railroad bridge while the train came over the top, shaking the bridge violently. Needless to say, in this situation they had little choice but to concentrate fully, lest they were to lose hold. In chess, in dancing, and in art work, there may not be the same urgency to maintain attention, but absorption in the goals of such activities often is described in equally strong terms.

It is easier to achieve order in consciousness in leisure activities such as bowling or watching a movie than in work or school. Therefore, it may seem that psychic negentropy must occur at the expense of society, and perhaps also, of the long-term welfare of the person. It is true that the most common settings for psychic negentropy are games, art, and sports. Warfare and crime can also provide powerful occasions for this kind of subjective state, as shown by their frequent use for television entertainment. For an adolescent, making wisecracks in class may be more enjoyable than taking the class seriously (Csikszentmihalyi and Larson 1978). Therefore, it might make sense to conclude that negentropic experiences are incompatible with community order and the goals of development because they drain attention away from more essentially productive tasks. This is the reason for the puritanical aversion to enjoyment that is expressed by the Protestant Ethic.

But the conflict is not necessarily unavoidable. There is no reason why inner harmony should be experienced only in marginal play situations rather than in work or learning. Work is potentially as enjoyable, if not more enjoyable, than play. Furthermore, it is impossible to conceive of socialization without at least some degree of fun. In a regimented educational system students will learn under compulsion, but unless they learn to enjoy learning, they will forget what they learned as soon as possible. Even Confucius, a model of pedagogical conservatism, sees "bursting eagerness" and "bubbling excitement" as prerequisites to real learning (Analects 7:8).

As Plato observed over two thousand years ago, the highest goal of education is to train youths to find "pleasure and pain in the right objects" (Laws II). The same conclusion is reached by one of the foremost contemporary geneticists, who believes that the best recipe for evolution is for mankind to learn to enjoy doing the things it must do (Jacob 1977).

The optimal state of consciousness—psychic negentropy—is not homeostatic. It does not come about because a former state of balance is restored, but because a new order among conflicting goals is created. When a young man recovers from being jilted by a girl for the first time, he does not return to his previous state of innocence. He must integrate new information about himself with previously held images and memories, and with future goals. Although millions have gone through this experience, for any given young person, restoring order in consciousness after being disappointed in love is a constructive, sometimes even a creative effort, which results in an organization of memories and goals that did not exist before. Psychic entropy cannot be avoided by returning to a previous state (although many try, and stop growing thereafter); the passage of time and the presence of new information constantly force us to create new order out of experience.

The pattern of psychic energy that is the self develops around organized experiences. One adolescent will find success as a flutist, another as a poet, another as a prankster. Some may find enjoyment in several domains; some may find it in none. Enjoyment shapes the growth of the self by focusing attention on goals that require increased skills for their achievement. The issue in adolescence is how to experience psychic negentropy in tasks that lead to a successful adulthood.

Adolescents and the Adult World

The problem is that there is so much competition for adolescents' limited psychic energy. Internal impulses clamor for attention: It's nice outside, let's take the bikes to the forest preserve. But requirements of socialization must also be heeded: If you don't read that biology chapter, you will flunk the quiz. A teenager who fails to listen to his inner voices will have trouble establishing a strong self. But if he ignores the values of society, he will have trouble later, because the habits of attention he has developed will not be sufficient to cope with the challenges of adulthood.

Just as the self evolves through ordered patterns of psychic energy investment, so do social systems. For example, a boy or girl become a "couple" or a "team"—in other words a social system—when they begin meeting more often than they would meet by chance. What keeps them together is the enjoyment they feel in each other's company. This in turn shapes their attention even more on the mutual relationship. Their thoughts, feelings, and actions will begin to harmonize in nonrandom ways. The attention they share coordinates their behavior so that they begin acting as a unit, and the growing relationship may in time become the seed for a marital couple and possibly the basis of a future family.

If an activity is organized so that it provides negentropic experiences, less external energy is required to motivate people to perform it. When work is enjoyable, there is less need for material incentives—money, power, recognition—to get people to do their job. In the past, married couples continued to live together because it was more convenient to face the world as a unit than separately; economic and social incentives kept the system intact even though the partners hated or ignored each other. In more recent time these external incentives have gradually disappeared, and the rate of divorce has skyrocketed. Presumably the marriages that survive are held together by the enjoyment the partners get from each other's company. Through attention attracted by negentropic experiences, a system of joint roles, norms, and values is formed that serves to hold together a social system in an internally ordered way.

This is as true of large systems as it is of a couple. Even huge institutions like General Motors or the federal government survive only as long as individuals agree to invest their attention in the system's goals. An institution that is no longer able to attract attention ceases to exist. For instance, an army that cannot make soldiers behave predictably will crumble into a disorganized collection of men. If the soldiers pay no attention to their officers, if the officers are no longer in touch with each other's plans, disorder or *social entropy* sets in, and the system falls apart.

The natural state of any social system is to be disordered. The goals of individuals inevitably begin to conflict, as each tries to satisfy his desires in competition with everyone else. If students are left to themselves, their attention will diverge from the single purpose set by the teacher. If teachers do not use their psychic energy to direct their classes, they dissolve into chaos. Each student has personal goals and brings to the class idiosyncratic desires and impulses. What is order for any given student is disorder for another, and what might be order for students as a group is disorder for the teacher. In any group of interlocking people, a basic tension exists that almost unavoidably leads to conflict.

Almost unavoidably, but not quite. For socialization is designed to reduce the tension and if possible alleviate the conflict. Socialization is a process whereby the goals of individuals are made congruent with each other and with those of the community. Effective socialization also reduces disorder within the psychic system of its members. Thus, socialization decreases entropy in the system made up by the socializer and the socializee. Effective socialization in the classroom means the educational goals set by the teacher also become the student's goals. The latter will have learned, as Plato hoped they would, to find pleasure in the right objects. If socialization is successful, every investment of attention strengthens the class while at the same time it makes the students' self stronger, because the two sets of purposes are now the same.

Adolescents need to learn patterns of thought and action that will enable them to contribute to the community. If they grow up lacking these skills, their peers will be unwilling to share material resources and to respect them. As adults they must be motivated to invest psychic energy into the institutions of society, lest the institutions disintegrate. The roles they now play as students, as family members, as friends rehearse the roles they must play as adults.

One of the most frustrating things about being a parent or a teacher is never being sure whether one is doing the right things. Only when the child in your care has grown up—when it's too late—do you know whether the education you provided was adequate or not. The same is true of the liberties we grant a whole generation of youth and the demands we place upon them. We do not know their effect until that generation has entered adulthood and begins taking over the reins of society. At that point it is too late to change anything. But if there is a barometer that indicates what adolescents are likely to become, it is the record of how they are living their daily lives in the present. The pattern of habits they are establishing, the activities they attend to, what gives them pain or joy: These are the best indications of the direction their growth is taking. How do teen-agers learn to get along with their parents? To enjoy school? To tolerate loneliness? To stand up to the pressure of their peers? These are the questions we shall turn to now, as we begin to report the results of our empirical investigation.

Chapter 3

Charting
Adolescent Life

BEFORE reporting what we learned about adolescents, it is necessary to give an overview of how the study was conducted. This chapter will describe the procedures used to collect the data, the community and the school of which the teenagers were a part, and how the various dimensions of experience were measured.

Old and New Approaches to Studying Adolescence

People studying adolescence have traditionally faced difficult methodological choices. On the one hand, they could do controlled psychometric research with standardized paper-and-pencil instruments to obtain data for large numbers of teenagers. This is the approach used in studies on self-image (Offer, Os-

30

trov, and Howard 1981; Simmons, Rosenberg, and Rosenberg 1973), relationships with family and friends (Brittain 1963; Kandel and Lessor 1969), social valences (Coleman 1961), and delinquent behavior (Gold 1970). In such research, high school students are typically led into the school auditorium and given extensive batteries of scientifically chosen questionnaire items, most commonly aimed at identifying individual differences.

The alternative to the psychometric approach has been direct observation. Under various guises, researchers have infiltrated high schools (Henry 1965; Cusick 1973), summer camps (Savin-Williams 1976), recreational settings (Hetherington 1972), and street corner hang-outs (Sherif and Sherif 1964), attempting to witness at first hand what goes on in teenagers' lives.

One approach provides a rigorous inventory of what teenagers say about their lives; the other provides an observer's interpretation of how they act, primarily in public.

Such methods, complemented by in-depth clinical interviewing, have revealed many important facts and trends about adolescence. But they have left an important aspect of this stage of life almost unexplored: how teenagers' subjective experience relates to the concrete events of their daily life, from encounters with friends to the long hours spent in classrooms, from the drudgery of helping clean the house, to the escape to their own bedrooms.

The approach we used, called the Experience Sampling Method, is a procedure which tries to accomplish this task, combining the strengths of previous approaches. It makes use of rigorous psychometric instruments which are administered not once but many times. It has the ecological validity of observational methods in that reports are made in their natural contexts and are not restricted only to public parts of life. Further, as will be demonstrated in a moment, the method can also provide an in-depth idiographic picture. But, while our method can be compared to traditional approaches, it is also fundamentally different. It is primarily aimed at the study of *experience*.

The word "experience" has two meanings that are useful to consider. First, it is used in everyday speech in reference to the raw emotional reality of what is (or was) in our immediate consciousness, whether it is the taste of a strawberry or the thrill of a roller coaster ride. We talk about the experience—what we felt and what passed through our mind—the first time we _____, or the night _____ happened to us. In a similar vein, we talk about and analyze our day-to-day experiences—with our family, with the boss, when exercising, or when making love. The *Oxford English Dictionary* defines this kind of experience as "the fact of being consciously the subject of a state or condition" (*OED*, Oxford University Press, compact edition 1971, p. 403, S.V. "experience").

The second and complementary meaning of "experience" relates to the outcome of that state or condition. It refers to the learning that has taken place, and sometimes to unplanned psychological consequences, as with a friend of ours whose unhappy experience with several love affairs made him increasingly bitter and cynical. The referent may be a single occasion in the past, but more often it is some segment of the past, a friendship, an opportunity, or a set of painful events. The *Oxford English Dictionary* defines this kind of experience as "knowledge resulting from actual observation or from what one has undergone." This meaning no longer emphasizes the immediacy of events, but rather their lasting developmental impact, the memory or knowledge they impart.

In attempting to understand adolescence, both connotations are essential. To attain an intelligent, constructive empathy with young people, we need to know the raw existential realities of their daily lives. To apprehend where they are headed, we need to consider the influence these realities are having on their development.

THE EXPERIENCE SAMPLING METHOD (ESM)

The research procedure we used is a method for gathering self-reports of the thoughts, activities, and feelings of persons through forty to fifty randomly chosen moments in their daily lives.

For one week, participants are asked to carry an electronic

pager, the kind doctors carry, and also a pad of self-report forms. At one random moment within every two-hour period a signal is sent to the pager, causing it to beep or to vibrate depending on the setting. The instructions are to complete a self-report form each time it does so. The person might be driving a car or listening to a lecture in class; when the pager goes off, if at all possible, the person is to fill out a report. The idea is to respond to as many signals as one reasonably can (Larson and Csikszentmihalyi 1983).

Adolescents participating in this research reported doing all the things they normally do, from cutting classes to teasing friends, from shopping for dental floss to watching the Miss America Contest. Because the schedule is systematic, it provides a representative sample of their life, a profile of what each teenager's daily experience is like. If a girl spends much of her time watching TV, this will show up in the activities she reports during the week. If a boy dislikes school, it becomes evident in the moods he reports when he is there. Across a large sample of people, the method provides a topography of daily experience— from the early hours of Monday morning to the late-night activities of Saturday night.

The ESM procedure is most easily understood by considering how it works for a single individual, such as Rob Miranda, a high school senior who lived with step-parents. Rob was a lanky, well-behaved boy, rather average in his studies. One puzzling thing about him when we first met was the contradiction between his soft-spoken, quiet manners and the rather conspicuous "greaser" outfit he usually wore. Was he as well socialized as his manner implied, or was he the rebel his style of dress suggested?

We explained the project to him, and to the rest of the group we studied, by stating our interest in teenagers' daily experiences: "What do you go through during a typical week? We want to get your story of what your life is like." To do this, we said, we had devised a new procedure, never before used with a large sample of young people.

With Rob, as with others, several days were provided for him to make up his mind about the study; at the end of this period we sat down with him to answer questions and discuss concerns he might have about taking part. Like most other teenagers, he appeared intrigued by the ESM procedure. David Elkind (1967) has suggested that adolescents carry with them an imaginary audience. This method gives them the opportunity to make that audience a little more substantial. So Rob agreed to participate in the study. On a Monday afternoon at the beginning of May, we went through the procedures and the self-report items with him in detail, then gave him the paper and self-report booklet.[1]

One week later, when he returned for the debriefing interview, his booklet contained self-reports on thirty-seven random occasions across that seven-day span, occasions when he had been sitting in class, eating with his family, discussing a date with a girl, and drinking beer with his friends. It had been a reasonably normal week, he explained, and the reports reflected most of the ordinary things he usually does. "You got everything," he said. At first the pager had attracted some attention from friends and family members, but they had quickly become used to it. As with other students, the process of filling out reports became routine and automatic, if not a bit dull. The procedure, he felt, had had no effect on his thoughts, feelings, or activities during the week. The method seemed to have fulfilled its objective, capturing a representative sample of his ordinary experience.

Rob's thirty-seven random self-reports, excerpted in Table 3.1, provide a picture of what his life is like, partly clarifying the original impression of incongruity. While he may have been soft-spoken with us, he appears to spend a large amount of time interacting with people; in fact, he is very seldom alone. A substantial amount of his waking hours are spent at home, often in conversation with his stepmother. While he drinks alcohol, rarely studies, and freely skips out of school for lunch on Wednesday, he provides no indication of a rebellious disposition: for exam-

1. For Rob Miranda, as for the other students, signals were sent between 7:30 A.M. in the morning to 10:30 P.M. at night. On Friday and Saturday nights the signals extended until 1:30 A.M.

ple, he hardly ever reports feeling angry or irritable. As will become apparent later, his moods are exceptionally stable, and they vary little from their typical positive level. He also reports being less self-conscious and more in control than other teenagers. A clinical psychologist might infer that Rob has responded to past family trauma by adopting a controlled, perhaps rigid stance, involving an excessive dependency on his new mother. However, to provide clinical interpretations is not our purpose.

What we want to demonstrate with this case study is the information the ESM procedure provides about an adolescent's experience. Where Rob spends his time, with whom, and doing what, are summarized in the graphs of Figure 3.1. This book, however, is not about lives of single individuals, but the patterns that appear when many adolescents are sampled. To do this, we drew on a set of ESM self-report data from a group of seventy-five adolescents.[2] The remainder of this chapter will describe the design of the study and the sample of experience that was obtained.

The Community and the School

No single community can provide a perfectly representative sample of teenagers from which to generalize to the mainstream of American youth. But the community bordering Chicago where this study was conducted comes close, given its heterogeneous population and its mixture of urban and suburban lifestyles. It is a community composed of a blend of upper-middle

2. In addition to the primary sample of adolescent experience, there are two other sets of ESM data that will be referenced here. The case study of Rob, and other similar case studies throughout the book, come from a two-year follow-up with 27 of the freshmen and sophomores from the original sample of 75 (Freeman 1982). We will also draw upon ESM data from research with 107 adult workers, obtained through five Chicago-area businesses (Graef 1979; Csikszentmihalyi and Graef 1980; Csikszentmihalyi and Kubey 1981; Csikszentmihalyi and Figurski 1982). This adult comparison sample of 40 men and 67 women, aged nineteen to sixty-five, serves as a contrast group for putting the lives of the adolescents into perspective.

TABLE 3.1
Rob Miranda's Week

The table summarizes some of the information provided by Rob for each of his 37 self-reports.

Day	Time	Location	Concentration (0–9)	Angry-Friendly (1–7)	Passive-Active (1–7)	Wish to be doing Activity (0–9)	Control of Actions (0–9)	What he was doing and with whom
MON	12:43	classroom	5	3	5	2	6	Checking test in business law with classmates
MON	18:41	basement	7	4	3	0	6	Talking to my mom, doing homework
MON	20:40	basement	8	4	4	1	4	Watching TV, talking to my mom
MON	22:25	bedroom	7	4	3	5	7	Watching TV, talking to my mom
TUE	8:43	classroom	5	5	3	2	8	Going over poems in English class with classmates
TUE	11:00	stnt. center	7	3	5	8	8	Talking to friends, working
TUE	12:35	classroom	6	3	5	6	8	Listening to a speaker in business law
TUE	14:04	classroom	3	5	5	1	6	Taking notes in Economics with classmates
TUE	17:16	kitchen	6	6	6	7	7	Eating dinner, talking to my mom
TUE	19:06	den	7	6	5	8	7	Talking to girlfriend on phone
WED	10:30	car	7	6	6	9	8	Going for lunch with friends
WED	12:19	restaurant	7	6	4	9	6	Eating with friends
WED	13:34	cafeteria	7	6	6	9	8	Talking with friends
WED	14:49	parking lot	7	6	6	8	8	Talking to a girl
WED	16:21	frnd's home	8	6	6	8	8	Talking to girlfriend about prom
WED	18:21	porch	8	6	6	2	8	Doing homework, staring off into space, alone
WED	20:51	basement	8	6	6	8	8	Watching Charlie's Angels with mother
THR	9:36	classroom	3	6	5	7	8	Reading in Spanish with classmates
THR	12:27	classroom	8	6	6	7	8	Taking notes in business law with classmates
THR	18:00	living room	1	6	1	8	8	Taking a nap, alone
THR	19:15	kitchen	8	7	6	8	8	Talking with mother about brother going to prom
THR	22:00	kitchen	8	6	5	2	8	Helping my mom clean, watching TV

TABLE 3.1 (continued)
Rob Miranda's Week

The table summarizes some of the information provided by Rob for each of his 37 self-reports.

Day	Time	Location	Concentration (0–9)	Angry-Friendly (1–7)	Passive-Active (1–7)	Wish to be doing Activity (0–9)	Control of Actions (0–9)	What he was doing and with whom
FRI	12:15	stnt. center	8	6	6	2	8	Talking with friends about a song
FRI	15:14	kitchen	8	5	3	6	8	Talking with mother about visiting aunt
FRI	18:47	car	7	6	6	9	8	Driving and drinking with a friend
FRI	20:15	car	6	6	6	9	6	Drinking and talking about Moll with friends
SAT	11:30	kitchen	7	6	6	9	8	Reading paper—about the Cubs, alone
SAT	13:00	outside	8	6	6	6	8	Bringing in things from the car with mother & father
SAT	21:26	frnd's home	8	4	6	7	8	Drinking and talking at a party with friends
SAT	23:22	living room	7	5	3	7	8	Talking with girlfriend about their relationship
SUN	13:20	outside	7	5	3	9	8	Reading, drinking pop with mother & father
SUN	18:15	park	8	6	6	7	7	Umpiring at a ball game
SUN	20:30	kitchen	8	6	5	5	8	Getting ice cream, doing homework with mother & father
MON	12:40	classroom	7	6	5	7	8	Going over homework in business law with classmates
MON	16:00	campus	8	6	6	9	8	Taking a look at a college campus with mother & father
MON	18:00	restaurant	8	6	5	9	8	Eating, admiring the girls with mother & father
MON	20:15	porch	8	6	5	9	8	Talking on the phone with girlfriend

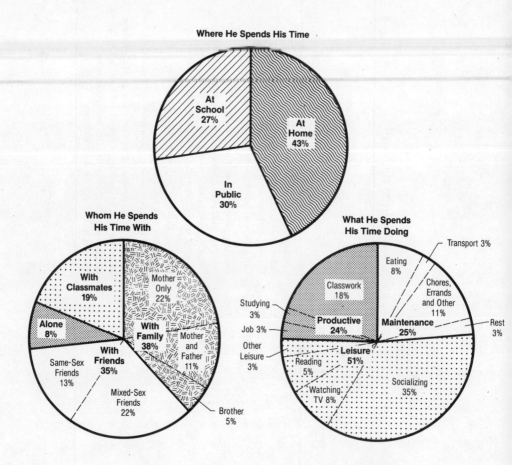

FIGURE 3.1
Profile of Rob Miranda's Daily Experience

class and lower-middle class families from a broad range of ethnic groups, including Italians, Greeks, Slavs, Blacks, and Asians
as well as Anglo-Saxon families. Some of these families have
lived in their homes for two or three generations; others are
newcomers with roots still in the city. While the community is
diverse, strong leadership and historical traditions have provided
a hedge against the urban decay and cultural normlessness that
have plagued neighboring communities. The presence of many
historical homes built by Prairie School architects contributes to

a definite sense of identity, facilitating a degree of community cooperation and organization that allow residents to live relatively ordered and flexible lives.

The school itself was seventy-nine years old when the study was conducted. It had served upward of 4,000 students each year since the 1920s. Constructed with a facade of evenly proportioned four-story arches, it was a symbol of neighborhood decorum and pride. The school was run in a very organized and efficient manner, described by some as "businesslike." Its faculty was highly professional, with 88 percent having degrees past their B.A.'s; many of the classes we visited were masterpieces of teaching artistry. The students' spirit of shared responsibility was illustrated by the fact that rows of original paintings line the hallways unmolested, a most unusual accomplishment in an era of endemic school vandalism.[3]

While adults in the community lived, to all appearances, in a harmonious world, the lives of the students were by no means free from the excesses and deviations for which teenagers are famous. A poll in the school, conducted at the time of our study by the student newspaper, indicated that 72 percent of the students had tried marijuana and 23 percent used it weekly. Official statistics showed rates of juvenile arrest somewhat above the mean for Chicago suburbs (United Way 1978). Within the school there were tensions and occasional fights between whites and the growing black student population, which numbered 271 at the time of the study. There was also an older, though less volatile, conflict between students from the northern, affluent half of the community and those from the southern, lower-middle class half. The lingering reputations of prominent artists and writers who had been residents also appeared to sanction a touch of Bohemia in the students' life styles.

But student life, on the whole, was not that different from what Coleman (1961) found in suburban Chicago schools, or from descriptions of other American high schools. Students were

3. The first contacts with the school were established by Patrick Mayers, whose dissertation describes the flow-like characteristics of classroom learning (Mayers 1978). For the actual study the field team in the high school was cosupervised by Reed Larson (Larson 1979).

more interested in athletics and in being popular than they were in their studies. Because of its size, there was no single social hierarchy, but several, oriented around athletics, student organizations, and various life-styles. In the terminology of Barker and Gump (1964) it was an "overmanned" school where extracurricular opportunities were taken by a minority of students who specialized in single areas of achievement, while a large number of students fell between the cracks, remaining unattached to any part of school life except their classes.

Outside school, the full range of opportunities a metropolitan area can offer was available. Students were members of church groups and community youth organizations; some joined specialized sports clubs and took dance lessons downtown. For informal recreation, they could go to the local shopping mall and the neighborhood forest preserves. Movie theaters, recreational centers, and a Great America amusement park also were available.

In sum, the school provided teenagers with a well-organized structure for the compulsory, adult-oriented part of their lives, and the community provided a wide array of additional opportunities for their discretionary time. This is the environment of constraints and opportunities in which they found themselves. Our research sought to discover what kinds of lives they carved out from it.

The population from which the sample was drawn is certainly not representative of teenagers growing up on Texas farms, in Appalachian hamlets, or even in the slums of neighboring Chicago. Adolescents in Africa, Southeast Asia, or the Soviet Union encounter even more radically different experiences as they grow into adulthood. Who, then, is this book about? Is it *only* about the seventy-five randomly selected adolescents we got to know intimately during the study, or do the findings generalize to broader categories of teenagers?

This question cannot be answered with any certainty. Our best estimate is that some of the patterns we will report, like the tension between family, friends, solitude, and educational institutions, are characteristic of all adolescents in any literate culture. Others, like the prominent part television and other electronic media have in daily life, are true for adolescents in most developed countries. Still other patterns, like some forms of family interactions and the emphasis on athletics and other organized extracurricular activities, are typically American. Finally, some of the findings are likely to be true only of middle-class, Midwestern, metropolitan teenagers in the last quarter of the twentieth century.

But what is universal about these adolescents seems to outweigh by far that which is unique. One of the authors spent his adolescence in various European cultures, living in widely different ethnic and social class environments. In some of these contexts, intellectual concerns were much more important to teenagers than they were in this American sample; in others, sex or sports were more prominent. The emphasis varied, but essentially the same mix of activities and experiences was present in the street groups of Naples in Southern Italy and in an exclusive Swiss boarding school. Drugs were not a problem in that generation, but alienation and apathy were probably just as prevalent.

In the last analysis, this book only claims to be an accurate map to the subjective experiences of the adolescents who were directly studied. With its help, the conscious experiences of other teenagers, in different places and different times, also will be better understood.

Description of the Study

The Experience Sampling Method is a means for people to provide an account of their typical hour-to-hour existence.

From the very first contact, we dealt with each student as a unique individual. With each, we discussed how the procedure would fit into their lives: How would their friends react? When might it be difficult to respond to the pager signals? How would the procedure fit into their lives? It was made clear that they had the right not to respond or even to quit the study at any point they decided. At the same time, we stressed how important it was for the research that they provide as close to a complete week of self-reports as possible. Relationship with students followed what Offer and Sabshin (1967) have described as a "research alliance," a mutual understanding about the means and goals of the study. Beyond this, however, we came to know many of them as friends.

The sample of the study is what is called a "stratified random sample." It was obtained by a procedure designed to get a random selection of students, with approximately equal numbers of boys and girls, equal numbers from all four high school grades, and equal numbers from two contrasting residential zones, a lower-middle-class sector of the community and an upper-middle-class sector.[4] How well the final sample of seventy-five students represents the population of the school cannot be fully established. As it got closer to summer, students invited to participate, particularly boys, became less willing to accept. One disappointing morning in late May, eleven out of eleven sophomores in one class declined to participate. Overall, of those invited, 60 percent of the girls and 45 percent of the boys invited completed the study. A fuller description of the sample and how it was collected is provided in Appendices A1 and A2.

In spite of attrition, it became clear that a wide variety of teenagers was represented in this sample. There were jocks and freaks, greasers and intellectuals, members of the "power elite" and of the "silent majority." In fact, the sample provided the full range of social types identified by researchers of adolescent subcultures (for example, Cusick 1973; Larkin 1979). Beyond these superficial tags it was apparent that each had a unique background and a personal set of goals, whether it was running the fastest 100-yard dash in the state, souping up a car, excelling in school, or just getting by. There were students absorbed in sail-

4. The lower-middle-class sector consisted of four census tracts in which the average 1970 income was $14,000 and 70 percent of the wage earners held blue-collar jobs. The upper-middle-class consisted of five census tracts where the average 1970 income was $25,000 and 50 percent of the wage earners held white-collar jobs.

ing and photography, friends' problems and family problems, love and getting high.

As described earlier in the chapter, students followed a procedure of carrying pagers and filling out self-reports at random times.[5]

One might think that a study like this would create unending disruption; it did not. Of thirty-six respondents questioned, only one said carrying the pager had any effect on his daily activity, only three said it affected their mood, and only four said it affected their thoughts. The effects they mentioned involved feeling self-conscious and thinking about when the next signal would come. As will become obvious later, these adolescents reported all the ups and downs one might expect—and some that nobody expected. Within the school there emerged a genre of beeper jokes, but aside from this the study went mainly unnoticed. While a few of these students reported that the paging became irritating after the fifth or sixth day, most of them said it was interesting and that they enjoyed taking part. Our biggest problem was mechanical failure of the pagers.

As important as the sample of adolescents is the sample of the experiences. How thoroughly does the final set of self-reports represent the students' daily lives? In total, the seventy-five students provided 4,489 self-reports.[6] The average student received and responded to 69 percent of the signals, a rate that reflects missing reports because of sleep, mechanical failure of the pager, and a wide variety of other reasons. A subgroup of thirty-six was asked what parts of their experience were inadequately sampled during the week. They indicated that socializing with friends may have been underrepresented, particularly on weekend evenings (Larson 1979), but there is little suggestion that any part of

5. Signals occurred once within every two-hour block of time except during school hours, when there was one during every forty-minute period to facilitate Patrick Mayers' dissertation on classroom experience (Mayers 1978).

6. In order to obtain sufficient information from each class, signals were sent every 40 minutes during school hours. To adjust for this disproportionate sampling, we have assigned a weight of one-third to these school self-reports, a weight which equalizes their frequency vis-à-vis nonschool self-reports (Mayers 1978). As a result, henceforward we shall be referring to a total sample of 2,734 self reports.

experience has been consistently excluded. The final sample of self-reports includes responses while in the bathroom, while using drugs, and while having sex. The students demonstrated an unabashed willingness to share their experiences.

The diligence with which the reports were completed is also reassuring. For 88 percent of the reports, the adolescents indicated that they had filled out the response sheet within ten minutes of the signal.

Undoubtedly, there are aspects of adolescents' lives that were poorly represented, some that one could not hope to learn much about with a method like this one. However, the large selection of daily life that was shared provides a starting point for an unprecedented understanding of what it is like to be an adolescent.

MEASURING THE EXTERNAL COORDINATES OF EXPERIENCE

Experience has both an external and an internal component that we wanted to capture. The external has to do with the frame of events and behaviors: with daily situations as they impinge on a person's consciousness. The internal has to do with the quality of consciousness: with how a person thinks and feels during daily life.

The external component was defined in terms of where the adolescents were, what they were doing, and whom they were with at the time of the signals. These three variables will be considered as the external coordinates of experience. The first, *location*, is based on the students' responses to the open-ended question, "As you were beeped, where were you?" To allow statistical analyses of these responses, answers were coded into twenty-six mutually exclusive categories, shown in Appendix B. Coders agreed on the same categories for 82 percent of their ratings. These twenty-six locations fit within three basic domains: Home, School, and Public. Rob Miranda, as you may recall, spent about half of his time at home, a fact that seemed to be characteristic of his life-style.

The second external coordinate is a person's *activity*. On a pager sheet, respondents were asked, "As you were beeped . . .

What was the MAIN thing you were doing?" Because activities (and people's descriptions of them) are far more varied than locations, coding of the responses to this open-ended question is less tidy. We developed sixteen mutually exclusive categories, shown and described in Appendix B; however, a rather heterogeneous mix of activities has been forced into some of these categories. For example, when Rob was visiting a college, this ended up in the category of "Chores, Errands, and Other Practical Activities." Nonetheless, the majority of self-reports fell easily into one choice or another, such as watching TV or studying. Independent coders agreed on activity categories for 80 percent of their ratings.

Coding problems did not arise with the third coordinate, *companionship*. Adolescents responded to the question, "Who were you with?" on a fixed checklist of possibilities such as parents, siblings, same sex friend. The various combinations of companions were classified into 3 mutually exclusive alternatives, fitting into four main categories: family, friends, alone, and in class. The following coding decisions were employed, based on preliminary analysis of the students' subjective states: (1) to include time with both family and friends in the category "with friends"; (2) to include times with pets in the category "alone"; (3) to include times talking on the phone as "with friends," even though "alone" had often been marked (see Larson 1979).

These coordinates differentiate important segments of experience that have been studied by other researchers. Television watching, playing sports, work, school, and especially relationships with family and friends have been the topic of many previous investigations. Few of the past findings, however, have been considered as parts of an integrated whole. A vast body of research on sports, for example, exists unknown to most students of human development, though it deals with an important part of many teenagers' lives. At the same time, the codings identify parts of adolescents' lives that have not been isolated before. Time alone, eating, and personal care are important segments of teenagers' experience that need to be understood as part of their total experience.

The challenge of this study is to see how these parts fit together, how they define a landscape of alternatives that help determine the overall quality of adolescent life. Where adolescents spend their time, what they do with it, and whom they spend it with demark a system of options, constraints, and potentialities that bear on lives such as Rob's, shaping both the immediate reality and the future growth.

MEASURING THE INTERNAL DIMENSIONS OF EXPERIENCE

Experience is information we find in consciousness when we turn attention inward. The states of consciousness are enormously varied, as the many descriptive terms used in everyday language suggest: pain, joy, desire, anger, concentration, fatigue, elation, boredom, love, fear, and so on. Each of these nouns refers to a slightly different condition. To make some order out of this bewildering array, psychologists have traditionally divided conscious processes into three main types: emotion, cognition, and will (Hilgard 1980). The first refers to the internal condition of consciousness as a whole—whether it is basically positive or negative. A negative emotional state means that negative feedback has been obtained, that the person has failed to meet some of his or her goals, thereby creating a disorder in the information-processing system. A positive emotion like happiness or joy indicates that the person's goals are being achieved. Cognition, the second dimension, refers to the activity by which consciousness interacts with the environment, and transforms meaningless stimuli into useful information. Will, or motivation, denotes the mechanism by which a person chooses goals in which to invest psychic energy and keeps the energy focused on the goal. Some investigators (for example, Piaget 1981), reduce these three dimensions to only two. They combine "affect" and "will," considering them to refer to the same energistic process, one distinct from structural cognition. Our approach, however, considers these as three separate aspects of the allocation of psychic energy.

As discussed, these dimensions of consciousness can be in either an entropic or negentropic state; they can either be random or weak, or harmonious and purposive. The question is, how does the quality of experience, along with the various dimensions of consciousness, change in the different contexts of adolescent life? Part III of this volume will focus on this issue. But the prior question that has to be answered is, how can the pager method be used to measure entropy and negentropy in consciousness? We now describe the ways these elusive phenomena were operationalized in the present study.

Affect and Activation. The easiest dimension to measure is the emotional, because it is the one that has been most extensively studied by other researchers. Past studies show that self-reported mood correlates with work performance (Hersey 1932), sociability (Wessman and Ricks 1966), altruism (Aderman and Berkowitz 1970), and physiological assessments of sleep (Kramer, Roehrs, and Roth 1976), as well as other behavioral and physiological measures. Past studies have also demonstrated that teenagers are capable of sensitive assessments of their emotional states (Wolman, Lewis, and King 1971; Ellinwood 1969). Kotsch, Gerbing, and Schwartz (1982) found that children as young as eight years old make consistent and reliable judgments about their emotions.

In this study we were concerned with two related dimensions of emotional state: affect and activation. To measure these, we developed items having opposite mood terms at opposing ends of a seven-point scale. One end of each scale represents the negentropic state (for example, happy, strong, free), whereas the other end represents the entropic state (for example, sad, weak, constrained). Students marked where they were on these scales each time the pager signaled. (See the self-report form, shown in Appendix A.3). Four strongly interrelated items dealt with affect and four with activation. We did not ask about states such as shame, guilt, and anxiety (Izard 1977), that possibly are an important part of adolescent experience but that are subject to repression and denial and thus are more difficult to assess. Our attempt was to study the level of emotional experience accessible to everyday consciousness.

Cognitive Efficiency. Cognition and information processing have been much studied, but very seldom in terms of variations in an individual's cognitive faculties. Most work in this area assumes that people always operate at their optimal level of cognitive efficiency. However, research that addresses these issues more directly, like the work on self-consciousness (Carver and Scheier 1981) or on the effects of fatigue on performance, has demonstrated that individuals fluctuate dramatically in their ability to process information. Cognitive negentropy varies substantially for the same person across time.

Drawing on available research and everyday language, we adopted four items dealing with cognitive process. First were the questions, How well were you concentrating? Was it hard to concentrate? and How self-conscious were you? The students responded to each on a ten-point scale from "not at all" to "very." In addition, students rated themselves on a seven-point scale in terms of "open" versus "closed." These items all bear on a person's ability to use psychic energy efficiently, even though they are not intercorrelated.

A person may concentrate his attention a lot—with ease when skiing down a slope or with difficulty when studying for an exam. Likewise, depth and ease of concentration both affect cognitive efficiency, but independently. The same is true of self-consciousness, which interferes with information processing by withdrawing psychic energy in order to monitor internal processes. Among the three items, concentration appears the most solid, given its correlations with the conceptually similar activation items, particularly with alertness. Nonetheless, the others should by no means be discounted. As we shall see, within specific contexts such as classwork and sports, the students' responses to them are quite revealing.

Intrinsic Motivation. There are relatively few precedents to draw from in regard to the mental faculty Hilgard describes as "will" or conation, a faculty he argues has been sorely neglected by psychologists (Hilgard 1980). This neglect is not surprising, given the difficulty of separating historic, concurrent, and goal-oriented elements of conation and of separating the deterministic from the volitional components of a person's actions. The concept of will is one philosophers have never been able to agree on. As with the measures of cognitive efficiency, we started from a weak empirical base.

Of the various aspects of will, we were most interested in how much a person actually wanted to do whatever it was she or he was doing—in other words, the extent of intrinsic motivation present. One of the central determinants of consciousness is whether we do want to do something or not. The philosophical question of free will is not at issue here; what is important is the phenomenological reality according to which we sometimes feel free and sometimes feel constrained in our actions. Therefore, we wanted to measure the degree of intrinsic motivation people reported in the various contexts of their lives.

Throughout the eight years of our ESM research one item has proven itself a most powerful descriptor of intrinsically motivated experience: "As you were beeped . . . did you wish you had been doing something else?" Responses are made on a ten-point scale, graded between "not at all" and "very much." This item seems to tap into a strong phenomenological reality, because responses to it show strong relationships with various contingencies of life and experience (Graef, Csikszentmihalyi, and Gianinno 1983; Rubinstein, Csikszentmihalyi, and Graef 1980). In different places we have referred to this item as a measure of "commitment," "involvement," and "intrinsic motivation." Its meaning fits all of these dimensions of a psychologically endogenous experience.

As supplementary measures of intrinsic motivation, we used respondents' ratings of their sense of control, freedom, and involvement. Although these four variables are often uncorrelated empirically, they do fit different facets of what a person who is intrinsically motivated should feel (Deci 1975; Lepper and Greene 1978; De Charms and Muir 1978). Given its more direct relevance to the concept of intrinsic motivation, we shall use the "wish to be doing the activity" item primarily, but we also shall consider the others whenever they seem relevant.

Other Items. In addition to these measures of mood, cognitive state, and motivation, a number of items dealt with other subjective variables. Respondents were asked to write down what they were thinking about at the time of the signal. These responses were coded into seventeen content categories, with interrater agreement of 83 percent. Other items involved ratings of the "stakes," the "skills," and the "challenges" a person found to be present in the current activity. Lastly, three items to be filled out only when a person was with others asked for ratings of the nature of the ongoing social interaction. They asked whether talk was "joking" or "serious," whether the goals of the people the respondents were with were "the same as yours" or "different from yours," and whether these companions were more likely to provide "positive" or "negative feedback." While there is no psychometric information about the validity of these items, various patterns of response suggest that they are meaningful.[7]

While these psychometric issues are important to consider, we hope they have not obscured the reality of what the method is attempting to measure: the ongoing reality of people's lives. Controlled, unvarying Rob Miranda hardly indicates the intensity of emotion experienced by some teenagers, an intensity evident not only in the extreme moods they reported, but also in their marginal comments, as well as the looks in their eyes when we reviewed their records at the end of the week. A dramatic example of this intensity is the self-report shown in Figure 3.2. The girl who provided it, normally calm and rational, was obviously quite unhappy and violently angry at her mother. When we reviewed the sheet with her, she was embarrassed but still virulent. One needs to keep in mind that the numbers in the statistical tables we present here are not mere "data," but reflect the passion and raw feelings of these teenagers' lives.

Psychological research ordinarily shuns subjective reports, preferring to base its conclusions on behavioral data. But when it

7. Elsewhere we have provided detailed information about the psychometric properties of the measures over a week of repeated use (Larson 1979). In brief, responses are quite stable. The means, standard deviations, and correlations of students' responses change only slightly from the first to the second half of a week. Differences between individuals are stable. Data from a two-year follow-up study demonstrate remarkable stability of individual response characteristics over two years (Freeman 1982).

comes to studying qualities of experience, there is no better source of information than what a person says about how he feels. There is no outside measure that can reveal what happens in consciousness. Even the best trained observer or analyst has no direct access to its content. Inferences about internal states made by outsiders are inherently less reliable than reports by cooperative subjects can be (Lazarus 1966; Mischel 1981). About fifteen hundred years ago, Saint Augustine, one of the great early psychologists, wrote at the beginning of his *Confessions:* "How do you know, when you hear me talk about myself, that I am telling the truth, considering that no man knows what is true of a man, save his own soul?" (Augustine A.D. 400). The point he made is still valid. Experience is known only to the consciousness of which it is a part. But if one is able to establish a trusting relationship with a person, one in which systematic distortions are unlikely, then the subjective report becomes the best—and only—measure of the quality of experience.

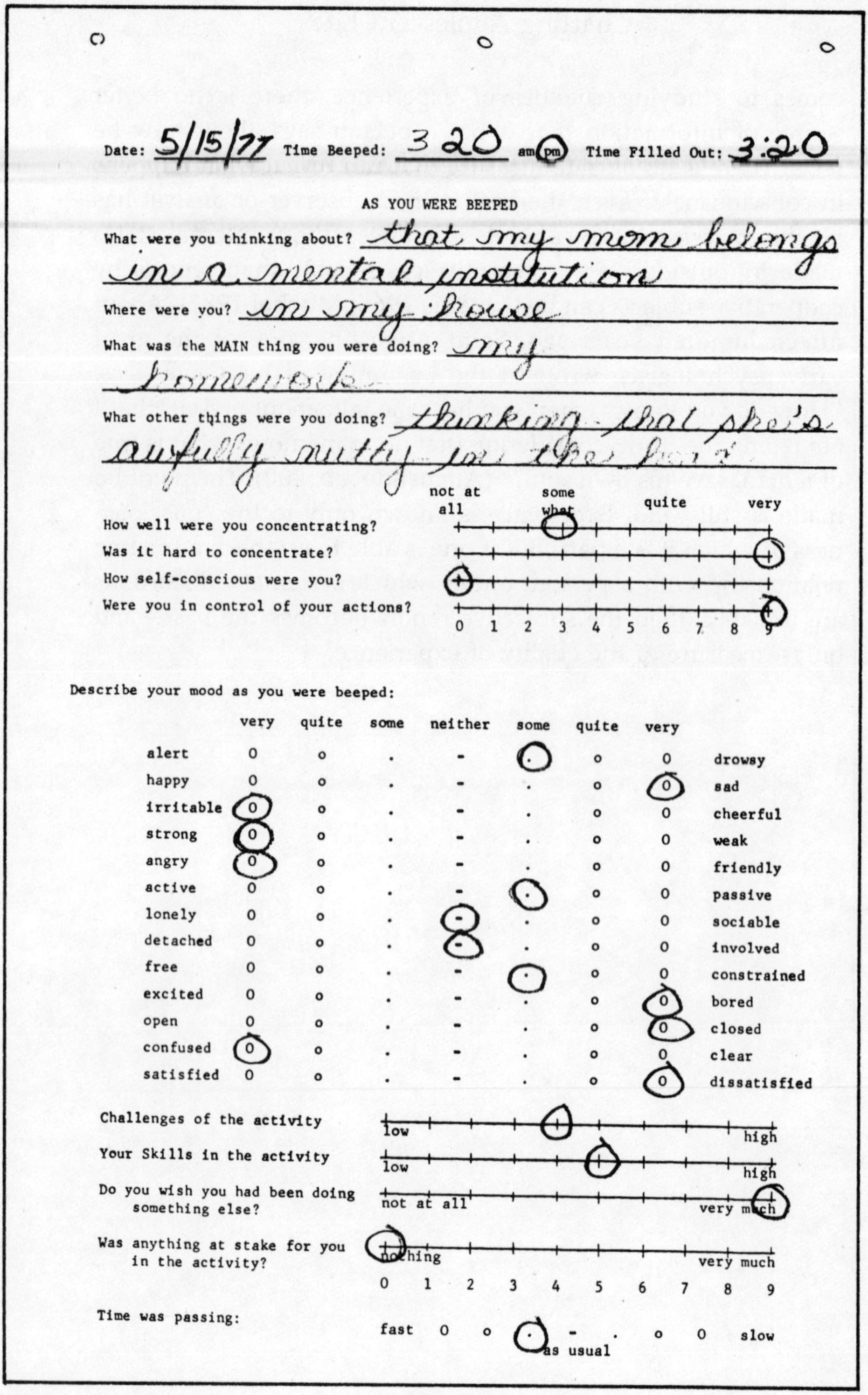

Date: 5/15/77   Time Beeped: 3 20   am (pm)   Time Filled Out: 3:20

AS YOU WERE BEEPED

What were you thinking about? *that my mom belongs in a mental institution*

Where were you? *in my house*

What was the MAIN thing you were doing? *my homework*

What other things were you doing? *thinking that she's awfully nutty in the ___*

	not at all	somewhat	quite	very
How well were you concentrating?		○		
Was it hard to concentrate?				○
How self-conscious were you?	○			
Were you in control of your actions?				○

0 1 2 3 4 5 6 7 8 9

Describe your mood as you were beeped:

	very	quite	some	neither	some	quite	very	
alert	○	○	·	–	⊙	○	○	drowsy
happy	○	○	·	–	·	○	⊙	sad
irritable	⊙	○	·	–	·	○	○	cheerful
strong	⊙	○	·	–	·	○	○	weak
angry	⊙	○	·	–	·	○	○	friendly
active	○	○	·	–	⊙	○	○	passive
lonely	○	○	·	⊙	○	○	○	sociable
detached	○	○	·	⊙	·	○	○	involved
free	○	○	·	–	⊙	○	○	constrained
excited	○	○	·	–	·	○	⊙	bored
open	○	○	·	–	·	○	⊙	closed
confused	⊙	○	·	–	·	○	○	clear
satisfied	○	○	·	–	·	○	⊙	dissatisfied

Challenges of the activity   low ——⊙———— high

Your Skills in the activity   low ————⊙—— high

Do you wish you had been doing something else?   not at all ————————⊙ very much

Was anything at stake for you in the activity?   ⊙ nothing ———————— very much

0 1 2 3 4 5 6 7 8 9

Time was passing: fast ○ ○ ⊙ – · ○ ○ slow
                              as usual

FIGURE 3.2

A Self-Report of an Angry Moment

```
******************************************************************
```

Think back on how you got into this activity.

How much choice did YOU have in selecting this activity?
(How easily could you have chosen to do something else?)

1) None   2) A little   3) Some   4) Pretty much   (5) Very much

Did you do it for

Your family?   1) Yes   (2) No
Your friends?   1) Yes   (2) No
Your future?   1) Yes   (2) No

Were there other things available that you wanted to do?   (1) Yes   2) No

Would you do it if you didn't have to?   1) Yes   (2) No

```
******************************************************************
```

Who were you with?

( ) brother(s), sister(s)   (bitch) (crazy person)
(X) parent(s) mother   ( ) friend(s)
( ) strangers   number ____ (initials __,__,__)
( ) alone   1) male(s) 2) female(s) 3) both
                             ( ) other _____

```
******************************************************************
```

Answer the following questions only if you were with other people:

Was somebody being the leader?   1) Yes   (2) No   she deliberately
Was it you?   1) Yes   (2) No   physically hurt
                                                    me + being mentally

Was talk: Serious   O   o   .   .   o   (0)   joking

In your activity the goals of [others] were:
the same as yours   .   .   o   (0)   different from yours

In this situation [were you more likely] to get negative or positive feedback
from the [people]
                    .   .   o   O   positive

```
******************************************************************
```

Great thoughts, nasty cracks, cartoons and jokes, excuses

help me I hate her
I hate her guts etc.
much I hate her she froze
help me my eardrum
she's please even I can't
mentally stand her
she's insane retarded
helpless

PART II

ENVIRONMENTS

Chapter 4

The External Landscape: What the Teenagers' World Looks Like

To understand what it means to be an adolescent, one needs to know first where adolescents spend their time and what they do with it. Where and how they invest their psychic energy determine the habits they learn, and in turn, the kind of people they are becoming.

Even the physical locations one happens to be in affect the quality of consciousness and the teenagers' development. The principal's office is a place most students would not visit voluntarily, whereas they would seldom need to be forced into an ice-cream shop. Each location offers some opportunities for behavior and has implicit limits on what can take place. Sitting in a pew in church makes spiritual reflection easy, but not much else; sitting in the stands at a baseball game makes spiritual reflection difficult, but many others things easy. The same argument holds for activities, and for whom one is with. Studying versus listening to music, being with a girl friend versus being with one's mom are different situations with different potentialities.

Thus the first step in mapping the daily experience of our adolescents is reconstructing the field of opportunities and constraints on which their lives are enacted—the places, activities, and social contexts they interact with during a typical week. We will be looking at the features of adolescent life an observer would see if he were able to follow them around. How much time do teenagers spend in places that reflect their own goals as opposed to those of others? How much time do they spend in educational versus recreational activities? And how much time do they spend with friends rather than with adults? Who an adolescent will grow up to be depends in part on the answers to these questions.

Locations

The paths of adolescents' daily lives pass through three main geographic domains. One might think of these as three separate countries, ruled by separate laws. The first is the home, where the adolescent must work out a way of life with his parents. The second is the school, where the teenager has little choice but to accept the norms of the institution. And finally, there are the public places—the parks, the buses, the supermarkets, the friends' houses where rules are varied and flexible.

Figure 4.1 shows where teenagers happened to be as they completed some 2,700 self-reports. This diagram gives a bare outline of the influences to which typical teenagers are exposed. The most pervasive context of their lives is still the home, where they continue to be in the dependent position of childhood, exposed to the formative influences of their family or origin. Another third of their waking life is spent at school, the institution which exists specifically to socialize them into the patterns of attention required by the social system. Given the fact that over two thirds of their time is spent in these contexts devoted to adult socialization, it is difficult to imagine at first how teenagers

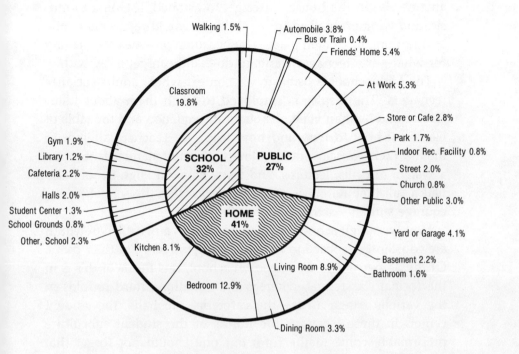

FIGURE 4.1
Where Adolescents Spend Their Time
Graph shows the percentage of self-reports in each location (N=2734). In this and the following figures, 1 percentage point is equivalent to approximately 1 hour per week, spent in the given location or activity.

would have a chance to develop goals divergent from those of adults. A closer look at Figure 4.1, however, might give some preliminary clues.

At home, adolescents spend the largest proportion of their waking hours (and also, their sleeping time) in their bedrooms. This begins to suggest that the home is not only a setting of family interaction but also a context of solitary withdrawal in which opportunities for individual development as well as for deviance are present. The 13 percent of time teens spend in their bedrooms may be used to read, reflect, and practice their skills, or it may be used to escape demands in hedonistic or lethargic relaxation.

One of the students in our study repeatedly slipped out of family interactions to go to his room to smoke hashish. He had devised a system whereby the smoke would not be detected by anyone else in the house. After getting stoned, listening to music, and lying on his bed for a while, he would rejoin his family as if nothing had taken place. The bedroom provides a sanctuary for whatever a teenager wants to do—and can get away with.

The high school is ostensibly a context where adults socialize teenagers. The faculty is employed to teach them about Julius Caesar and Nathan Hale, the quadratic equation and the table of elements, how to type and how to drive. Teachers attempt to modify their consciousness in line with adult standards through a system of drills, lectures, and tests. Belmont High School also had a full time narcotics officer who prowled the school to discourage students' involvement with drugs.

However, high school can also be seen as a place where youth are constantly exposed to the socializing influence of their peers. Of the 31 percent of time spent in school, two thirds of this is in the formal classrooms, whereas the remaining third unfolds in the various fringe areas—the cafeteria, the halls, the student center. In these locations the norms of the student subculture presumably come to the fore; but one should not forget that even in classrooms students outnumber teachers by at least twenty to one. Despite the status and power teachers have in the classroom, one wonders to what extent the sheer numerical superiority of students helps to structure their attention in patterns consonant with that of peers rather than adults.

In this school, like many others, parts of hallways were claimed by different competing groups. Cliques of jocks and debaters, of Italians and Blacks established their personal spaces. One of the most vehement self-reports we obtained during school hours was from a girl in the middle of a fistfight, defending her group's turf. One of her friends had been challenged, and as a leader she ferociously entered the fray. This event stood out as more significant than anything else that had happened in school that day.

The public locations through which adolescents move are not easy to assign either to the world of adults or to that of peers. When they are working at a part-time job the attention of teenagers is structured in terms of adult goals. The rest of the locations might represent either adult or peer influences. Stores, churches, and restaurants demand adult behavior; drive-in movies, discos, and rock concerts reinforce the values of the youth culture. A similar ambivalence is characteristic of the time spent traveling in cars. On the one hand, driving a car requires conformity to adult patterns of attention—one could make a case for the almost universal socializing power of a driver's license in America: A teenager must learn to attend and adapt to the behavior of other drivers, to require a voluntary restructuring of attention along prosocial lines. On the other hand, driving also gives one license of a different kind—to indulge a need for power and speed, to withdraw from the eyes of adults, to park at night with a lover. The automobile provides teenagers an unparalleled opportunity to act out their wishes. As we shall see, older adolescents are allowed to spend more time in these more negotiable public environs.

The first glance at the geography of teenagers' lives begins to reveal the opportunities and constraints shaping their existence. The home looms most prominently, offering both interaction with the adults responsible for one's life, and a solitary refuge. Second is the school, a regimented engine of formal training, paradoxically inhabited by thousands of relatively unsocialized peers whose influence might conflict with that of the institution. And finally, there is the multifaceted context of the public sphere, offering examples of adult behavior as well as opportunities for spontaneous, unsupervised activities. Adolescent experience is split. Much of their life space appears to be dominated by adult values; at the same time, there are numerous locations where the influence of peer values is predominant, or where a person can find a measure of freedom from all "others."

Activities

This basic split becomes even clearer when one considers the activities in which teenagers spend their time. While place delimits actions—it is difficult to have a beer party in a classroom—what one is doing defines the focus of one's thoughts more precisely. For example, a boy in his bedroom might be doing homework or listening to a tape recording of "Kiss." Which one it is makes a substantial difference to the kind of self he is cultivating.

The issue is how much of their psychic energy adolescents invest in educational activities, and how much in leisure activities. The mix is crucial for the kind of adults they will become; habits learned in adolescence are difficult to break. In some contemporary cultures adolescence is seen as a period of constant preparation for adult roles, where every ounce of energy must be spent in training for work or study. The "examination hell" of Japanese high school graduation casts a long shadow over the preceding six years of life, and this sense of externally imposed competition limits the activities of teenagers in most technological societies. How do ours spend their time?

Figure 4.2 shows what activities were reported in response to the 2,700 random signals. Twenty-nine percent concern what might be classified as productive activities, primarily ones related to school work. An additional 31 percent concern various maintenance activities, activities that are needed to keep the body functioning in an acceptable way—such as eating, resting, bathing, and dressing. The rest of the times, teenagers were engaged in other activities, such as talk, sport, and reading, which can be classified as leisure.

Strictly productive activities take up relatively little time. Actual schooling, that is, classwork or studying, occupies only one quarter of the waking hours, and this for only nine months of the year. Time spent studying is literally an investment, the fruits of which will be reaped later in life. But it is interesting to note that, according to the testimony of our respondents, of the 20 or so hours a week in classrooms, only 4 are actually spent listening to teachers (Mayers 1978). A greater proportion, 5 hours per week, is spent listening to other students in class or in discussion groups. Thus, direct adult socialization is relatively rare even in the classroom. By far the largest type of academic activity is individual study, which takes up 13 percent of total waking

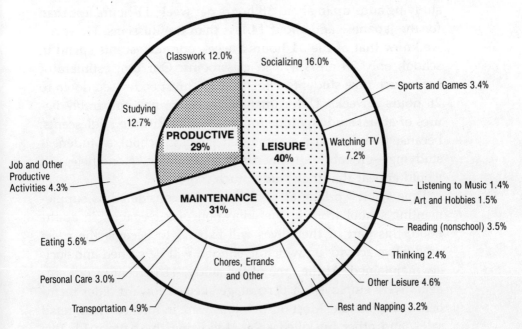

FIGURE 4.2
What Adolescents Spend Their Time Doing

time. The smallest, but perhaps the part with the greatest impact, is the two hours a week spent taking tests; these are the occasions on which teenagers are evaluated to see whether they have learned to structure their psychic energy according to the patterns adults consider necessary.

The time our teenagers spend studying is substantially less than what is common in some other technologically advanced societies. Japanese students, for instance, spend about 59 hours a week in school or studying (Japanese Finance Ministry 1980). In Soviet Russia the figures are 50 hours for boys, 53 hours for girls (Zuzanek 1980, p. 370). It should also be noted that the school year is much longer in these countries than in the United States. The Japanese school year is 243 days, while in the United States it is generally 174 (Stigler, Lee, Lucker, and Stevenson 1982.) Thus Japanese children spend 69 more days in school each year in addition to spending more hours studying each day when school is in session. In our sample, school and home studying adds up to about 38 hours per week, 11 hours less than for the Japanese and about 14 less than the Russians. However, we know that of the 31 hours a week our adolescents spend in school, only 20 are spent in classrooms. Our best estimate of how much time students actually study must be revised down to 26 hours a week.[1] Unfortunately, there are no comparable figures of actual studying time for Japanese or Russian adolescents, because their statistics assume that when in school, a student is studying—probably an inaccurate assumption. Nonetheless, it would appear that they study much more.

Time spent working at a job might be considered as supplementing school work in the education of a teenager. In adulthood, this part of their lives will expand to become the main productive activity by which livelihood will be earned and society maintained. At the time of the study, 41 percent of our students were employed, a percentage skewed toward older members of the sample. Most of their jobs were in food services, retail sales, and other unskilled areas, following the pattern for this age group (Greenberger and Steinberg 1981). They reported spending between 5 and 33 hours per week at their jobs, for an average of about 18 hours a week (or 7.4 hours when computed over all students). These figures correspond closely to national figures.[2]

Compared to other industrialized societies, however, this is quite a heavy time investment. The average high school student in Japan works much less: only 1.75 hours a week (Japanese Finance Ministry 1980). And work as an activity category does not even appear in Russian students' time budget. Thus, the little time American adolescents spend studying is at least partly compensated by direct experiences in adult roles.

1. In a recent pilot study using the ESM with comparable high school students in Milan, Professor Fausto Massimini and Paolo Inghilleri found that Italian students spend 27.5 hours a week actively engaged in study, a proportion almost exactly like the one reported here.

2. For instance, Greenberger, et al. (1980) found that 36 percent of Orange County, California tenth and eleventh graders were holding jobs, and that the average employed adolescent reported working between 20 and 24 hours per week, or about 7.9 hours per high school student.

The External Landscape

If we consider school work and employment as a whole, the total percentage of time teenagers spend on them is equivalent to the amount of working time reported by our sample of 107 adult workers. School, study, part-time and voluntary work combined add up to the amount of time average adults spend working. The sum total, however, still does not match the amount of time Japanese and Russian youth devote to formal socialization.

This finding raises questions about how well our youth will compete as adults with their counterparts in other parts of the world. Are young people investing enough psychic energy in the complex patterns required to become productive adults in an increasingly technological environment? To deal with this question we need to take into account what they are doing with the other parts of their lives.

The second broad type of activity teenagers pursue consists of daily maintenance tasks. These include perhaps the most realistic necessities of life, the kind of things we all have to do simply to keep going, to take care of the basic survival requirements as defined by needs and by the culture. The habits teenagers develop in this area of their lives often create conflicts with their parents, and give shape to what their future will be like. How important food, rest, or personal appearance are going to be later depends on how much psychic energy is invested in them during these years.

On the average, our teenagers reported 6 hours a week eating, and 3 hours resting; these tasks are needed to restore the body's energy level. Five hours a week were spent walking and driving—moving the body from one place to another by foot, car, bicycle, train, and even skateboard. Another 16 hours were reported in various other practical activities, from helping around the house to shopping and straightening things out. This included brief practical activities done for oneself, like "unlocking my locker," as well as extended projects done as a contribution to the household economy, like cleaning the bathroom or mowing the lawn. Other research has established that most American teenagers *do* do some household chores (White and Brinkerhoff 1981). Finally, about a half hour each day was spent on personal appearance: grooming, dressing, bathing, and primping in the mirror.

On the whole, very close to one third of the teenager's life is devoted to tasks of maintenance, somewhat less than our data suggest they will devote as adults, when they will have children to care for (Csikszentmihalyi and Graef 1980). In this category, our students are very much like the Russians, who also spend about 50 minutes a day eating and half an hour a day on personal care (Zuzanek 1980, p. 370). It might seem that these figures should be the same everywhere, because the activities they refer to are dictated by biological needs. But even in this area culture does make a difference. Japanese students spend considerably more time on bodily needs: 1.5 hours a day eating and a full hour grooming, twice the time allocated by the two western samples (Japanese Finance Ministry 1980, p. 10). No doubt Japanese mothers have fewer concerns about their teenage children properly digesting their food or looking neat.

Of course, these activities differ considerably from each other. For instance, eating is not just a physiological necessity—an annoying but obligatory refueling stop; for most people it is a pleasurable experience in its own right, and an occasion for relaxing social interaction. Presumably, this is especially true for the Japanese. Housework, on the other hand, is generally seen as a necessary evil without redeeming intrinsic features. Despite such differences, maintenance activities socialize adolescents into coping with basic survival necessities. Some of these are relatively unproblematic: No teenager needs to be taught to eat or to walk from place to place (although they might differ from their elders in terms of when and how to eat or walk). Other tasks, such as housework or grooming, provide classic occasions of conflict between parents and children; typically, the latter cannot understand why it is such a big deal to take the garbage out every day or to have a neat haircut. Part of their socialization consists in learning to feel internal discomfort at the sight of what the culture defines as disorder, and in learning to invest energy to maintain their physical environment in harmony with social expectations.

The largest proportion of time, 42 hours per week, is spent in the third category of activities, those we have labeled leisure. This includes times in school when students are not studying. Thus, adolescents spend almost half of their waking time in self-chosen activities, where they can allocate their psychic energy in goals that are not determined either by survival necessities or by future productive aims. Almost half of their time is relatively "free." This is far more than diary studies have shown for other technologically developed countries. In East Germany, for example, the leisure time of tenth grade boys is estimated at about only 26 hours a week (Micksch 1972). In the Soviet Union, high school students' free time is identical—26 hours a week (Zuzanek 1980, p. 370). In Japan, the leisure time of students is estimated at about 28 hours (Japanese Finance Ministry 1980). Of course, diaries are very rough measures compared to the ESM, and they almost certainly underestimate the amount of time that is actually free. Nevertheless, our adolescents clearly dispose of more leisure than their counterparts in other developed countries.

Within leisure, the largest single activity is socializing, which takes up one sixth of waking time. If one includes the times when talking was secondary to activities like studying, watching TV, eating, and so on, one finds that teenagers spend one third of their day conversing with others, by far the single most prevalent activity in their lives. (The students named talk as a secondary activity for 17.6 percent of the self-reports.) Of course, talk is a very broad label; it can mean a great variety of things, from the earnest intimacies of lovers, to rambling chitchat about last night's game, to the planning of a drug sale. Three times as much of it occurs with friends as with parents or other adults; 13 percent occurs by phone. These teenagers report much more time talking than the adults we studied, or than Japanese, West German, or Soviet youth. What is significant about this large volume of time is that it is spent in direct communication with others, involving the exchange of ideas, impressions, and feelings as well as conveyance of values, standards, and norms. It is "socializing" in both senses of the term

After talking, the next largest leisure pursuit is watching television, an activity diametrically opposite in that it involves no reciprocal exchange. About 1 hour per day is spent viewing TV as a main activity; approximately 1.5 hours per day is added when TV is secondary. For this amount of time, adolescents absorb the packaged, storybook version of the world the media has prepared for them. In most cases the students did not indicate what they were watching, suggesting a lack of commitment; the shows they did mention read like then current Nielsen ratings for 1977: Johnny Carson, The Fonz, Carol Burnett, and the news. The adults we studied reported almost the same amount of TV watching, as if there were a prescribed amount of time in our society that people are supposed to be plugged into the world TV presents. It is interesting to note that in Japan and the U.S.S.R., as well as in our sample, high school students spend about the same amount of time—about 2 hours a day—involved in the mass media (TV, radio, newspaper, magazines, movies).

About 1.25 hours each day is spent in more active, more structured leisure. Sports and games, arts and hobbies, reading, and listening to music together account for 9.8 percent of teenagers' time. While they are voluntarily chosen, they represent culturally defined, almost classical leisure pursuits. The first, sports and games, can be divided into that which is adult-organized, mostly for school teams, and that which is spontaneous and informal. This study having been performed in the spring, baseball, softball, and track are most commonly mentioned, but bicycling, basketball, and swimming are also well represented. Boys report more participation in sports; girls report more participation in the next category, art and hobbies, in which dance, playing musical instruments, and singing are most frequently mentioned. These activities are similar to sports in requiring participation in a predetermined system of rules, but they differ in their orientation toward open, self-defined goals rather than narrow, competitive goals. Certainly, both may produce learning as a result of intrinsically motivated actions taking place within a frame of preexisting constraints.

The portion of time spent reading for leisure (3.5 percent)

mainly involves the reading of magazines and newspapers. Contemporary books are mentioned (*God Bless You, Mr. Rosewater* and *The Electric Kool-Aid Acid Test*), but most of the reported reading seems to involve brief encounters with the comics, Ann Landers, or news stories.

Listening to music, like reading and watching TV, involves passive exposure to a prepackaged experience. However, most music is "packaged" by young people rather than middle-aged adults, thus making it less of a socializing medium for grown-up roles (Larson and Kubey 1983). The students mentioned listening to groups with names like "The Grateful Dead" and "The Deevolution Band," groups whose songs were often at odds with adult culture. For instance, one popular teenage song had the refrain: "We don't need no education, we don't need no mind control." It is amusing that Confucius saw music as the most difficult and advanced of art forms, capable of being appreciated only in old age. Along with sports, listening to music was far more common for adolescents than for our sample of adults. Music is now considered to be part of teenage metabolism, although its role in socializing—or unsocializing—adolescents is a common matter of debate. In this respect, our adolescents are very different from their U.S.S.R. or East German counterparts, who are rarely exposed to subversive messages in the media.

What remains under the heading of leisure might primarily be thought of as "idling," involving no predefined structure and little physical activity. From these responses we separated out the instances in which activity was specifically identified as "thinking" or thinking about something, occasions when directed cognition was indicated. Much of what falls into the other leisure category is more passive and undirected, such as staring, fiddling, "just sitting," and doing nothing. A small number of occasions, twenty, when our subjects were spectators at a sporting or cultural event, also has been included here, but in general these two categories of activity might be thought of as time between other things. We have found this to represent a substantial portion of time, both for adolescents and adults.

Attempting to place this great volume of leisure into perspective, sociologists have often noted that adolescence is a relatively empty part of the life-span in terms of social demands. An adolescent is not likely to be spouse, parent, breadwinner, or civic leader. This lack of demands explains why students have about 10 percent more time in leisure than adults, a portion of time the adults spend in child care and additional household tasks. In this sense, adolescents are indulged. One prominent sociologist has suggested that our culture defines the role of the adolescent as having fun (Parsons 1942). While there are other societies that give even greater liberties to the young—Winnebago boys were apparently relieved of many responsibilities so that they could stay up at night courting girls (Radin 1920)—free time is certainly not a universal luxury of this age period. Even within Western society, such freedom was not common one hundred years ago for those youth who worked in the fields or in the factories.

If there is a rationale in our society for adolescents' surfeit of leisure time, it is that social interaction and play provide preparation for a richer adulthood. Such an argument, however, rests on suppositions about the nature and quality of that social exchange—and with whom it is done. The final contextual variable of adolescent experience, and perhaps the most important one, is with whom adolescents spend their time. It is other people who socialize us by the support and feedback they provide. As George Herbert Mead (1934) pointed out, it is by relating to others, either concretely or in imagination, that we develop the attentional patterns we call the "self."

Companions

Teenagers spend much of their time in locations supervised or structured by adults, but they spend relatively less time actually involved in adult-oriented activities. When we know whom teens spend their time with, the reason becomes apparent.

Adults as a whole invest very little time in being with young people. While our society is supposed to place a great emphasis on education, adults actually put relatively little of their energies into it.

The self-reports indicate that students seldom are in the company of adults (see Figure 4.3). One fifth of their waking hours is with the family and only a portion of this is with parents; other adults add only an additional two percent to this total. One fourth of the day is passed in solitude, theoretically outside the reach of socializing influences—except as these are mediated by the books read, the records listened to, or the memories reflected upon. A full half of the week's waking hours are spent with peers—partly in the classroom and partly with friends outside of class.

In terms of sheer amount of time, peers are by far the greatest presence in an adolescent's life. It is with them that a boy or girl

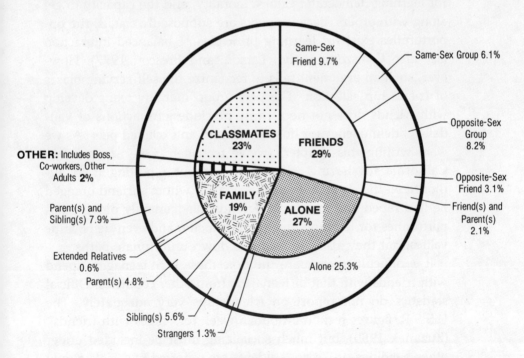

FIGURE 4.3
Whom Adolescents Spend Their Time With

spends the most time: talking, joking, experimenting, getting feedback on who he or she is. The time with peers clearly has to be separated from time "with friends": classmates are assigned (usually by computer); friends are chosen. These peers are more likely to be competitors than companions; the feedback they provide is likely to be less supportive.

Time with friends, in comparison, involves purely voluntary associations and activities that are chosen rather than imposed. In contrast to classmates and family members, friends can be freely chosen by teenagers, hence we can expect teenagers to gravitate around people who reinforce the self they wish to be (Kandel 1978). In this sense it is bias feedback—whether a hippie, a greaser, or an intellectual, a person is likely to choose friends who say what he or she wants to hear. Recently, James Youniss (1980), basing his work on the ideas of Sullivan and Piaget, has argued that peers are better than adult companions for learning democratic values, morality, and the capacity to get along with others. Because peers are supposedly equals, the opportunities exist for learning principles of balanced interaction (see also Csikszentmihalyi, Larson, and Prescott 1977). However, such an argument fails to recognize the self-serving biases of friendship selection. The peer-group morality teens develop with friends does not necessarily preclude joint actions of vandalism, delinquency, or hostility toward an excluded peer. As we were writing this chapter, twelve teenagers were arraigned in California for having witnessed—without reporting it to authorities—the mutilated remains of a girl whom a friend bragged he had raped and murdered. Friends may certainly provide opportunities for learning loyalty, reciprocity, and even democratic values, but they also can lead one down unfortunate paths.

It is difficult to compare the time these U.S. teenagers spend with friends with that of teenagers from other countries. Official statistics do not report on friendships very adequately. The U.S.S.R. figures reckon 2 hours a week for "hikes with friends" (Zuzanek 1980), but much socializing must be included under other headings. In Japan, students are reported to socialize only for about 2.5 hours per week (Japanese Finance Ministry 1980,

72

p. 11). Figures for our teenagers show about 20 hours per week of socializing. Perhaps much of this discrepancy is due to different ways of measuring "socializing," but even so it is unquestionable that our teenagers spend more time in each other's company than is the case in other modern societies.

In all societies since the beginning of time, adolescents have learned to become adults by observing, imitating, and interacting with grown-ups around them. The self is shaped and honed by feedback from men and women who already know who they are, and can help the young person find out who he or she is going to be. It is therefore startling how little time these teenagers spend in the company of adults. In the sample of 2,700 reports, they indicated only five times that they were alone with teachers, five times with a boss, fifteen times with grandparents or aunts, and nineteen times with other adults. The total adds up to only 1.6 percent of their time, a portion not evenly distributed across individuals. Time with parents was, of course, more frequent, but in a follow-up study in which we asked separately about each parent, among 1,000 self-reports only ten times did teenagers report being alone with their fathers, and five of these occasions involved watching TV. In other words, one might expect the average adolescent to spend one-half hour each week, or 5 minutes a day, interacting exclusively with their fathers. "My dad would work twenty-four hours a day if he had the energy," said one boy. One wonders how much actual communication occurs in such brief snatches of time. Occasions alone with their mothers were about four times more frequent, and several teens described having regular long conversations with them about friends, feelings, almost anything. Mothers seemed more receptive to sharing experiences. The total time spent exclusively with a parent or parents is about 5 percent (Figure 4.3). For an additional 7.9 percent they are with parents and siblings together.

Contact with teachers occurs almost exclusively in the impersonal class format, where the teenager is part of a large group facing the single adult. Except in special education classes, a student competes with dozens of others for a teacher's attention.

Almost never did these students report talking personally to a teacher (0.2 of the self-reports); their only contact with them was as authority figures. The school had many excellent faculty members. Some were dearly loved by their students; nonetheless many were perceived negatively by students, as in the following acrid description provided by one fellow:

> She's a real pain in the ass, to put it mildly. She's the kind of person who's gone through menopause three times by now and shows it. She's not mean, she just doesn't really grasp the feelings of her students. She's more or less aloof from the whole class; it's hard to talk to her on a one-on-one basis.

When students did develop rapport with a teacher, it was usually defeated the next year when new class assignments were made.

It was surprising to find from the interviews that more than one half (56 percent) of the students reported having at least one friend over the age of twenty, but the self-reports showed that they spent relatively little time with them. Youniss argues that adults are ill-suited as companions because they are unequals; but the posture of inequality is certainly more attributable to the adults than it is to the teenagers. It is clear that the potential for cross-age friendships does exist; in fact, in most other societies teenagers have much more contact with elders, working side by side in the fields or in apprentice relationships. Not only work but forms of leisure are typically designed to integrate the young with the old. In our society, however, the structure of daily life is characterized by "age segregation" (Whiting and Whiting 1975; Bronfenbrenner 1979), which makes the integration of attention across age boundaries more problematic.

In our society the most frequent alternative to interacting with friends and family is to spend time alone, an alternative not admissible in many cultures (Malik 1981). These adolescents reported spending a remarkable 25.6 percent of their time by themselves. Solitude occurred primarily at home and quite often in the privacy of a bedroom. A common response to the pager was: "In my bedroom alone, lying on my bed, listening to music." Studying, watching TV, doing chores were other activities that commonly filled this part of their lives. One girl reported several occasions when she escaped to the attic to play her guitar; another mentioned dancing around the house when her parents were out; and the boy described earlier smoked bongs of hashish alone in his room. But the great majority of times alone were low key.

This unstructured time, devoid of direct feedback from others, might be seen as a wild card: It can be used constructively or wasted in idleness. On the one hand, we have found solitude to be a frequent state of students and scholars, a useful aid to thought and to work; on the other hand, we have found it common among persons with psychological problems of adjustment—for example, persons with eating disorders, who fill it with food obsession (Johnson and Larson 1982). That such an alternative fills one quarter of teenagers' time is consonant with the value placed on individualism in our society. We will discuss its special opportunities and constraints more fully in Chapter 9.

In sum, the social world of teenagers is divided, like their spatial environment, into three distinct contexts: an "unstructured" sphere in which each teenager experiences life alone; a "structured" sphere in which the goals of family and school make demands on their attention; and a sphere in which what will happen depends on constant negotiation with friends. As we shall see later, this third context of socialization is the one which adolescents experience as the most negentropic, the one in which they feel most happy, alert, and intrinsically motivated. But this is also the context that parents and teachers distrust and fear, because it competes with adult socializing experiences for the teenagers' attention. Adults are afraid that the lives of their sons and daughters will be shaped by the spontaneous goals of youth and fed by affirmative feedback, while at the same time these same sons and daughters will resist being shaped by the goals around which adult life in our culture is built. The paradox is that adults themselves are prepared to invest relatively little of their own time, attention, and wisdom to provide the bridge. Except by parents' manipulation through external rewards and punishments, teenagers are more or less left on their own to choose among the directions available to them.

The Rhythm of the Week

Free time and external obligations do not alternate haphazardly in the lives of teenagers. They fit together into a weekly cycle of activities and social relationships. Phenomenologically, the week breaks up into a more "structured" segment that runs from Sunday evening to Friday afternoon, when school lets out for the weekend; and a less structured period running from Friday evening to Sunday afternoon. Each weekday is further divided into approximately equal halves, a more structured period from nine to about three, and a relatively freer period of roughly the same length afterward.

Whom adolescents are with across the hours of the day shows this cycle most clearly. Interactions with friends occur across all hours of the day for all days of the week, but it is Friday and Saturday nights when they are most prevalent (see Figure 4.4). Solitude occurs in between, at times not taken by schoolwork, meals, or occasions out with friends.

Another pattern is shown by the daily and weekly change in the proportion of productive, maintenance, and leisure activities (Appendix D.1). In accordance with the modern separation of work and leisure (Dumazedier 1974; Csikszentmihalyi 1981), these parts of an adolescent's life are segregated, with productive work being first both in importance and time. Adult requirements fill the first part of the day; personally chosen activities come only afterward. Adolescents are most likely to be involved in productive activities around midmorning on weekdays (although, even at that time, the probability that they are is only 60 percent), least likely around midevening on weekends. Maintenance activities are most frequent on weekend mornings, while leisure reigns past 4:00 P.M., especially on weekends.

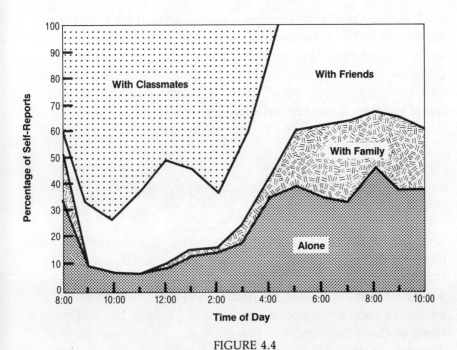

FIGURE 4.4

Shifts in Companionship across the Weekday*

*The 2 percent of time teenagers reported being with "other companions" is not included in this Figure.

The transition between structured time and free time is often enacted with drastic rites of liberation, particularly on Friday afternoon. Outside the school, souped-up cars begin to congregate as the last period of class is underway. Teachers report that less work gets done in this last hour, because kids' minds are already elsewhere. When the bell rings, hall monitors have their hands full maintaining order, keeping people from running, yelling, or lighting up cigarettes inside the school. Some students head off to public parks or someone's basement to start drinking beer or smoking reefers; shortly thereafter, they will be on the phones, trying to find out where the party is tonight, whose parents are out of town, and how to get more beer or dope. Other students will walk casually home from school with friends, perhaps a new beau; some will head for dance class, scouts, or a job; and some will seek privacy and solitude to discharge the tensions and pressures of the week.

Thus, the experience of adolescents is divided into phases of structured and unstructured social relationships alternating on a daily and weekly rhythm. This pattern is, of course, superimposed on a broader yearly cycle that includes a summer vacation and various holidays, which may be used for leisure or additional structured, productive activities.

Differences Among Adolescents in the Use of Time

Thus far we have talked about the patterns of adolescent life as if all teenagers did exactly the same things in all respects. In reality some spend more time than others in structured environments, in adult-oriented activities, and in interactions with adults. In turn some spend less than the norm. We will look closer at these differences in Part III of the book. Here we shall consider whether these are systematic differences across demographic subgroups. The question we asked was, to what extent do various kinds of teenagers (differentiated by age, sex, and social class) differ from each other in the way they structure their lives?

The answer to that question is that their lives follow astonishingly similar patterns. There are very few differences due to these variables. As one would expect, age is related to most of the significant differences. Separation from one's family and increasing involvement with peers is dramatically documented by the reports of our respondents. High-school freshmen reported 25 percent of their time with their families; seniors only 15 percent. Part of the reason was that, with age, parents granted them more liberties: curfew hours were moved back, expectations that they be with the family for meals were relaxed. Another reason was that sometimes families had shrunk due to older siblings leaving or parental separation: "Everyone's gone, I don't really have a family these days," said one senior in this situation. There were also cases of open conflict with parents that had been hidden at earlier ages, as in the following description from a senior boy:

The External Landscape

I don't hate them. I love my family. It's just that I don't like 'em. In the long run I love 'em all, but I can't tolerate being with them, except for my sister whom I haven't seen in two years.

We're spending less and less time together, mainly because I don't want to. I can understand how they feel, all of a sudden their kid doesn't want to spend time with them—but we're at each other's throats, especially me and my mom. We're both very stubborn people and we never give in, *ever!*

With the decline in family time at home, there is an increase in time with friends in public. Freshmen spend 18 percent of the time in public, seniors 30 percent. Amount of time with friends, especially talking with them, increased from each high-school year to the next, for an overall change of about 10 percentage points, equivalent to 10 hours per week. Our data are, of course, cross-sectional rather than longitudinal; nevertheless they confirm the findings of others (Douvan and Adelson 1966; Dunphey 1963). Typically, juniors and seniors describe much greater sophistication and differentiation in their friendships. Often they'll relate how they have disassociated themselves from some crowd that "wasn't me," and now have closer friends, including perhaps a boy or girlfriend, who more directly reflect the life they want to lead. There might be a church group they appreciate for serious conversation, a clique they hang around with for "good times," and a couple of intimate friends for sharing personal feelings.

What is perhaps most notable is that these are the *only* changes. Freshmen do not differ significantly from seniors in how much they study, work, rest, or watch TV; how much time they spend alone, and so forth. The only age differences relate to the increasing amounts of time spent away from home and family, in the company of friends in public places.

Boys differ from girls on even fewer points. Whatever difference there might be between the sexes at this age in terms of feeling or thinking, they are not reflected in how boys and girls spend their time, where, and with whom. The largest difference is in the amount of time spent on sports and games: For boys this is almost 6 hours a week, for girls it is half that time. In contrast, girls spend about 3 percent of their time making art or music, boys a little more than half of that. Clearly, the boys are learning to structure their psychic energy in traditionally physical and competitive patterns, while girls are investing theirs in aesthetic goals more compatible with traditional feminine roles. Girls also spend, on the average, 2.5 hours more than boys each week talking to adults (primarily their parents); thus they are presumably more exposed to adult socializing influences. It is interesting to note that girls do not spend significantly more time with adults than boys; contrary to young women of previous generations, who were more restricted in their movement, they are just as often found outside the home. But when they are in the company of adults, they still interact more with them than boys do.

In other countries, sex differences almost certainly would have been more pronounced. In East Germany, for example, female high-school students spend over twice as many hours doing household chores as male students, and spend significantly fewer hours in leisure (Micksch 1972). In Japan, girl students work *ten times* as much on household chores as boys—the former spend 3 hours a week on the average, the latter only 20 minutes (Japanese Finance Ministry 1980, p.10). Such sex-role-related differences, which are even larger in more traditional societies, are almost entirely absent here.

The teenagers in our sample were not extremely different in terms of social class; perhaps due to this fact, only one variable differentiated between the pattern of the two classes. Students from the upper-middle-class part of town spent an average of 3.5 hours per week making art and music, those in the lower-middle-class part spent only 1.7 hours. Combining this finding with the sex difference noted above, it appears that involvement in the arts is a prerogative of higher-status girls, and it is negligible among boys of the lower-middle class. But otherwise, class differences had no impact on the time allocation of teenagers, despite what one would have expected from the literature that stresses the importance of social class on adolescent experience (for example, Havighurst 1976; Hollingshead 1949).

The obvious characteristics that should have affected how adolescents spend their lives—age, sex, and class—turn out to have little impact. The general constraints of the culture end up structuring the allocation of psychic energy in similar ways, and individual differences within each group cancel out whatever trends might be due to these general characteristics. The main findings are what one would expect: Boys are more involved with sports, girls, with art and music, and upper-status students are more involved with aesthetic pursuits. Perhaps the most significant finding is that with age, teenagers spend more time outside the influence of adults: They spend more time in public and with their friends. Aside from these contrasts the lives of different groups of teenagers unfold in relatively similar patterns.

Freedom versus Structure

What have we learned about adolescents' experience? We have seen that the external framework of teenagers' lives can be mapped out in terms of three related coordinates: where a teenager spends time, doing what, and with whom. Appendix D.2 shows how these three overlap with each other, and demonstrates the diversity of young people's experience.

Each of the three coordinates separates time use by the degree to which it is structured by society versus the degree controlled by adolescents themselves. (In Appendix D.2 this axis is represented by the hatched cells). At one extreme are contexts that attempt to socialize teens formally into productive adult roles, to shape their attention in accord with the complex demands of adult life. At the other extreme are contexts in which adolescents use time as they wish; these permit self-directed personal growth, but also mere wasting of time, and, in some cases, the development of antisocial patterns.

It would be fascinating to know what teenagers from different cultures or periods of history would have said if they had been paged every two hours. How different were the lives of the leisurely Samoan adolescents Margaret Mead described (1928), or the endless days endured by working-class teenagers during the industrial revolution? In the Samoan case we would likely have found that girls spent much of their time confined to home, babysitting and performing household chores, while the boys wandered freely, fishing, swimming, and hunting in groups. In the latter case, we would have found most of the teenagers' waking hours taken up by factory work, with little time for interaction with peers, formal education, or leisure pursuits.

The life space of contemporary American adolescents is more heterogeneous. Our students report a greater variety of settings and activities than one might expect in the lives of young Samoans or nineteenth-century teenager laborers. But how does this variety—this balance of home and school, work and leisure, solitary pursuits and social intercourse—shape experience and how does it prepare adolescents for the lives they will lead as adults? According to Mead, Samoan adolescence prepared teens well for life within the leisurely, traditional culture, but left them unprepared for the coming onslaught of Western culture. Adolescence in a factory prepared youth for not much more than a bitter adulthood in a factory. The demands of modern society are broader and more complex than for any prior group of young people who have entered it. Survival as an adult in American society requires the capacity to function effectively in many different settings; being able to contribute to society requires an even greater mastery. Does the experience of adolescents provide the background to thrive in such a world?

If we are to judge by our data, these teenagers have a great deal of leisure. Relative to what they will face later in life, and compared to what youth in other technological societies report, their low participation in school work and their abundant leisure is a great indulgence. But, emphasizing only the quantity of their leisure ignores the quality of what teenagers might actually be experiencing in each context. How does each event or activity impact adolescents' consciousness? Does it inspire or enervate, does it help the person's evolving membership in the human race? Or does it degrade it? If time in classroom is spent in alienated worry and boredom, then the Soviet or Japanese may be at a great disadvantage. If it is with friends and alone that teenagers concentrate most and feel most alive, then these may be contexts of decisive developmental importance, and American youth may have the advantage. We need to know what adolescents typically experience in each of these contexts.

Chapter 5

The Internal Landscape: What the Teenagers' World Feels Like

Where teenagers spend time, doing what, and with whom provides a first approximation of what their lives are like. This knowledge gives a surface account of where and how the attention of adolescents is invested. But to get a meaningful picture of their lives one also needs to know how they actually experience events. As they pass between school and home, between work and leisure, between friends and family members, when do they feel a part of what they are doing, and when are they unwilling participants?

The term psychic entropy describes times when things are not going well, when a person feels lonely or tired, when an activity seems less than intriguing, or when concentration just is not there. How prevalent is psychic entropy in adolescents' experience? Is it more frequent at this stage of life than it is in adulthood? Is it more common for boys than for girls, for lower- than for upper-middle-class youth? The basic question is whether the life adolescents lead—the life society structures for them—provides opportunities for them to become alive.

To grow up one must experience negentropy—the opposite of entropy—in at least some aspect of existence. Unless teenagers get first-hand evidence that there is order and enjoyment in life, they become cynical and disillusioned, ready to catch at fleeting pleasures without concern for their own long-term well being, or that of anyone else. This sense of spontaneous involvement may come in mastering mathematics, in athletic achievement, or in being a successful lover. If adolescents experience it in school we can have confidence that they will develop to be adults who are motivated to contribute to society. But if they show enthusiasm only in antics with friends or in socially disruptive activities, then we must be much more concerned about the people they will turn out to be.

This chapter will examine when entropy and negentropy occur in adolescents' lives. In which of the contexts discussed in the previous chapter do teenagers feel dispirited, and in which do they feel alive? We will look most closely at intrinsic motivation as perhaps the best single indicator of harmony in teenagers' consciousness. Our measure of this dimension is the students' rating of how much they "wish" to be in their current activity. In other words, how much are they doing something because they have to, versus because they are truly invested in it? In addition, we will also consider the students' reported emotional states and cognitive efficiency. How regularly do they experience positive affect, feel activated, and concentrate on what they are doing?

The first thing we will do is compare adolescents with adults in terms of motivation, and then contrast different groups of teenagers with each other. Then we shall turn to the main task of the chapter, which is to evaluate the experience teenagers reported within the specific contexts of their lives.

How Do Adolescent and Adult Experience Compare?

Unfortunately, we do not have experiential reports from the Japanese and Soviet youth discussed in the previous chapter. It would be most valuable to know their levels of motivation, happiness, and concentration in daily life in order to compare them to American teenagers.[1] We can, however, compare our adolescents to the adults we have studied (see footnote 2, chapter 3). Do the students experience their lives as more entropic or negentropic than the average adult? We will look first at motivation, then at moods, activation, and concentration.

In response to the question, "Do you wish you had been doing something else?" our students gave the full range of answers. Twenty-five percent of the time they indicated a complete wish to be doing what they were doing, but for the rest of the time they reported various degrees of wishing to be doing something else. In other words, for only one-quarter of their lives was motivation wholly intrinsic. The adults, most of whom worked in rather ordinary secretarial or blue-collar jobs, reported complete intrinsic motivation 40 percent of the time, a substantially higher proportion than that of the students. The average adolescent had a mean score nearly a full-scale point lower than the average adult (Appendix D.3). Teenagers seem to experience less investment in their activities than this group of working-class adults. Day in, day out, they appear to be more alienated from what they are doing; their personal goals are not in harmony with their actual behavior.

The picture concerning emotional order is not as negative. In the great majority of instances, students indicate their moods to be favorable. On the affect scale, they report positive states in 71 percent of the cases. Furthermore, for 5.5 percent of the time they are as happy, cheerful, sociable, and friendly as the scale

1. Daniel Offer and colleagues have collected cross-national survey data which suggest that American youth are happier than youth in many other countries, including Australia, Ireland, and Israel (Offer, Ostrov, and Howard 1981).

86

allowed: an essentially "perfect" feeling state. These students don't lack happiness in their lives; there is an emotional richness to their experience. Similarly, on the activation scale, they report positive states about 60 percent of the time, including forty-three occasions (1.8 percent) when they are as fully active as the scale permitted. Thus, despite deficits in their motivation—a lack of harmony between goals—teens usually report emotional harmony. They might not be committed, but they are reasonably content.

Now, how do they compare to the adults? First, the adolescents' average responses to the affect items do not differ significantly from those of the adults (Appendix D.3). In fact, adolescents report more occasions when they feel themselves to be at the positive extreme than grownups (Larson, Csikszentmihalyi, and Graef 1980). On the activation items, however, their means are somewhat lower in spite of their youth. Surprisingly, they report being less strong, active, and alert than adults in the forty-to-sixty-five age range (Csikszentmihalyi, Graef, and Larson 1979). Similarly, they report levels of concentration that are significantly lower than those of adults. They appear to be less able or willing to mobilize their psychic energy. These data suggest that they attend to the world less often and see it less clearly, because unless a person can concentrate on what is around him, unless he can actively focus his attention upon things, he is but passive recipient of disordered information and stimuli.

To summarize, the largest difference between adolescents and adults is in their motivation. It is perhaps because they feel less free in choosing their goals that they show less activation and concentration. They do not use their mental capacities to the fullest because they are less involved in what they are doing. We should note also that the basic pattern of states holds across age, sex, and social class of adolescent groupings.[2] Girls are no happier than boys, upper-middle-class teens are no more motivated than those from less-advantaged backgrounds.

2. In a three-way multivariate analysis of variance with individual means for intrinsic motivation, affect, activation, and concentration as the dependent variables, none of these demographic variables showed a significant effect.

These findings suggest that adolescents are not living their lives as fully as they might be. Of course, the differences between adolescents and adults may reflect unavoidable developmental differences, but it is likely that they are due, at least in part, to the particular pressures at this age period. While adolescents may be afforded a great deal of leisure, they are also burdened with many choices and demands. They are novices in an extraordinarily complex society which provides few breaks for those who have not mastered its ways. True, they are as happy as adults, but at the same time they are alienated from what they are doing and less involved in it. Does this alienation affect their capacity to grow into adult roles?

Perhaps the important question is where adolescents experience these different states. There definitely *are* times when they feel motivated and active. The question is, how are these occasions distributed across their lives? Do at least some of their enjoyable experiences occur in conjunction with productive activities? This is the major topic we turn to now.

Intrinsic Motivation in Different Locations

The last chapter has shown that adolescents spend their time in three basic domains: home, school, and public. The greatest proportion of their waking hours (41 percent) is spent at home, with this time divided between the more public rooms of the house, where they are subject to parental influence, and retreat to the privacy of the bedroom. School is the second most frequent domain, with the majority of time here spent in the highly structured context of the classroom. The remainder (27 percent) is spent in various public locations, subject to varying degrees of adult supervision. If socialization were efficient, intrinsic motivation should be as high, or higher, in the environments structured by adults as in peer-dominated environments, because the former are the ones oriented to growth and development. However, this is not the case. In general, whenever teenagers are in an adult-oriented location like the classroom, the job, or a church, they report wishing to do something else. Adult-structured environments appear to conflict with the goals of teenagers, thereby introducing entropy in their motivational state.

The levels of intrinsic motivation reported from each location are charted in Figure 5.1. There are enormous differences between contexts (more than one standard deviation in some cases!) such as those between classes and jobs on the one side, and public parks on the other. Looking across the bottom and then the top of this chart, it is apparent that the lowest motivation occurs in those places which are most structured by adult society (class, job, school halls, school library, church) and the highest motivation occurs in those which are furthest from adult control (the student center, the lunchroom, the basement, parks, and friends' homes). The pattern looks almost conspiratorial, like what one might expect from members of an underground political group: They report acting willingly only outside the reach of the oppressive regime, when huddled in basements, out in the woods, or gathered in numbers with their fellow oppressed in the student center or lunchroom. Other times they may go along, but in their hearts they wish they were elsewhere. It is almost as if barbed wire were separating the two domains.

This kind of geographical representation of young people's lives (with hints of the same imagery) has been suggested by Kurt Lewin (1938, 1936), Roger Barker (1968) and by recent adherents of the environmental psychology movement (for example, Moos 1979). In various ways they have pictured the life space of children and teenagers in terms of a topography of experiential settings, each associated with specific constraints and opportunities. In Lewin's view of the world, adolescents have the status of marginal people because so many settings exclude them: They are not allowed to participate fully in adult settings; within the school and home they remain in the role of children, a position they often resent. One might conceive of adolescents' daily lives in terms of a color-coded map with bright and dark shadings indicating where they are likely to feel

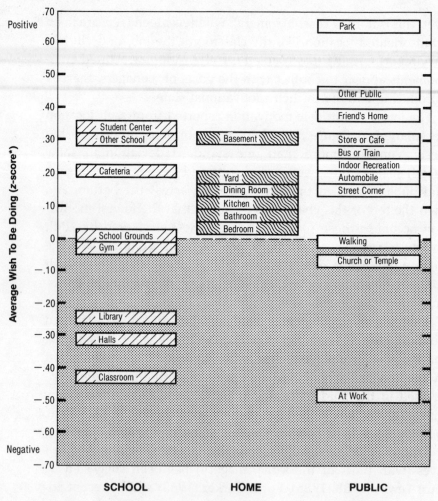

FIGURE 5.1

The Relationship of Intrinsic Motivation to Location

*A z score is a raw score which has been statistically transformed to make it comparable to other scores. All z scores have a mean of 0 (zero) and a standard deviation of 1.0 for each person. In this Figure and in the following ones, a difference of 0.15 is usually statistically significant. For example, when students are in the cafeteria, they are significantly more motivated than they are on the average; when they are in the library, they are significantly less motivated than on the average.

accepted and where they are not. Each location could be described in terms of the multifaceted terrain it presents: the challenges, excitement, affect, and other features associated with being in it (see Appendix D. 4).

In reality, a teenager's physical environment is actually one of the less important correlates of subjective state. Rather, it is what they are doing and whom they are with that most influences the nature of their experience.

Intrinsic Motivation in Different Activities

What one is doing establishes the frame and focus of attention. It defines goals, the appropriate actions, and the meaning of one's efforts. Therefore, teenagers' activities should make a great difference in terms of how they feel. What activities do they want to do most? Which ones are they least involved in? These are extremely important questions to answer. If adolescents experience growth-oriented activities as entropic, it means that their development into adulthood will involve conflict, and socialization will not be effective.

Figure 5.2 shows how the three basic activity categories are rated in terms of intrinsic motivation. When engaged in productive activities, teenagers usually report that they wish they were doing something else. When engaged in maintenance, teens experience positive motivation in two activities, while three other are associated with neutral and negative motivation. In leisure activities, as one might expect, teenagers report the most positive motivation, although here too there is a wide range.

The general pattern is for teens to be least motivated when doing things they have to do in order to become productive adults. One girl relates that she dislikes her job because the adults she works with are "full-timers"—they are "just living day by day." (Adults also report lower motivation at work, although it is nowhere near as low as that of the adolescents [Larson, Csikszentmihalyi, and Graef 1982].) This girl is also upset because the manager has been picking on her and seems to give advantages to males. The best times at work occur when the manager is away. Another girl who works at a fast food restaurant told of catsup fights and joking about customers when the boss's back is turned.

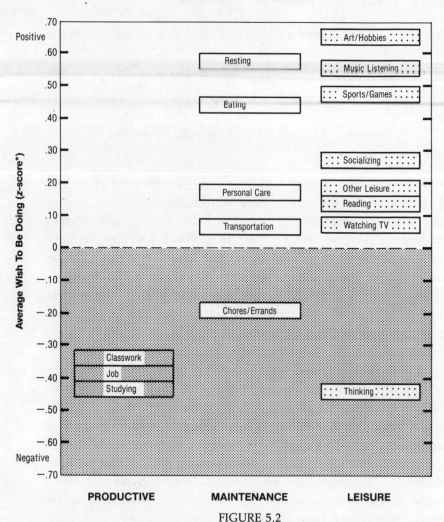

FIGURE 5.2

The Relationship of Intrinsic Motivation to Type of Activity

This lack of involvement in productive activities raises troublesome issues for those concerned with adolescent development. We will consider schoolwork in Chapter 10, but now let us look at the findings related to work at jobs.

Employment is often lauded as an opportunity for youth to develop their identity and firm up career objectives (Shore 1972; Coleman et al. 1974). Such praise rarely takes into account the fact that work available to teenagers is almost always menial and undertaken with little genuine commitment. Given the negative pattern of motivation we have found, it is noteworthy that employment among high school students has increased steadily since 1940 (Greenberger et al. 1980). While youth employment is not necessarily detrimental to sound development—Supreme Court Justice William O. Douglas worked at several jobs concurrently through high school and college to support his mother—there is increasing evidence of adverse effects: that it is damaging to school performance, teaches new forms of delinquency, and even undermines interest in future career development (Steinberg 1982; Greenberger and Steinberg 1981). "This job is strictly for morons," says a bright young girl, beeped as she is replenishing the shelves of the drugstore where she works. "Is this why I am studying French and calculus?" It is possible that teenagers are being socialized at an early age into a cynical, resigned acceptance of jobs that have no intrinsic rewards to offer. We shall present more data on their experience in the next section.

A few students have had the good fortune to experiment with work that gave them a sense of challenge and satisfaction. One boy became a skilled carpenter, helping out a neighbor, and another enjoyed preparing confections in a bakery. Traditional craft-type jobs seem more conducive to intrinsic motivation than the more modern clerical or service jobs that are usually open to teenagers.

The goals of maintenance activities tend to be more spontaneous than those of productive ones, hence it is not surprising that the students report greater intrinsic motivation when doing them. These activities split, depending on whether they involve body maintenance (eating and resting) or the everyday conduct of life (personal care, transportation, and chores). The former, which involve primary needs, are highly motivated. Rarely do students wish to be doing something else *less* than when they are sleeping and eating, although these activities are imposed on them by physiological necessity. Sleep was described as a very sweet activity, and the students were usually not too happy when the pager interrupted an afternoon nap. Eating was also praised by many students, who related love affairs with french fries, cream pies, and deep dish pizzas.

The other maintenance activities appear to be less spontaneously motivated. They involve social requirements of living, such as preparing food, driving a grandmother home, weeding the garden, or ironing one's shirt. These are activities done to meet cultural demands and support other activities; they fulfill important needs, but the students perceive them as less pertinent to themselves than activities they do in response to equally rigid physiological needs, like eating or resting. Teenagers were most outraged when they had to do things simply "for show," such as straightening out their rooms or cleaning the blinds. "What f_____g difference does it make if the tables are shiny?" a boy asked to oil the furniture grumbled. For most adults, order in the home is a very important sign of order in consciousness; but very few teenagers see it that way. For them, concern with externalities is a hypocritical evasion of what is really important—namely, their inner feelings.

Leisure activities almost always have voluntarily chosen goals. However, students do not invariably experience intrinsic motivation when engaged in leisure. For example, reading and TV watching are on a par with maintenance activities such as transportation and personal care—the students report no great investment in them. Our previous studies have suggested that people typically read or watch TV only when they have nothing better to do, as a way of avoiding the even more entropic condition of utter boredom (Csikszentmihalyi, Larson, and Prescott 1977; Csikszentmihalyi and Kubey 1981). The students repeatedly described TV as "stupid" or "phony." Neither TV watching nor reading are undertaken frequently as an activity teenagers really *want* to do.

"Thinking" is the most entropic leisure activity; in fact it may be wrong to call it leisure at all. Generally, teenagers resort to thinking only when something goes wrong. A boy lies in bed, talking to himself and "brooding" about his looks; a girl feels lonely and longs to be at her boyfriend's house; a boy wonders "How can I convince a friend that I am not an idiot." Many of these occasions involve anticipation of the future: "Thinking about what I was going to do this weekend"; "Thinking about school next year"; "Lying in my parents' bed, thinking about

94

being married to Alphie." For adolescents, thinking as a primary activity is usually a response to a problem that must be solved; as such, it is an occasion for psychic disorder. It is something you must do, but wish you did not have to. Therefore, thinking for teenagers is imposed from outside, and the teen must invest psychic energy in it under duress.

Let us now turn to the leisure activities in which adolescents genuinely feel motivated, the parts of their lives in which they come alive and feel invested in what they are doing. Understanding these will be crucial to comprehending where teenagers' lives are headed.

The most intrinsically rewarding leisure activities turn out to be ones that are highly structured activities in which teenagers can use their skills within an organized framework. Art, hobbies, and sports allow students to pursue definite goals that are freely chosen. Teenage music, like thinking, often deals with emotional problems. Yet, the sad lyrics refer to someone else's life, and listening to the song is a way of bringing order to one's goals through identification with people like oneself (Larson and Kubey 1983). It is striking that the three most intrinsically motivated activities are not free and spontaneous, but involve external rules and challenges. True, teenage art and music often involve rebellion against adult society; particularly, their music has been accused of being primitive or regressive. But even this rebellion represents a participation in a wider community and a public system of symbols. Art, music, and sports require going beyond the egocentric, impulsive activities of childhood; they demand discipline and engage adolescents in cultural systems, but unlike the activities imposed by school or job, they are undertaken willingly.

Thus, it is *not* primarily passive, hedonistic activities that are seizing adolescents' attention. Nowhere did the data indicate that sex, drugs, or random talk motivated these students most. Rather, it is things like sports, hobbies, and music that they really wish to do. These activities, *much less* common among adults, might have a particularly significant role in the experiential transition into adulthood, because they are the only ones that provide adolescents with challenges and with intrinsic rewards at the same time.

In sum, the general pattern confirms what was anticipated in the previous chapter. There *is* a cleavage in adolescents' lives between what they have to do and what they want to do. In activities specifically oriented toward adult socialization, they appear restless and uncommitted; their motivation is not in tune with what is required of them. However, it is not instinctual or libidinal activities that they wish to do most (except eating and resting). Rather, their favorites are "transitional" leisure activities that engage a person in a structured system of participation.

Additional Dimensions of Experience

Two more dimensions round out the portrait of each activity. The first, affect, combines the student's feelings of happiness, cheerfulness, sociability, and friendliness. The other, activation, combines their feelings of strength, excitement, activeness, and alertness. The objective is to achieve a more complete picture of the typical experience for each of the activities just considered. Will these two new dimensions tell us the same things we learned when looking at motivation—that activities structured by adults are entropic, and those chosen by adolescents are fun? Or will they show something different?

To bring together the different dimensions, we have included them into a three-dimensional graph, shown in Figure 5.3. Each activity is represented here by a bar. The height of the bar represents intrinsic motivation—the variable treated in the previous section and Figure 5.2. Therefore, we will focus mainly on the two dimensions that make up the base of the graph.

The first impression one gets is that these two new dimensions are strongly correlated. If an activity makes teenagers happy and cheerful, chances are it also makes them active and alert. The ultimate example of this is playing sports (up in the right-hand

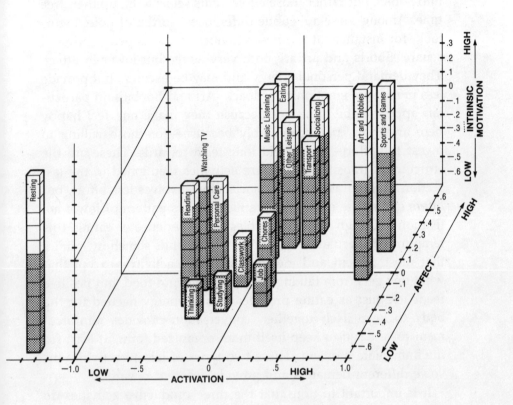

FIGURE 5.3
The Subjective Landscape of Adolescents' Activities
Figure is based on data found in Appendix D.4.

corner), which is rated equally high on both dimensions. Teen-agers typically report both positive affect and activation in this kind of experience. At the other extreme is "resting" (down at the lower left) which is rated very low on both affect and activa-tion (perhaps as a cause rather than a result of their resting). Most of the other activities are spread out between these two extremes. The general message is that feeling happy and feeling active go together for teenagers.

Most of the pursuits that make teenagers happy and active involve leisure: they are not the activities designed to turn them into adults, but rather those adolescents select to fill up their free time. Among these are subtle differences worthy of note. Let us look, for instance, at the best activities in the upper right-hand square. Sports and art are both very active but lower in affect. They demand personal energy and may be exciting, but provide less immediate emotional feedback. Art and hobbies, in particular, appear to be done not because they make one feel happy here and now, but presumably because—for those willing to invest the effort—they yield long-term rewards. These are the structured "transitional" leisure activities mentioned in the last section. In contrast to them, socializing involves less effort, but offers immediate emotional gratification. Its pattern of lower activation and high affect resembles the experience of eating. It is tempting to speculate that talking with friends somehow mimics that most ancient and indispensable oral activity—except that what one gets from talking with friends is not food, but positive feedback. Just as eating provides caloric energy needed for the body to keep itself together, conversation provides reinforcement for the self to keep itself in an organized form, at least for the immediate moment. These two types of leisure activities involve different demands and provide different rewards.

It is important to note that the three productive activities do not lie in the extreme negative area of the graph. Classwork, studying, and working at a job do not represent the most emotionally entropic experiences in these kids' lives. Many students, for example, told us they liked some of their classes: They were interested in the topic, liked the teacher, and enjoyed discussions with their friends. Likewise, some spoke of positive feelings at work: "It makes me more independent, my mom isn't standing over me," said one girl. But the bars for these three activities are very short. This means that teenagers do not wish to be doing them—a finding we discussed in the previous section. Yet while they wish they were doing something else when in class or at work, apparently this does not stop adolescents from feeling happy and active.

Perhaps the most encouraging message of Figure 5.3 is that these productive activities are not at the entropic end of the continuum. It is true that classwork, homework, and part-time work are dismally low in intrinsic motivation; students are unwilling to do them. Yet they are happier doing classwork than watching TV, reading, thinking, grooming (personal care), or resting. They feel more active studying and working than watching TV, reading, thinking, grooming, or resting. It is when they are working toward a goal in a structured activity that they feel best.

This raises the possibility that productive activities, which represent the socializing goals of the adult world, are not entirely in conflict with the spontaneous interest of adolescents. Returning to the graph, we might visualize the task of socialization as that of raising the height of the columns marked "Studying, Classwork, and Job." If students were to endure classwork more willingly, for instance, it would not be a much worse experience than listening to music. What prevents teenagers from getting more involved in the tasks of adulthood, even though these are not that unpleasant? This is the real question educators and adults concerned with the orderly progression of generations need to answer. Because as long as teenagers feel a discrepancy of goals in productive activities they are not whole; the split in their consciousness generates psychic disorder.

How Moods Change with Different Companions

How important are friends to the well-being of adolescents? Do they ever enjoy their families as much as their peers? Companions are important because they determine, to a large extent, the kind of feedback a person receive. Friends, family, teachers, and strangers react quite differently, and provide much different support and reinforcement.

According to Figure 5.4, adolescents wish most to be with friends, least with classmates, while family and solitude are in between. The four categories are more distinct from each other

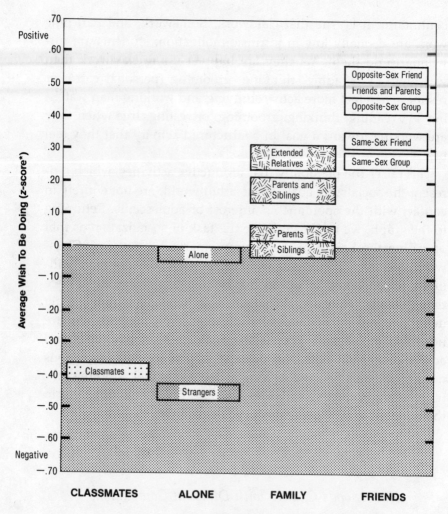

FIGURE 5.4
The Relationship of Intrinsic Motivation to Companionship

than was the case for environments or activities. But do these differences really depend on whom teenagers are with? Or are they due to the different activities they are likely to do with different people?

The answer to both questions is yes. They do more leisure activities with their friends and they wish to be doing *any* activity more when they are with them. Let us show how this works for three activities, taking studying first.

100

The Internal Landscape

When they were studying, adolescents gave the least colorful reports: Usually, they identified what they were doing with the single world "studying," sometimes two words, "doing homework." One might think that the experience of studying would be the same in all of these circumstances; however, this is not so (Appendix D.5). Studying with friends is quite a positive experience. In class, alone, or with the family, it is uniformly negative. It feels worst to study alone, perhaps because it provides so little feedback. One girl wrote the following when she received a signal while studying one night:

> This homework is driving me up a wall—I am just sick of it. It is boring and useless and I wish I could do something else—anything else!! I HATE HOMEWORK (especially when my sister doesn't have any).

As a substitute for the companionship of friends, teens often report having the stereo or the TV going when studying alone.

Moods might be better while doing homework with friends, but one wonders how successful this studying really is. Solitude induces more negative moods, but ultimately, students may find it to be a more effective learning context. In fact, cognitive efficiency is highest when studying alone, although not significantly. With friends there is the advantage of being less bored and stagnant, but the drawback is described by one junior preparing for a test: "I can't study with Aria here. How can I keep my mind on what I'm supposed to be doing instead of *what I want to do?*" (his emphasis).

Activities classified as "Chores, Errands, etc." also occurred across all four categories of companionship. There is some difference in content among them: When with family or alone, a teen is more likely to be doing chores, whereas with friends he or she is more likely to be doing errands. Class activities in this category include "figuring out how much I was going to get paid this month" or "going through my purse." However, all of these situations are similar in their mundane, practical objectives. It is striking, then, to see how significantly different the experience of doing chores or errands is, depending on whom a person is

101

with. When doing them with friends, students report positive motivation, affect, and activation (Appendix D.5). When doing them alone or in the presence of classmates, these states are negative.

The difference companionship makes is shown by the way activities were described and by the kind of comments that were added to the self-report forms. Alone and even with family, descriptions tended to be very matter-of-fact: "shopping for deodorant," "cleaning my hamster cage." With friends, there was some indication that the activity had been converted into more than a mundane chore: Driving becomes "cruising," shopping becomes "checking out the women at Marshall Field's," doing yardwork gets converted into a game. Humor, intrigue, and excitement are added to what otherwise would have been a dull task. Friends enliven any activity, although perhaps at the expense of the effectiveness with which tasks are carried out.

The same pattern recurs in other activities. Watching TV also gets progressively worse as one moves from family to solitude; with friends, conversation and joking help to bring on better moods. There are only two exceptions to this trend. One is art and hobbies, where solitude is highly beneficial; adolescents work at them better alone than in company. The other is socializing, which will be described next.

When teenagers socialize with friends, they talk about different things than when they socialize with family members. With friends, talk is typically joking and buoyant; it deals with topics such as sports, relationships, gossip, and general goofing around. With family, particularly during the relatively few talks with parents, the interaction is more serious and topics include college, work around the house, the state of the world, and the family vacation. Nonetheless, talking with family is nearly as positive as with friends (Appendix D.5).

A few students described rousing nightly discussions around the dinner table. A girl reported debates on politics in which each family member would have a turn to express his or her views. An open politeness prevailed which allowed each to hold and to develop independent opinions. Disagreements were translated into good-natured teasing in a way that defused tension and did not injure any one's self-esteem. Other students made allusions to running jokes they had with their families— ongoing comedies about relatives, family life, or the world. But certainly, many students lacked open channels of communication with their parents. Considering how pleasant and potentially valuable this context of experience is, it seems a pity how seldom adolescents and parents found time for talking together.

Talk with family might be grouped with the transitional activities, like sports and hobbies, described earlier in the chapter. These were activities where adolescents found enjoyment within a structured system of rules and constraints. Likewise, talking with the family involves participation within the parents' world of discourse, a world which is presumably more rational and goal-oriented than the one shared with peers.

The Integration of Experience

Figure 5.5 shows the effects of what adolescents do, and with whom, on their motivation. It shows the clear effects of whether the goals of an activity are free or imposed on how adolescents feel when they are in it. There is a gradient from low to high motivation moving from productive to leisure activities. There is also a gradient from being with classmates to being with friends. The graph would be similar for affect and activation. It is in personally chosen contexts that teenagers report feeling happier and more energetic, as well as most motivated.

If present well-being were the only thing that mattered, one might conclude that adolescents should spend all their time in leisure with friends. But, of course, there are other issues to consider; especially, are they getting prepared to lead productive and meaningful lives in the future? Are they developing the knowledge and control they will need as adults?

Contradictions between present and future well-being surface

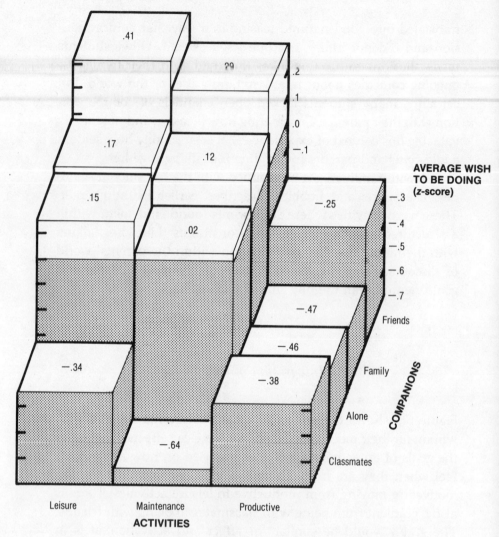

FIGURE 5.5
*Intensity of Intrinsic Motivation in Different Activities and
with Different Companions*

even in the students' description of how they feel right now.
They report most focused thinking in different contexts from the
ones in which emotions and goals are most in harmony. As
shown in Figure 5.6, *it is in productive rather than leisure activities that concentration is highest;* it is lowest with friends. The
gradients of Figure 5.5 and Figure 5.6 are almost opposite. Focused thought and good feelings occur in different situations.

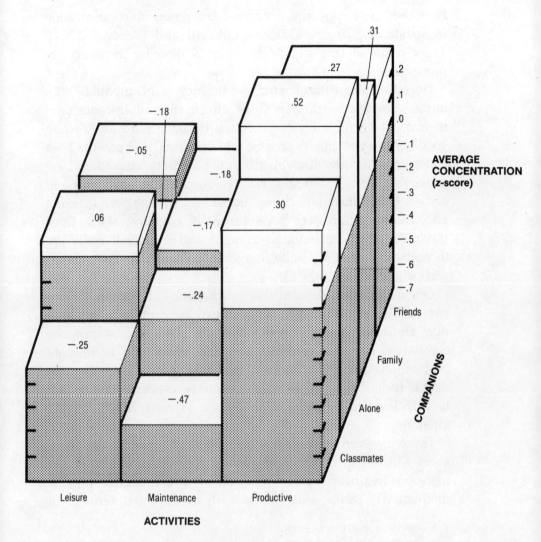

FIGURE 5.6
*Intensity of Concentration in Different Activities and
with Different Companions*

Numerous examples illustrate this pattern. Taking tests, students report high concentration combined with low motivation and affect. Although it is something they do not want to be doing, they are usually able to get their brains working on the challenges teachers present. At the other extreme is their reported experience while drinking alcohol or using marijuana.

Here they are happy and motivated, but report no concentration to speak of (Larson, Csikszentmihalyi, and Freeman 1984). These mind-altering chemicals explicitly disorder their thought processes.

Does this mean that cognitive efficiency is incompatible with intrinsic motivation and positive affect, that adolescents (and their mentors) must choose between thinking hard and feeling good? In the past, many rectors, schoolmarms, and parents have chosen the former, thereby justifying Spartan educational regimes that disregarded students' feelings. In the late 1960s and early 1970s, education chose the second alternative, stressing affective education over development of cognitive skills. Does this mean that concentrated thought and emotional order are incompatible, that a wholly harmonious consciousness must always elude adolescents?

Our data do not support this conclusion. The two are *not* incompatible. Within any given context, concentration, motivation, and affect are positively related. In class, for instance, the correlation between concentration and motivation is strongly positive, even with occasions of test-taking included.[3] If a student is feeling good, he is more likely to be concentrating than if he is feeling sad. Negative states appear to interfere with paying attention.

There are even stronger associations across people. The teenagers who report the highest average concentration also report more positive overall affect and activation and higher intrinsic motivation.[4] Thus, while the socially constructed settings of

3. ($r = .32$, $p < .001$, $df = 5236$).

4. The correlation of average concentration with average affect was $r = .24$, ($p < .05$, $df = 74$) with average activation $r = .47$ ($p < .002$, $df = 74$), and with intrinsic motivation $r = .09$ (*n.s.*, $df = 74$).

For the reader unfamiliar with statistical terms, a brief glossary might be useful from this point on. The symbol r stands for a coefficient of correlation between two variables. It can range between the values of -1.0 and $+1.0$; the larger it is, the more highly the two variables are related to each other. The symbol df is short for "degrees of freedom," and it refers to the number of people or observations measured (number is also expressed as N). Perhaps the most important symbol is the so-called p -value, which expresses the probability that a certain pattern or relationship could have happened by pure chance. The smaller the p, the less likely that the relationship is due to chance, and hence it is considered to be more significant. For example, the correlation between

teenagers' lives tend to erect barriers between the emotional-motivational and the cognitive dimensions of experience, these states are not contradictory; they are complementary.

The optimal conditions for growth clearly involve maximizing harmony in all dimensions of consciousness. One cannot allow disorder to disrupt either emotion, cognition, or motivation. Sacrificing one is detrimental to the others. The challenge of growth is to find opportunities for a synergistic nurturing of all potential forms in which psychic energy is manifested.

In this chapter we found a number of activities, such as sports, games, hobbies, and conversation with family, in which high motivation occurred in conjunction with opportunities for learning cognitive discipline. These are all activities that also elicited high ratings of concentration. Part III will begin to explore these opportunities: Where, within the contexts of family, friends, solitude, and classrooms, do adolescents come fully alive? Where do emotion, cognition, and motivation work together? It is a very difficult question, one to which only tentative answers can be offered. But before dealing with this issue we need to look more closely, in Chapter 6, at the texture of daily experience. It is important to consider how these experiential patterns unfold in an adolescent's life from one hour to the next.

---

concentration and affect ($r = .24$) could have happened by chance five times out of a hundred. The correlation between concentration and activation ($r = .47$) could have happened by chance fewer than twice in a thousand tries. Therefore, the relationship between concentration and activation is stronger than that between concentration and affect, although both are statistically significant. The symbol *n.s.* stands for a relationship that is not significant in statistical terms.

Chapter 6

Peaks and Valleys: Variability in Daily Experience

ADOLESCENT LIFE, as we have been describing it, might seem rather bland. It may appear that teenagers lead routine lives, responding in stereotyped ways as they move through the day. A statistical focus on *average* experience creates the illusion of teenagers leading a regular and regimented life. But when we look at an individual's experience across time we get a very different picture: The regular patterns break down into a quick alternation of activities and moods.

In a matter of minutes, a teenager can switch from elation to the deepest blues, and then back again. If it is true that a mature person is one who can keep his emotions on an even keel, then the quick changes in consciousness might be a sign of immaturity, or a lack of control over psychic energy. But do adolescents actually switch back and forth in their moods more often than adults do? If so, what might be the causes of this emotional variability? And does it have bad consequences for future development? These are some of the questions we now address.

To gain a more dynamic view, we shall present sequences of reports from the lives of a boy and of a girl showing some of the patterns of change that are common to most teenagers. These case studies also illustrate how the moods change as the adolescent steps in and out of contexts that are under adult control. It is at the interface between the world of teenagers and that of adults that the order of consciousness gets reshuffled.

Greg and Kathy—the two students about whom we shall be talking—also illustrate an important difference in the functions that mood variability has in the lives of adolescents. Because Greg has not yet developed any long-range goal in his life (except for "having a good time"), a bad mood simply means that he is not enjoying himself. For Kathy, who is determined to be a good student and a skilled musician, a bad mood often means that she is falling short of her goals. Thus, for Kathy, a negative emotion contains information she can use to develop her skills. These two ways of using negative feedback imply quite different strategies of growth: In the first case, frustation only weakens the self; in the second, it has a chance to make it stronger.

A Week in the Life of a Head

Greg Stone, 16 years old, considers himself one of the "heads" in the school. In former times he would have been a beat or a hippie. In dress and behavior, he lets it be known that he has rejected the goals of the school and the straight community. Greg's week is as full of excitement as any other student's, but the harmony of his consciousness is dependent on his environment. Only when he is acting out freely with friends does Greg come alive; in school and at work he falls into something close to hibernation. If he continues this way it is difficult to imagine how he will ever become spontaneously involved with the roles that are part of adulthood. From the evidence of his responses, Greg is being dragged into maturity against his will.

The study was conducted shortly after release of the movie *Animal House*, a film that has had a strong influence on many teenagers, including Greg and his friends. His self-ratings of mood (which are the sum of the affect and activation dimensions of psychological state), reflect the spontaneity of this "animal" spirit—at the same time showing the predictable influence of various contexts on the quality of his experiences (see Figure 6.1).

But the week starts out on a pretty dull note. In all but one of the first ten reports, he indicates being "very bored" or "quite bored." This is because the first two days Greg gets paged at work and at school, and fails to find much that is exciting or challenging in either place. At work, he says, "My mind just kind of goes blank." He is a bit embarrassed when the pager goes off while he is rearranging women's gynecological products (Figure 6.1, fourth item). In chemistry he has an altercation with the substitute teacher after he leans over and turns down the volume of the film they are watching.

The high point in this period is when he is walking home with a girl whom he is starting to consider his girl friend. The fact that he is currently paired up with someone else, but wants to go to the prom with this girl, will be a source of concern for him as the week moves along.

The next series of reports indicates dramatic fluctuations in his experiential state. Wednesday morning he wakes up in a good mood. He fills out a report at 7:30 while eating breakfast and talking with his sister. But the chemistry class is pretty dismal. "I always get confused when he (the teacher) starts talking. I don't figure it out until two days later. He just starts talking and talking." Not too much later, however, Greg is with friends out on the school mall and back in a good mood. He is admiring some graffiti he had written previously ("*Q:* Are we not men? *A:* We are DEVO!") Looking at it, he says, reminds him of the song these lyrics are from, and that cheers him up. But next, 45 minutes

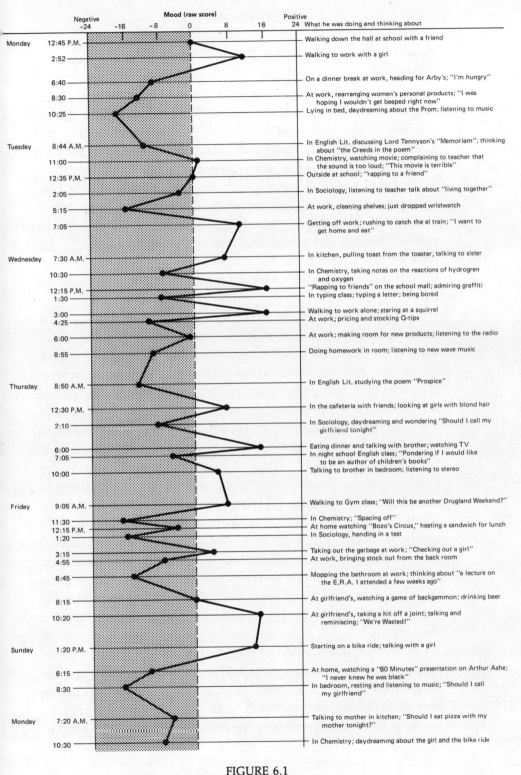

FIGURE 6.1

The Week of Gregory Stone

Chart shows Greg's mood score for each of his self-reports.

later, he is in typing class, and his emotional state is again in disarray.

At 3.00 P.M. his mood is back up; he is very happy and cheerful, even though he is alone and walking to work. This, he explained in the interview afterward, was because he had just kissed his girl friend (the new one) and is feeling elated. But then work and the rest of his evening are dull.

Thursday, his moods again vary considerably. One of the lowest points is in sociology class when the teacher's discussion of girls' problems in dating has triggered thoughts about how he can tell his old girl friend they are not going to the prom. He feels guilty, but has made his mind up not to take her. "Suicidal" is the word he uses (with a touch of exaggeration) to describe his mood.

That night he starts to make plans for Saturday, when the school is holding the annual Senior Banquet to honor the graduating class. At 10:00, when Greg is signaled, he is debating with his brother how to obtain yellow chemical wet suits to wear to the event (this is the costume worn by the rock group DEVO). He will not succeed, but other friends have come up with an equivalent idea, wearing togas as in *Animal House*. The weekend looks promising.

For Greg the weekend starts on Friday morning. "Every Friday I get up and put on this song 'Drugland Weekend.' If I listen to the song in the morning, I'll have it in my head all day." At 9:05 when he is signaled, that is what he is thinking about and his emotional tone is pretty positive. The song, however, is not powerful enough to carry him through chemistry and sociology, where his mood falls to its typical low state. In between these two classes he goes home for lunch. "Friday my Mom works. No one is home, so I can get home and mix a quick drink or smoke a quick bong."

Friday night after work he goes to his old girl friend's house and his mood, given the circumstances, is surprisingly high. He hasn't told her yet and everything is okay. They are drinking beer and playing backgammon with this girl's female friends. Later he is even more elated. He reports feeling a little uncom-

112

fortable being with all these girls, but he is smoking a joint and "the night is developing." He doesn't receive any more signals, but reports afterward that it was a "craaaazzzy night."

Unfortunately, in the craziness he lost the self-report booklet, hence we do not get his reports on the next night, which sounds as if it was even crazier. Suffice it to say that the Heads and the Jocks reenacted the antics of *Animal House* at the Senior Banquet. Greg expressed disappointment that he was not able to give us first-hand reports on his experience, "It was a *very* good Saturday," although at least one other student, who was not part of the rival groups, reported having a "lousy time" because of the commotion they caused. (The experience of this student, Jerzy Madigan, is reported in Chapter 11.) After being kicked out of the banquet, Greg goes to his old girl friend's house again, and they spend the night drinking and partying with friends (her parents are out of town). He goes home as the sun is rising at 4:30 A.M.

Sunday morning the old girlfriend calls while he is at church, and tells Greg's mother that she has found the pager booklet. He describes the events that follow:

> This is a weird story. . . . She was going to Lake Geneva that day, so I came home from church and I called her. She had already left. Well, my other girl friend's phone number is there (points to the last page of the self-report booklet) and that's the only place that I had it. I was going crazy, because I'd promised her I'd go bike riding that day, and I figured there'd be no way I could get in touch with her. Anyway. So I go up to the one girl's house, and I was just hoping she'd left the door open . . . and it *was* open. So I flipped to the last page, and I dial the phone up real quick. It was great! So I went over and we went bike riding. This was the day I asked her to the prom, which was really weird because I was with the other girl all day the night before, and then I ask this girl to the prom.

When he is paged at 1:20 he is biking with the new girl friend and feels very cheerful and free. That evening, however, he is quite tired, and at 8:30 he is deliberating how he is going to tell his old girl that they are not going to the prom.

Greg's life swings back and forth between slow, tedious times at work and school, when he is unchallenged and turns his mind off, and fast, excited times with friends, when he feels truly himself. In school we often see these two states switching rapidly, as he moves between classes and friends. At work the boredom completely takes over, while during the times he is with other young people excitement and cheer set in.

Greg does not lack negentropic experiences, times when he is involved in what he is doing, and enjoying it. He finds challenges in the forbidden activities of drinking and smoking pot, he relishes the cat-and-mouse game with his girl friend, and he looks forward to the unpredictable developments of each crazy night. None of these, however, takes place in a context where Greg might learn to act the way adults in our culture are supposed to. The use of disciplined skills—whether in school, with a musical instrument, on a job, in sports—leaves him bored, if not stupefied. Certainly he is learning from his enjoyable experiences, and a cynic might claim that he's learning the most important skills for later life: how to have a good time regardless of what it costs to others, without being bothered by rules or responsibilities. It is the attitude that prompted Lasch (1979) to call ours the "culture of narcissism": a widespread belief that short bursts of pleasure interspersed with apathy are the best recipe for living one's life.

Yet it is apparent that Greg takes relish in his personal narrative; like some kind of Rabelaisian folk hero, he seems to have sense that he is performing for an audience. In fact, he was so disappointed that he had lost the booklet on that "great" Saturday that he persuaded us to let him carry the pager for the following weekend, and he provided us with additional reports of rapidly fluctuating moods, coupled with beer drinking, smoking pot, listening to a tape by Elvis Costello, a brush with the police, and general rowdiness.

What about this boy's week is uniquely adolescent? The alteration between boredom and excitement is not typical just of adolescents. Many adults show similar shifts in state as they pass between different parts of their lives. What distinguishes Greg's week from that of a typical adult is how quickly the moods change, and the extremes of dejection and exhilaration they involve.

For Greg, life is still open, full of options. The responsibilities and commitments of adulthood are still foreign to him. His week is one long life-style cavalcade: changing girl friends, trying on new behaviors and identities. In all likelihood, he will with time make a few choices among these options and "settle down" to the responsibilities of a worker and family man. If everything goes right, he will learn to enjoy practicing a skill, a trade, or a profession; he might even get to enjoy the company of a steady woman friend. Then his life will become more predictable, with fewer "crazy nights," "weird stories," and perhaps with fewer "*very* good Saturdays." Perhaps the secret of adolescent development is to achieve this transition so that the second half of life is as lively as the first, instead of being poisoned by regret and frustration. In Part IV we shall explore further how teenagers manage this delicate transition.

A Week in the Life of a Teenage Virtuoso

To balance the somewhat rebellious picture presented by Greg, let us look at a youngster whose life is focused on a clear goal and oriented toward adult accomplishments. Katherine Tennison is a junior with a serious commitment to orchestral performance. She concentrates her attention on developing academic and musical skills. She has clear goals that provide direction to her psychic energy. In many ways, Katherine's consciousness is much more negentropic than Greg's; yet even her moods are constantly buffeted by changing conditions. But while for Greg bad moods are a signal for tuning out the adult world, for Kathy they are a warning that she must redouble her efforts to succeed. Greg wastes his frustration, while Kathy puts hers to good use.

Throughout the study Kathy was getting ready for a weekend concert. Her reports reflect how she is preparing for this event, as well as the other normal things that go on in her life. Figure 6.2 shows the path of her overall moods.

The first time she is signaled, she is at lunch in the cafeteria with the usual group of friends. "It is pretty much the same as every day," she says. They are joking, and her mood is positive. Later that afternoon, she receives the second signal while walking home from school, and we begin to see the influence of the upcoming performance on her emotions. Her mood is substantially lower: "I was kind of worried. It was one of those nights I had a lot of homework, and I had to be at rehearsal and wasn't sure how long it was going to last. I figured I would finish it all; it was more how I was going to be the next morning."

The rehearsal itself brings positive moods. At the next report she is leaving for it in a cheerful state. She reports that there is also something else affecting her. "It was the first time I ever got the car by myself. I knew everyone was going to stand at the window as I pulled away." She is happy and excited, but she is also self-conscious and a little worried.

The next signal comes later that night as she is returning home and just as she has gotten herself into an embarrassing jam. In order to open the garage door, she had to remove the keys from the ignition, but when she got back in, the keys would not turn to unlock the steering wheel. And, of course, "My Dad was standing on the porch watching me." Furthermore, she had promised to be home by 10:00 P.M. and was now late. But hurrying seems to have gotten her flustered. She was irritable and angry, she said, because what she was doing was "pretty stupid." While driving initially had been very exciting, now it became the cause of unpleasantness.

In spite of the frustrations and pressures of the night, during most of the next day her moods are remarkably positive. She feels good during history and gym classes. The high point comes while practicing the violin alone in her room at 5:24 P.M. She is playing something she really enjoys, and reports emotions about as positive as they could possibly be.

An hour and a half later, however, her mood has crashed disastrously; she is very irritable, detached and bored. The ex-

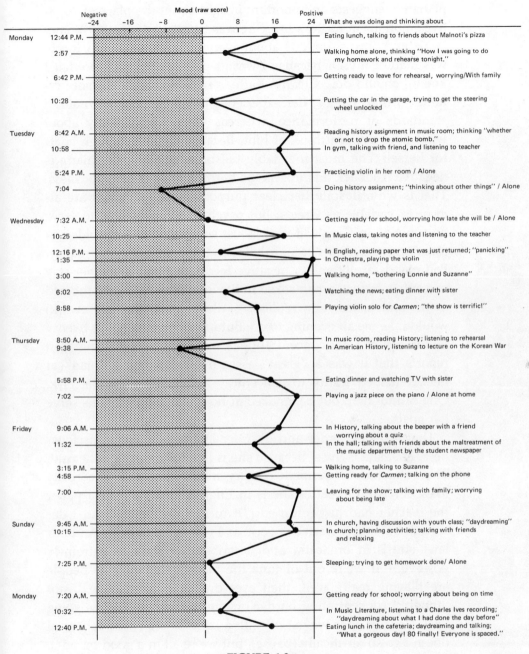

FIGURE 6.2
The Week of Katherine Tennison
Chart shows Katherine's mood score for each of her self-reports.

planation suggests an important insight about the place of negative emotions in Kathy's life. She was trying to do history homework, and "I was thinking about everything else except history! I was mad at myself because I wasn't paying attention to what I knew I should do." Clearly, Kathy's superego is much more tyrannical than Greg's; her experience is affected by internalized standards of performance, whereas Greg worries only about what others might think of him. Because Kathy sets high goals for herself, she must inevitably fail occasionally. The failure is negative feedback that upsets the harmony in her consciousness. That is why, despite her clear purpose, Kathy's moods are almost as variable as Greg's. But psychic entropy seems to serve no function in Greg's life—it is just something to be avoided or forgotten; in Kathy's case, it helps to improve her performance. Bad moods are literally "negative feedback" that helps her stay on course. In fact, when asked in the interview how long the bad mood had lasted, she replied, "I thought it (the homework) would take me all evening to do. But I finished it in about twenty minutes once I got concentrating. I was very happy." She even reports that it was a "great" assignment. Becoming "mad" at herself helped Kathy to concentrate successfully on the task. One cannot help but be amazed at how well her emotions serve her goals.

The next day, order and disorder alternate in her consciousness. First she is upset because she is late for morning rehearsal. Then she has a twentieth-century music class that she really likes. Shortly thereafter she is in English stewing over a paper the teacher had just returned ("It turned out better than I deserved, but still it wasn't as good as I wanted it to be"). An hour later she is in orchestra and describes her state as extremely positive. ("If we're out of tune the mood gets better. If people are playing really well, then everyone gets uptight, well, not 'uptight,' concentrating harder on the music because it's going well. Usually once we get off into a sociable state, the rehearsal doesn't go so terrifically (pause), but we're all in a good mood"). Her emotions are together, but her concentration is lower than usual.

At 3:00, she is walking home with a friend and her state is still positive—though her friend is not pleased that she keeps stopping to tie up her backpack. Supper with her sister takes place in a neutral state; then at 8:58 the pager signals in the middle of a rehearsal as she is playing a solo. Her affect is positive, but she feels self-conscious and not strong.

Her emotions continue to fluctuate. On Thursday she reports a very low mood in history. The teacher is lecturing on the Korean War, a topic that does not interest her. In the evening she has the house to herself and has a great time playing the piano: "I can never practice jazz when the others are there." Friday, Sunday, and Monday we see more changes in her mood. (Saturday, she took the SAT's and turned the pager off.)

To some extent her moods follow the contextual norms discussed in the last chapter. Like Greg she is happy with friends, neutral with family, and tends to be down when alone or in class. But there are glaring exceptions: Kathy has positive times in school and when playing music. She has chosen for herself some goals from among those her culture approves, and she is voluntarily investing her attention in them. Her psychic energy is purposefully channeled, and she is learning to enjoy being an adult.

Each context is associated only with the likelihood of a certain mood. It is not the context itself that determines whether a teen is happy or sad, but the way he or she uses the constraints and opportunities in each. Friends present a certain set of limitations and possibilities. Class balances the chance of learning against severe constraints on behavior and emotions. Being alone is a drag if one doesn't know what to do, but a great opportunity if one wants to play jazz on the piano. Each context is associated with a set of potentialities, an experiential envelope. An adolescent may or may not succeed in using what each has to offer.

What is striking about both of these teenagers is how quickly their emotional states change. At one moment Kathy is in despair over homework, convinced it will take all night; 20 minutes later, it is done, and she is happy again. Greg's changes seem even more dramatic, jerking back and forth between boredom and happiness throughout the day. At one moment they are using superlatives to describe their positive feelings. But elation suddenly drops away, and they are using superlatives to describe anger, loneliness, and boredom. And, of course, this negative mood is again short-lived; they bounce back and forth incessantly.

For both Greg and Kathy, emotional disorder is characterized by a momentary disruption in the psychic energy: for the hedonist Greg, it is manifested as boredom and passivity; for Kathy, with her professional goals, it is expressed as frustration leading to anger and irritability. But the long-range effects of bad moods are likely to be quite different for the two youngsters. Kathy seems to have learned how to harness frustration in the service of her goals.

Mood Variability in Adolescents and Adults

When mood shifts from happy to sad, from alert to drowsy, it is not a trivial change that takes place. One's entire consciousness becomes revised and restructured; what gave pleasure a moment ago may now be a nuisance. A contrasting set of information has been brought out from memory and loaded into attention. It is like putting on a pair of distorting glasses that invert one's vision, so that what was up now appears to be down, and what was on the right side now shows itself on the left. True, the effects of moods are temporary, but that makes them no less real for the person subject to them. And moods may have long term effects. A bout of depression or anger might lead to a rash act with extreme consequences, while a spell of profound joy may be remembered forever, providing solace whenever the going gets rough. For better or for worse, mood states constitute a person's "being in the world" (as Heidegger [1927] called it), the totality of conscious awareness present at a given moment of time.

Peaks and Valleys

It is from this perspective that we need to consider the pattern shown by Greg and Kathy. Their emotions are often extreme and erratic. While these swings are partly related to situational contexts, they are largely unpredictable and often seem out of control. Are these fluctuations markedly different from those of adults? To answer this question, one might consider three separate aspects of mood fluctuations, each representing a different aspect of variability.

The first aspect to take into account is the *width* of the mood changes. Both Greg and Katherine oscillate between extreme highs and extreme lows; is this in any way typical of adolescents in comparison with adults? The results suggest that it is; on nearly every mood item, adolescents reported a significantly wider variation than adults (Appendix D.6). During an average week, both boys and girls reported more emotions at both ends of the scale. They are less anchored in a familiar, middle-level, base-line state than adults; they are more prone to swerving to one extreme or the other. In contrast to their elders, adolescents are more likely to experience euphoria, to catch a glimpse of a world in which everything is perfect. However, they are also more vulnerable to sudden incursions of pain caused by unexpected events. Unlike adults, they are less protected by the accumulation of experiences. In sum, extremes of order and chaos more often rule their consciousness—but this conclusion is significantly modified by the next finding.

The second dimension of variability to be considered is the *duration* of these emotional states. We selected the occasions when adolescents and adults reported the most extreme moods to see how long they lasted. Adolescents' extreme moods turned out to be remarkably short-lived. Within 45 minutes of being either very happy or very sad, they were back near their average mood level (Figure 6.3). In contrast, adults were still significantly happier than usual two hours after an exceptionally happy mood, or still sad two hours after a really sad time. All their extreme moods lasted much longer than the teenagers'. Therefore, while adolescents may experience a wider range of states, these are short-lived; they are more like flashes of emotion.

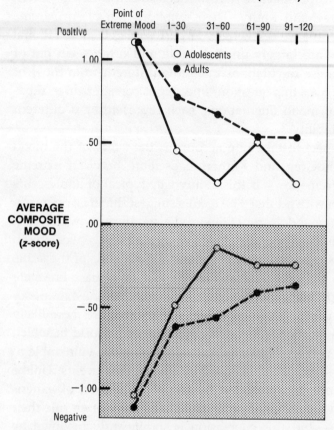

FIGURE 6.3
The Rate of Decay for Extreme Moods
(Adapted from: Larson, Csikszentmihalyi, and Graef 1980)

The flux, however, is not necessarily wild or chaotic. The third index of mood variability, *predictability*, was a measure of how well the environment predicted emotions. Specifically, it was an index of the proportion of variance in a person's mood which could be explained by knowing what he or she was doing. On this index, adolescents and adults were comparable. Overall, the adolescents' states were no less predictable than those of the adults (Larson, Csikszentmihalyi, and Graef 1980).

In other words, the variability of teenagers seems to be associated with what they do, as much as with how they process experience. If they are more emotional, it is partly because they are exposed to more varied environments than adults are. In fact, teenagers move from one context to the next more rapidly than adults, and thus their emotions have a greater chance of being affected by situational factors. (Appendix D.7). Whether it is because they have not yet chosen a pattern for their lives, or because society makes fewer demands on them to conform to a predictable set of activities, adolescents are less firmly rooted in their environments. Therefore, their emotions shift more readily with the restless pattern of their lives.

Variability in mood in adolescence often has been thought to resemble pathology, both by psychologists (A. Freud 1958; Lewin 1938), and by laymen (Hess and Goldblatt 1957; Musgrove 1963). The great swings in mood that clinicians, educators, and parents note with alarm tend to be interpreted as dangerous lack of control, as a sign of a weak ego—thrust this way and that by powerful libidinal urges. However, the results from the present study do not support this interpretation. Adolescents whose moods change most, report being as happy and as much in control as their steadier peers, and they appear to be as well adjusted on other measures (Larson, Csikszentmihalyi, and Graef 1980). Quick shifts in emotions are not necessarily associated with deleterious effects in the long run. They do not represent pathological disequilibrium. Nonetheless, as Greg and Kathy showed, they are a central feature of adolescent life, a typical aspect of their ongoing experiential world.

Is There Order in Adolescents' Experience?

What the mood swings do indicate is the inconstancy of the adolescent personality. The teenager in school appears to be a different person from the one coming home with his friends. Moving from one situation to the next, each teen's moods and cognitive states fall into constantly changing configurations like bits of colored glass in a kaleidoscope.

We began this chapter hoping to find the threads of continuity that tie an adolescent's life together, the stable woof and warp that unifies experience in geometry class with experience in getting stoned with friends or in playing a violin. However, in the two case studies considered, there was scanty indication of such threads. The only unifying elements were the student's general orientation and goals. In the lives of these two teenagers and in the sample as a whole, what is most conspicuous is the lack of continuity, the fragmentation and instability of consciousness.

Adolescent variability is sometimes attributed to the biological changes of puberty, which immediately precede the high school years. Puberty brings major increases in the body's base level for several hormones, including sexual ones, and, perhaps most significantly, adrenal hormones, which play a central role in arousal (Petersen and Taylor 1980). It is possible that adolescent variability reflects the trial-and-error efforts to adjust to a body with new shapes and new needs.

However, many scholars, particularly anthropologists, have been unwilling to accept this explanation. Margaret Mead concluded that there was little evidence of emotional or behavioral variability among adolescents in the Pacific island cultures she knew. She and many others have argued that the tribulations of puberty are due to unique features of Western culture. Mead stressed the conflicting messages given to young people in our society—that they should be responsible yet fun-loving, child-like yet mature—and the overwhelming range of expectations placed upon them. Ruth Benedict (1938) has argued that we impose on adolescents the requirement that they reverse major elements of their personality between the childhood and adult years. Talcott Parsons (1942), Kurt Lewin (1938), and many others have proferred similar explanations for the turbulence of adolescence in our society.

Our data lend credence to this socio-cultural perspective. The emotional changes adolescents in this study show are related at least in part to the conflicting experiences in their lives. At one moment they are sitting in class, expected to learn materials (and earn grades) that will have a crucial bearing on their future life; the next moment the bell rings and they are with friends, impelled by an expectation to have a good time. In the past, adolescent boys and girls were placed in separate schools, with the intent of focusing their attention exclusively on education. Now boys and girls are thrown together, in part to accentuate the competition between educational and peer-related goals. Extreme variability in consciousness is the result.

In the twentieth century, young people have inherited expectations that attempt to merge the Protestant work ethic with a belief that the rewards of heaven are accessible on earth. They are expected to take adult responsibilities seriously and at the same time to reap the celebrated pleasures of youth. Some adolescents, such as Greg Stone, cope with this double expectation by giving up on the former. At work and at school he "blanks out" his mind, wasting hour after hour in passive boredom. Others, such as Katherine, focus all their attention on the latter. She has devoted herself totally to the different path of succeeding in the world of orchestral music. The solutions they have chosen only seem to intensify their emotional variability. In a sense, both their goals are unrealistic. Greg expects too little from adult life, Kathy expects perhaps too much. As they pass from context to context, their consciousness responds to the transition as a wind-chime responds to a shifting breeze.

The central question is how this variability relates to personal growth. Many psychologists recognize that conflict is a necessary condition of growth. "Dialectic" psychology is one of the contemporary perspectives that emphasize how one cannot change without stress: The impetus for growth usually comes from a challenge that cannot be avoided (Riegel 1976).

The swings of emotion are probably neither good nor bad. What matters is *how* teenagers respond to the challenges of their unpredictable environment. Those who learn to control psychic energy to make their goals come true will become confident, competent individuals. But we shall save until Part IV the discussion of optimal growth.

The more immediate question concerns how adolescents get through each day. In their kaleidoscopic reality, what are the sources of order? How do they make sense out of daily experiences? Building a lasting pattern of purpose requires that they perceive some regularity in their hour-to-hour interactions. But is there enough stability in their encounters with family, with friends, with school, for them to construe a modicum of psychological order within those domains?

To answer this question we must abandon the view of each context as a fixed environment, as a rigid experiential template. Order in daily experience is not given by the consistency of each context, but by the range of possibilities each present. In the family, for example, there is an array of opportunities for either positive or negative feedback. One can be praised for taking out the garbage or yelled at for tracking dirt into the house. One can find enjoyment in a weekly game of backgammon or continuous grief in an inability to get along with a younger brother or sister.

To make sense of the possibilities in an adolescent's life, we are going to discuss each of four major domains as an experiential system, an organization of constraints and opportunities. The sharpest divisions in teenagers' experience correspond to whom they are with: Being with friends is the most freely chosen part of their lives; being with classmates—in class—is the most constraining. What is the systematic structure of interactions in those two domains? The family is the other major social context and seems to be neither as exciting as friends nor as dull as school—what is the balance of constraints and opportunities here? Finally, there is the mysterious context of solitude, which fills one quarter of waking time. When alone, there is no one else structuring a teenager's attention—what threats and rewards are encountered here?

Part III will analyze the experiential dynamics and analyze the potential of these four systems. Then it will be possible to come back to the issue of development and the question of where opportunities for long-range growth exist within fragmented daily existence.

PART III

INTERACTIONS

Chapter 7

Familiar Aggravations: Relations with Parents and Siblings

OF the four major contexts of adolescent life—solitude, family, peers, and school—the family plays in many ways the most important role. Financially and legally, if not emotionally, adolescents still depend on their parents for basic survival necessities and self-definition. At the same time, both they and their parents know that this dependence is about to end, and that in a few years the young men or women will have to become responsible for their own subsistence.

The family is the context of origin; it is where an infant spends all his or her time and first discovers the joys and limitations of reality (Berger and Luckmann 1967). In the home, youngsters find the earliest support for their developing selves: The love and attention of parents is the first proof that they exist and they

129

matter. At the same time, the home is also where some of the most bitter battles unfold between adolescents and their parents, as each attempts to define where the teenagers' psychic energy should be directed.

What kind of an adult an adolescent will become depends to a large extent on the balance between these two aspects of the home environment. A youth who can use the opportunities for growth without paying too high a price in the struggle for autonomy will be well on his or her way to maturity. Teenagers in this sample spent an average of about 20 percent of their waking hours with their families. But one of the largest age differences also was found in connection with time spent with family: The figure for freshmen was 25 percent, for seniors only 15 percent. This trend toward redirecting psychic energy away from members of one's family to one's peers and to the wider world is, of course, what most scholars have seen as the main developmental task of adolescence (for example, A. Freud 1958; Blos 1962). The normal transition for persons of this age is to become gradually free from dependence on one's parents, while at the same time developing a positive attitude toward family life and one's future procreative role (Havighurst 1948; Hill 1980).

The question is, what kind of a system is this receding context? What effects does the family have on adolescents' well-being and development as they pass in and out of the family context several times a day? In this chapter we will look at the experiences adolescents report having with their families, in order to understand more clearly the main sources of psychic entropy and negentropy in this context.

Before turning to the analysis of the data, however, it might be useful to review some of the characteristics of the family as a social system. A brief theoretical and historical glance might help to explain why some structural characteristics of families produce disorder in teenagers' consciousness, and tension in the relationship.

Institutional Constraints

It is well known that interaction between parents and adolescent children is far from smooth. Although psychologists, writers of fiction, and popular wisdom might have overestimated the amount of stress actually occurring between parents and teen-agers (Douvan and Adelson 1966; Offer 1969), there are some design features of families in general, and Western ones in par-ticular, that make a certain amount of conflict inevitable. These features were clearly identified for the first time by Davis (1940).

According to his analysis, there are five main structural factors that promote conflict in families. The first is the *rate of socio-cultural change*. When this rate is high, each generation is ex-posed to widely varying social and historic conditions, almost as if they belonged to different cultures. The impact of this societal change manifests itself through a second factor, occurring within each family, *decelerating rates of change among the adults*. The consequences of putting these two trends together is that as par-ents learn new ideas at a slower rate, their children still learn and change quickly; if the culture produces new information rapidly, a gap is bound to open up between what parents and their children know, and between their views of the world. Third, as teenagers are reaching new physical powers, their par-ents are just beginning to experience the first twinges of physical decline. This *contrast in the trajectories of physical and sexual pow-ers* induces jealousy and competition; at the very least, it means that not only are teenagers in a difficult stage, but so are their parents (Bossard and Bell 1955; Conger 1977, p. 246).

Davis also argues that there is inevitable *conflict between adult realism and youthful idealism* within the family. By virtue of lon-ger life and hence more abundant experience, parents tend to have a more jaded, more "realistic" outlook on the world. Adults learn that their desires are more often frustrated than fulfilled. This tacit knowledge tends to conflict with the "ideal-ism" of teenagers, who still expect their goals to be easily realized. Ironically, this discrepancy is often due to the efforts of parents to shelter their children from the impact of entropy. The result is that children frequently think their parents are cynical because they lack enthusiasm for the beautiful goals that they, the children, believe are so easy to reach.

The final design feature Davis singles out as a source of family tensions is the *unequal authority wielded by parents and children*. This, too, is an inevitable and hence universal characteristic of family life. Adults have important privileges concerning sexuality, property, and control over behavior from which adolescents are, and to a certain extent must be, excluded. But this necessarily makes youth outsiders within the very bosom of the family; it forces them into an adversary position, where they perceive their interests as divergent from their parents'. In other words, as Marx and Engels proposed, differential control over the means of production (and reproduction) recreates, in miniature, the class struggle within the family (Tucker 1978, pp. 85, 159, 734 ff.).

Given this list of opportunities for conflict, it seems a miracle that there is not more turmoil between parents and children. The reason is that there are also factors that mitigate the entropic features of family structure. Of these Davis mentions three: (1) family authority becomes internalized in childhood as the only reality; (2) children learn to identify with their parents despite all the differences between them; and (3) there is a growth of reciprocal power relationships, which slowly emancipate the children from parental authority.

To these one might add the weight of external rewards that keeps teenagers docile in most cultures: The realization by youth that, in the long run, they will reap economic and social benefits by maintaining close ties with their families. This, of course, is more typical of stable, traditional cultures where there is a passing of roles, responsibilities, and possessions from one generation to the next, but even in our culture there are benefits to young adults for maintaining friendly relations with parents.

Some critics of American family patterns have pointed to a form of stress peculiar to our times: the disproportionately high expectations we place on the nuclear family, and hence the almost inevitable disillusion that ensues. Because of the increasing impersonality, competitiveness, and instrumentality of work and public life—so they argue—the family remains the only "haven in a heartless world" (Lasch 1977). Many parents experience their strongest emotional rewards within the family, and thus come to depend on it to stabilize their personality. Because of the importance the family assumes as a source of psychic negentropy for parents, they are especially threatened by any conflict with each other and with the children. The widespread permissiveness of parents is due to their fear of antagonizing their offspring: "The parent, in his need for love . . . tends more and more to become almost driftwood in the tides of the child's demands" (Henry 1965, p. 138).

At the same time, while increasing psychological demands are placed on families, fewer and fewer of them are surviving as traditional systems. In 1960, about one out of ten adolescents was living in one-parent families. By 1980, the ratio of single-parent families had more than doubled. The proportion of teenagers that will live in "broken" families by the 1990s is estimated to range from one third (Glick 1979) to 45 percent (Weitzman 1978), to the majority of all American children (Brandwein 1977). It is not surprising that in recent years the very survival of the family has been questioned (Cooper 1970).

However, it is very unlikely that the basic design of the system will disappear. Whether a society can afford to have a majority of its youth growing up in one-parent families remains to be seen. The few times in recent history that conscious attempts were made to weaken the family, as in Soviet Russia, the Israeli Kibbutzim, or the Chinese communes, the problems thus created seem to have outweighed anticipated advantages. It is interesting to note that, at least in the Soviet Union, the greatest impact was not on small children, but on adolescents. After the Revolution, Soviet policy makers made every effort to destroy the family as a viable entity in Russia. A major goal was to remove youth from the authority of their parents, and to redirect their loyalties from the family to the Socialist state and its representatives. The attention of Russian adolescents was to be restructured so that their psychic energy would no longer be invested in their fathers or mothers, but in the officers of the Party. In the two decades or so that this policy was implemented, juvenile delinquency on an immense scale became a severe problem in the Soviet Union. The policy makers realized that extrafamilial institutions could not replace the family as a context in which socially negentropic goals are passed on from one generation to another. Therefore, by the late 1930s, the Soviets reversed their efforts to undermine the family, and tried instead to co-opt it for their larger political goals (Coser 1951; Bronfenbrenner 1967).

Of course, this historical event does not "prove" that the family is indispensible to the functioning of society. It could be that the spontaneous development of capitalist ingenuity will succeed in making obsolete the family where the conscious efforts of a communist society have failed. In any case, never in the long and complex history of mankind has there been a time when people lived outside a family system. So the question is not whether there will be a family or not, but rather what forms it will take. And admittedly a lot of leeway is possible on this score: We simply do not know what the limits are beyond which a family is no longer a family. Are two parents necessary? This is no longer true biologically. Is it necessary psychologically and socially? What activities can adolescents and adults share together? What opportunities are there for them to enjoy each other's company? Is there anything meaningful in the day-to-day interaction or is the family just a relic of previous times that serves necessary custodial functions? All these questions, which nowadays make sense, would have made none a few generations ago—illustrating the extent to which the family system has already been transformed.

The Quality of Family Experience

The teenagers we studied had been growing up in greatly varied families: Some had all the structural features of traditional families, others involved idiosyncratic arrangements. We had information on the family composition of sixty-three out of the seventy-five adolescents. Of these, thirteen, or 20 percent, lived in single-parent families (all but one of the single parents was a mother). This proportion replicates exactly the census figures for the period.

A few families were racked by constant dissension and occasional violence, while a few others were distinguished by remarkable harmony and mutual understanding. The results reported in Chapter 5 suggest that the home context is, on the whole, a balance wheel in the emotional swings of adolescent life. Being the context where the first emotions are experienced, it serves as a benchmark against which newer ones are compared.

Part of the reason for this intermediate emotional tone follows from the activities teenagers do with their families (see Figure 7.1). About half the time is spent in routine maintenance activities like eating, running errands, or doing chores around the

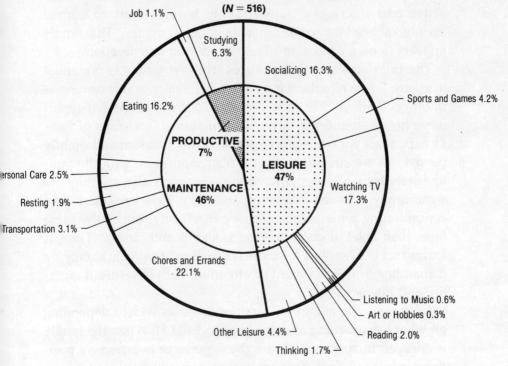

FIGURE 7.1
What Teenagers Do with Their Families

135

house; and the other half in leisure activities. At first sight, this pattern appears quite similar to what teenagers do with friends. But, on closer inspection, the maintenance and the leisure activities are different in the two contexts. For example, "transportation" (much of it between leisure activities) accounts for almost one third of the maintenance activities with friends, whereas it rarely seems to take place with the family (only 3.1 percent of the time). In contrast, doing chores is the single most frequent activity adolescents do when they are with their families.

Leisure is even more different between the two contexts. With parents and siblings, 21 percent of the time is spent in *active* pursuits, including "socializing," "sports," and "art or hobbies," while with friends this active leisure takes up 44 percent of the time—more than twice as much. If one adds up the *passive* leisure activities (watching television, listening to music, reading, and daydreaming), the percentages are 22 percent with family, and 7 percent with friends. Clearly, leisure with peers is strongly active and interactive, while family leisure tends to consist mainly of noninteractive, unchallenging activities. The family appears to be a context of maintenance and regeneration.

The full pattern of typical states with the family is presented in Figure 7.2. While there is as much variability in this context as in others (Larson 1979), the averages for most of the self-report items hover around the mean. The emotional landscape of family experience for teenagers appears slightly pleasant and slightly passive. As we already know, intrinsic motivation with the family is relatively higher than average. Teenagers also say they are significantly less self-conscious and they have an easier time concentrating when surrounded by the family; but at the same time, their level of concentration is significantly lower. Thus, it seems that the family allows the restoration of psychic energy by demanding little investment of attention, both in terms of quantity and intensity.

Of course, the quality of experience varies widely depending on what is happening at home (Appendix D.8). When the family is engaged in sports or games, the experience is extremely positive across the board: Teenagers concentrate more than average,

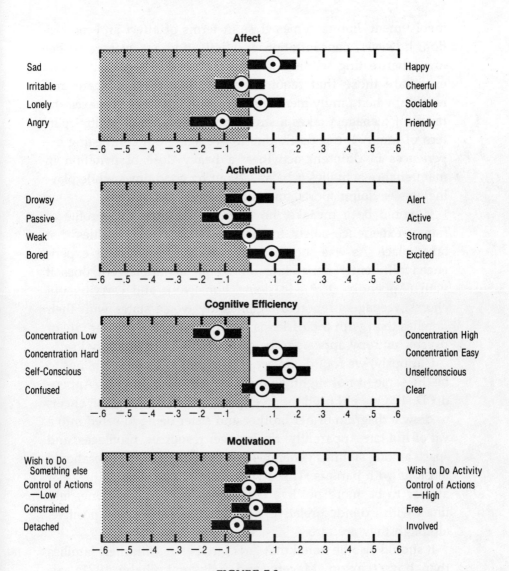

FIGURE 7.2

Quality of Experience with Family

The bars indicate the average self-ratings (mean means) for the 75 adolescents and the 95 percent confidence interval for each average.

their activation level is very high, they are happy, and the motivation is intrinsic. It is tempting to conclude that "the family that plays together, stays together"; no other activity is as unequivocally negentropic, and therefore as conducive to spontaneous

137

involvement. Eating comes close in terms of affect and motivation; however, concentration and activation are average or below when eating within the family context. The worst experiences are those that require privacy, like personal care and reading; when family members are around in these contexts, the mood of teenagers takes a strong dive. The overall neutral pattern of family life is partly due to averaging out contrasting experiences in different activities; a heavy dose of irritation in maintenance activities is balanced out by good times while playing games, doing sports, and eating.

It would be a mistake, however, to attribute this profile of family experience solely to the constellation of activities that takes place. As was shown earlier, the same activity is experienced differently depending on whom an adolescent does it with (Appendix D. 5). In doing homework and carrying out chores, teenagers reported significantly worse states with their families than with their friends. In other words, a greater rate of psychic entropy appears to be associated with the family itself.

Curiously, we found adolescents' moods with their siblings to be the same (it not slightly worse) as with their parents (Appendix D. 4). One girl used the free space on one of her pager sheets to draw a diagram of her brother and sister being lowered into a vat of hot tar. Apparently, rivalry over resources, privileges, and space among siblings generates as much conflict as generational tensions with parents. Times with parents and siblings together appear to be more positive than times with either alone, and times with extended relatives stand out as particularly positive, although they are rare.

It should also be noted that girls fare better with their families than boys (Larson, Mayers, and Csikszentmihalyi 1977), although, for the most part, the differences are not quite significant and appear to diminish with age. The largest difference by gender is that girls more often reported themselves to be "the leader" when with their families, suggesting that they feel more incorporated into the family's goals. However, instances of conflict for girls are just as common. For them, as for boys, the context of friends is experienced as a much less entropic setting.

Friction appears to be an endemic feature of family life. The neutral pattern of average states with family partly reflect a stalemate between entropic and negentropic forces. It would appear that the institutional burdens placed upon family life—the generational differences, the conflicts over values and resources, and the differences in status, as described by Davis—produce somewhat of an emotional deadlock. The forces that will propel adolescents out of the family are in full operation. But the way teenagers part ways with their families is critical; after all, not only will the relationship go on under new guises, but most of these adolescents will attempt soon to reconstitute families of their own.

Sources of Family Conflict

When teenagers are with their families, negative thoughts outnumber positive ones about ten to one. Here is a sampler from what our respondents wrote down after the question: "As you were beeped, what were you thinking about?" when they were interacting with family members. Each of the responses that follows was given by a different adolescent.

"Why my mother manipulates the conversation to get me to hate her"
"The bullshit exiting from my sister's mouth"
"Why my brother was scraping the breading off a perfectly good veal Parmesan"
"How much of a bastard my father is to my sister"
"How ugly my mom's taste is"
"How incompetent my mom is"
"My bitchy mom"
"How pig-headed my mom and dad are"
"How much I really don't like my sister's hair"
"My aunt talks too much"
"About my mom getting ice cream all over her"
"How f____g stupid my mom is for making a big f____g fuss"
"My brother taking all my possessions"

This litany of complaints shows the kinds of tensions endemic in family interaction. They usually do not involve important matters. Instead, the conflict seems to hinge on questions of taste, like scraping the breading off a veal cutlet, or the shape of a hairdo, or the dripping of ice cream over clothes. But these reasons might not be as trivial as they sound, because they represent the strain that results when young persons are attempting to develop their goals and values—in short, those expectations by which the negentropic condition of their selves will be defined. A word that makes no difference to an adult can threaten a teenager's whole, precariously constructed self system. Asking a boy who has spent many days practicing a song on the guitar Why are you playing that trash? might not mean much to the father, but it can be a great blow to the son. The so-called "growth pains" of adolescence are no less real just because their causes appear to be without much substance to adults. In fact, this is exactly what the conflict is all about: What is to be taken seriously.

If a girl decides to become a dancer, she is not only choosing a hobby, but also a goal that for a time will define who she is. To take her goal lightly amounts to discounting the importance of her self. At a time when identity is still fragile, young persons can resent bitterly such threats to their psychic integrity.

Adults and adolescents live in separate, if overlapping, realities. Jessop (1981) found remarkable discordances between parents and children on basic facts about family life. They had much different versions of what was going on. The generation gap consists in differing beliefs about what is important, what counts, what is real. Socialization aims at restructuring adolescents' reality to resemble that of their parents, but teenagers often resist, and the conflict does not always end with their surrender. Often enough, the reality parents hold to be true is changed instead of the child's (R.Q. Bell 1968; Bell and Harper 1977).

The issues that cause conflict are very different from each other on the surface, but appear to grow out of the same roots: a contest for the power to define the content of consciousness. Let us take as an example one of the young men in our sample, Jerzy

Madigan, an active athlete in high school. Of all the experiences he reported during the week, the one where he was feeling the worst occurred on a Sunday morning at 10:15 as he was sitting in a car with his parents, driving to church. Here is what he says about the event:

> I never want to go to church, but I'll go. Finally I get a Sunday off; I don't have to work, so I can sleep a little later. But now I've got to go to church. I've got to wake up earlier than if I'd had to go to work.
>
> They always wake you up, and they're always cheerful, and you go "oh, no!." They act cheerful, but they are really hostile if you don't want to go.
>
> Right then I'd just asked them to turn the channel. They were listening to some opera stuff. They just ignored me; you know, because we were parking and everything. Still, they could have acknowledged me. That's why I was so upset. I went, "Jesus Christ, at least they could answer me."

In this short statement (from Larson, Csikszentmihalyi, and Graef 1980), Jerzy identifies four types of conflict, each involving an effort on the parents' part to structure his attention (that is, to socialize him), and Jerzy's resistance. First of all, the parents insist that their son go to church instead of sleeping. This, of course, involves a rather massive change in Jerzy's consciousness. It means that for several hours he has to attend to something that conforms to his parents' goals rather than to his own. Listening to a sermon, all dressed up and looking reverent, is typically an unwelcome socializing experience for most adolescents. Second, the parents want their son to act as if the interaction were negentropic—they expect Jerzy to be cheerful, as they ostensibly are. Again, he is asked to change his consciousness to suit the parents' goals. Third, they wish to control the son's auditory input by playing opera rather than the kind of music he is spontaneously interested in. These three instances of competition for Jerzy's attention set the stage for the fourth, and most intense conflict: When he tries to have his own goals acknowledged, he is ignored. This amounts to a denial of his existence as an autonomous individual, to his effective exclusion from the system. The message being conveyed is: Things will happen the way we want them to happen, and your desires make absolutely no difference. No wonder that Jerzy was "so upset." By not answering, his parents symbolically made him disappear from the world for the time being. As an example of socialization, this episode is fairly typical.

The most negative experiences occur when the spontaneous goals of adolescents are at odds with goals parents set up to channel the psychic energy of their children. To have to follow parents' orders, such as picking up clothes or doing homework, is bad enough as far as most teenagers are concerned, because these activities temporarily preempt control over their psychic energy. But doing these things at least leaves the mind relatively free. It is even worse when the parents attempt to control the inner workings of consciousness as well, by instilling guilt, or by requiring specific conformity ("You have to do it *exactly* this way...."). Then the child loses even the inner experience of freedom. By not being able to establish his own goals, he cannot get positive feedback—therefore the order of the self is weakened.

It is significant that in the episode just described, Jerzy was suffering from a hangover acquired from drinking beer the night before. A junior girl, whom we shall call Alice, found herself in a similar situation. She spent Saturday with a girl friend, going to a dance and then spending the night at her friend's house, talking in bed till three in the morning, sharing joints of marijuana and plucking her eyebrows. Next day, Alice and her mother just couldn't get along: The mother insisted that she do homework and housework, and tried her best to make Alice feel guilty. It was just too much for Alice, in comparison with the carefree times she had passed with her friend the night before. When she responded to the pager around 3:00 P.M., she reported the worst moods of the week. This is what she was thinking about: "That my mom belongs in a mental institution. I hate her guts. Help me, I hate her so much. She deliberately hurt me physically and mentally. She broke my eardrums. She's mentally retarded. She's helpless." The mother, far from being mentally retarded, is a successful professional. But all is fair in the war of defining what shall be real, even projecting insanity onto one's adversary—this is the ploy that Berger and Luckmann (1967) call "nihilation."

Of course, there is usually fault on both sides. In an interesting longitudinal study, Steinberg (1981) found that as boys approached puberty, there was a *mutual* breakdown in communication. Both boys and their parents interrupted each other more frequently in conversation and provided fewer explanations for their behavior. Adults bring their own stubborn reality into the family situation, a reality with a grounding in their own daily experience, and in their past experience as teenagers—twenty to thirty years earlier. The fact that a parent might bear heavy career responsibilities does not exempt him or her from investing psychic energy into the family relationship. Unfortunately, parents' expertise in other domains may make them less able or less willing to listen and be attentive to an adolescent's point of view.

Adolescents complain most about their fathers being insensitive—and rarely available. Girls in particular report that their dads are aloof and provide little personal support (Wright and Keple 1981). For instance, one girl in our study is riding in the car with her father, and feels extremely "irritable," "angry," and "dissatisfied." Why? Because her father had insisted she go shopping with him even though she was hungry and would have liked a snack, and because her father stopped the car with a jerk at the stop sign, just as "he always does." The father is probably unaware of this peculiarity in his driving habits, but it grates on the daughter, who is angry for being helplessly subjected to his idiosyncrasies. Much tension in the family results from the way parents eat, dress, talk, or blow their noses—teenagers feel they are stuck with having to pay attention to irritating mannerisms over which they have no control. Becoming independent means having a choice over what one pays attention to. The dependent situation of adolescents often puts them in positions where they feel hurt by their parents even when hurting them is the last thing their parents mean to do.

It is unfortunate that we did not have the parents carrying

pagers along with their children. It would have been possible to see how their thoughts and experiences coincide. Some authors have suggested that adolescents fare well in family interactions compared to what their parents go through (for example, Lidz 1969). What could a mother and father feel when driving a hungover, intransigent son to church? How well does a parent stand up when her daughter is accusing her of being insane? And what burdens in their own daily experience cause them to be insensitive or petulant toward their children? Ultimately, adolescents' family experience needs to be understood in terms of all the parties involved.

All in all, the kind of family conflict our teenagers reported is of the "normal" variety; it involved mostly tensions built into the family structure itself. But if these conflicts were the only substance of family life, the institution would quickly fall apart at the seams. According to the second law of thermodynamics, it is the nature of physical systems to come apart—to move toward a state of randomness and disorder. However, some physical systems (for example, life forms) have means for counteracting this constant decay. Processes of entropy are clearly evident in adolescents' relations with their parents. The question is what, if anything, occurs in these interactions that keeps the family together as an ordered social system?

Negentropic Family Patterns

In dwelling on the dramatic instances of conflict, it is easy to overlook the constant material and psychic support that the family provides, as a matter of course, in the lives of teenagers. The family is a bit like good weather, which is usually noticed only when it fails. It is true that adolescents are positively gloomy with their families compared to how they feel with friends; on the other hand, they are radiant with the family in comparison with how they feel in solitude or in classrooms. By and large, the family seems to provide a setting of neutrality where teenagers recover in relative safety and warmth from the highs and lows of daily life.

The routine of family life with its emphasis on maintenance makes the experience of strong positive feelings difficult. Many teenagers complain that father comes home from work tired and irritated, and he "takes it out on us." The same is true for mother if she works; if she is a housewife, she is often dulled by the monotonous, unchallenging rounds of household duties. The teenagers are often exhausted from the demands of school or the excitement of peer activities. It is not surprising that the most rewarding and memorable family experiences tend to occur on holidays and vacations. As one girl who is very close to her family said: "It's mostly when we are doing something other than the usual thing that we get along so well."

It is a strange paradox of modern life that for members of a family to really be together, they have to leave home. Under ordinary circumstances, parents and children rarely do things together, except at meal times. Ever since work and school have pulled adults and children away from the home, conflicting schedules keep family members circling around each other in eccentric orbits. These orbits tend to intersect only when one or the other member is exhausted by his or her other roles. Thus, relaxed togetherness is available only in extraordinary circumstances, usually when the whole family physically moves away from its home base for a day on the town, an outing, or a prolonged vacation. Away from home, the family operates on the same schedule, and each member is likely to attend to the same stimuli, and therefore share the same experiences.

In the interviews, many teenagers described their warmest memory as involving a trip with their family. The typical scenario included a circle of relatives sitting around a fireplace after a cold and active winter day spent outdoors, eating a homemade meal, joking with each other, or singing and playing a game. This archetype of family harmony, reminiscent of a Norman Rockwell illustration, seems to be a very important component of our teenagers' past experience; it is a memory that serves as a cornerstone for their self-concept, a benchmark that indicates what kind of life they would like to live in the future.

In calling such family patterns negentropic, we do not mean solely that they make family members feel good, think more clearly, and so forth. We also mean that there is a structure to the interactions that allows for the perpetuation of those qualities. The main features of such a negentropic interaction pattern are clear: The psychic energy of the separate individuals is directed to a common goal, which involves an activity that provides positive feedback to everyone. This harmonious activity is frequently in contrast to some previous one that was quite strenuous—like hiking, sledding, fishing, or swimming. The rewards often include joint sharing of food or warm drink. The whole atmosphere is suffused by the good will generated when people feel at peace with themselves and with others. It is the kind of experience that makes families enduring.

These warm experiences are obviously not limited to vacations and outings. At home, too, there are times of almost perfect harmony. The most frequent context for harmonious interaction is at dinner, when moods are mellowed by food and there is often bantering around the table. Occasionally it occurs when everybody is watching television. A girl describes her family's weekly watching of *Masterpiece Theatre* as follows: "There is then a communicative silence. Our thoughts are focused on the same thing—we are all interested. We discuss the show afterwards—what happened to all the characters and such." It is a good description of a negentropic social system, in which several people freely focus their psychic energy on the same goal, and they exchange information about their common experience. The discrepant views of reality, so commonly a cause of conflict, become, in such instances, a source of sharing and growth. Differences complement each other rather than occasion friction; the shared goal unifies the psychic energy of family members in a meaningful interaction.

But the main purpose of the family, at least from a functionalist perspective, is not to make children feel good, but to socialize them. Parents are supposed to substitute goals that are socially valued for the goals their children choose out of spontaneous preference. This inevitably involves imposing sanctions on the range of behavior which does not fit within acceptable norms (Larson 1983). Thus, family life amounts to a continuous compromise: Positive feelings, rooted in mutually reinforcing interaction, alternate with negative feedback required for socialization and for the simple task of getting along on a day-to-day basis. The result is an average lukewarm climate.

Varieties of Family Experience

The importance of the family context becomes evident when we begin comparing adolescents whose experiences in this context differ. Quite a number of studies have shown that disorder in family relations relates to adolescents' well-being (Elder 1963; Loeb, Horst, and Horton 1980; Offer, Ostrov, and Howard 1981; Rosenberg 1965). Here we shall consider the correlates of adolescents' investment of time in their family, and of the quality of affect they experience in this context. For instance, is a teenager who spends more time at home likely to do well by societal standards?

In our culture, perhaps the most highly valued goal held out for a middle-class adolescent is academic success. It is very clear that teenagers who spend more time with their families (and less with their peers) achieve better grades in all their school subjects (Appendix D.9). They also are absent from school less often and are rated more intellectually involved by teachers. Apparently, the family does fulfill its socializing function, at least as far as scholastic achievement is concerned. Just sheer exposure to family improves performance in school—or perhaps those who do better in school experience less conflict with family goals, and thus are willing to spend more time within its confines.

What is interesting is that this same group—those who spend more time with their families—also are rated by teachers as having lower *social* involvement in class, implying that they may be less able to relate to peers, or less interested in doing so. More importantly, they show less variability in affect, implying that they have less of the feistiness that makes dealing with adults problematic. It would appear that the family has a suppressing effect on extreme emotions, either through negative sanctioning or through the positive support it provides. Douvan and Adelson (1966) found that girls who spent extra time with their families were less autonomous: They relied more on external authority, had less to say in family decision making, and were more often punished. Spending time with family seems to signify acceptance of social goals. The family stands for the straight and narrow route to adulthood.

The quality of the home experience was also related to school achievement. Those teenagers whose moods were relatively better at home than anywhere else made higher grades in school. This was not due to their higher intelligence, because SCAT scores (School and College Ability Test) had been controlled for in the analysis; it suggests, rather, that youngsters who enjoy their families tend to be overachievers. Furthermore, adolescents who are happy at home tend to be happy at school—a correlation that does not hold between mood in school and the other major contexts: solitude and peers. It appears, then, that how a child will feel in school is related most to home experience. And since how happy or friendly a student feels in school is in turn correlated with the grades he or she gets (Mayers 1978), the family atmosphere influences performance in school indirectly as well as directly.

For most adolescents, it is clear, the experiential terrain of the family represents the smooth institutional path to adulthood. Some chose to follow it; others choose more circuitous and rocky courses. But what happens when the family deviates from its prescribed institutional form?

Conventional wisdom assumes that when one parent dies or leaves, the effects of growing up in a "broken home" will be generally negative on the children.[1] And, in fact, early research

1. A "broken home" has been, until recently, a "fatherless home" nine times out of ten. This is in part due to the earlier mortality of adult males, but more importantly to their greater readiness to abandon children and spouse. How much of this is due to gender-linked genetic selection, as sociobiologists claim, and how much to differential sex-role socialization, is still a moot point.

showed that teenagers who grow up without fathers commit more juvenile crime, do worse in school, are more likely to become addicted to drugs; and if girls, to become pregnant before marriage. However, on closer inspection, all of this pathology that originally was attributed to "broken homes" seems to be caused by other forms of social entropy that underlie both the father's departure and the children's behavior. To put it simply, men who are unable to get integrated into the socioeconomic system tend to leave their families more frequently than men who can function within the system. If the children of the former turn to crime and drugs, it is not because their father has left, but because of the poverty and the lack of skills that caused the breakup of the family in the first place and then later the children's deviance.

Recent research has begun to point out that, while single-parent families present a "high-risk situation for parent and children" (Hetherington 1979), not all the effects need to be negative. R. S. Weiss (1979), for instance, concluded on the basis of extensive interviews that children living with one parent might benefit from the adult responsibilities and participation in decision making that the separation thrusts upon them. Such children might mature earlier, and accomplish the transition to adulthood with fewer conflicts between the world of peers and that of grownups.

We had the opportunity to check whether the experience of growing up with one parent is in any way different from that of growing up in a traditional family. By and large, the thirteen teenagers who lived with only one parent did not differ substantially from the fifty who lived with both. They did just as well in school and reported just as many friends. Surprisingly, those differences that did exist were all in favor of the children from single-parent homes (see Appendix D.10).

When thousands of self-reports were averaged, it was found that children from one-parent families rated themselves overall as significantly more strong, free, clear, and skilled; and they tended to see their goals as more congruent with those of the people around them. The major difference between the two groups is in terms of the variable "clear-confused." Apparently,

149

living with only one adult simplifies a teenager's perception of what a situation requires. Inevitable conflicts between the demands of two parents might contribute to a teenager's sense of confusion. On the whole, all of these dimensions of experience point to the single-parent child feeling more mature and autonomous. It is as if a single-parent family system provides a more favorable context for an adolescent who is already in the process of leaving that system.

Of course, this does not mean that one-parent families are "good for" adolescents. All too often the breakdown of a traditional marriage results in severe stresses—loss of income with consequent change in lifestyle, loss of status, and so on. The mother and children may have to move to less expensive living quarters in a less desirable neighborhood (Tessman 1978). These material dislocations add to the original emotional turmoil that the separation usually entails. It is remarkable that despite such stresses the teenagers in this sample showed no adverse effect of parental separation; indeed, that the few differences were in a positive direction.

Although we were initially surprised by these findings, on second thought they are not that mysterious. Single parents, lacking an adult companion to share experiences, will naturally turn to their teenage children as an ally in running the household and in carrying the psychological burden of their lives. Because of this, such teenagers experience greater maturity and responsibility than their peers living with both parents. In effect, they graduate into adulthood before their peers; thus they feel more strong, free, and skilled. It is mainly the girls of single-parent families who show the increase in positive experience. This presumably is because the single parent at home is almost always the mother, and mothers tend to turn to daughters rather than to sons for support when alone.

Other intriguing differences between the two groups, pointing in the same direction, are that teens from single-parent homes feel significantly less happy and active when they are with friends, and they say half as often as teens from traditional families that they do what they are doing "for friends." In other words, the paradoxical effect of living in a "broken home" is to get more strongly attuned to grown-ups. Teenagers tend to get emotionally separated from their peers as they get inducted into the adult world where they must replace a missing parent. Thus, even in this atypical form, the family context thrusts adolescents toward adulthood.

Of course, our data cannot even suggest whether these effects are permanent or not. The real test, presumably, is how teenagers will act once they grow up and take their place in the productive and reproductive process. Will early maturity confer any lasting advantage to those growing up in single-parent families? Or will that experience of clarity and strength turn into liability later in life? Only a longitudinal study that followed children for several decades into adulthood could answer such questions.

The Family as an Opportunity for Growth

The family always has been viewed as the smallest subsystem of society. Like any other social system, it exists only insofar as individuals expend psychic energy toward a common set of goals. When parents and children cease to pay attention to each other's goals, the family breaks up as a viable unit.

One can speak of a "strong" family when the psychic energy of its members is predictably determined by common goals as these are interpreted by its leader, usually the father. A good example, which one still encounters quite often, is the power of Japanese families over their children. Urged by a paternal telegram, a thoroughly modern, young, physics student at a U. S. university will drop his career and return to Japan in order to marry a girl his parents have chosen in his absence. The strength of the family does not always manifest itself at an overt, conscious level. In fact, the Freudian perspective argues that our psychic energy is controlled to a great extent by patterns established in childhood by mute struggles with our parents. The superego, or the internalized version of what as children we thought our father wanted, is one way the family determines the shape of its children's consciousness, even if unwittingly.

In either case, it is by being socialized in the family that each generation learns to invest its psychic energy in patterns that replicate more or less closely both the adaptive and the neurotic patterns of the previous generation. Social structure is passed on through the family. This is the pattern that seemed to exist for the adolescents in our study who spent much of their time with their families.

But a systems perspective allows us to see the family from a different angle as well. It suggests the dimension of entropy—negentropy as a useful way to view family interaction. A family where individual goals conflict with each other is one in which entropy is high: much psychic energy is wasted in arguments, fights, and defensive maneuvers. If the psychic energy of the members runs out, or gets attracted to other less entropic relationships, the family simply falls apart. Like every other system, the integrity of the family is always threatened by a return to randomness, or chaos. In terms of a family, this means that its members cease to see each other at predictable times, do not invest attention in each other's goals at more than chance levels, fail to share experiences except accidentally. In other words, their interaction loses its predictable order, so that the individual members now relate to each other only as any two people chosen at random from the community would.

Alternately, members of an entropic family may continue to live together and spend time together, appearing to be "strong," but in reality sapping each other's energy and destroying each other's lives. For example, Douvan and Adelson (1966) describe the "American Gothic" archetype, families in which "affect is expressed with great restraint, if at all, but where family dramas of great intensity and bitterness are enacted (p. 138)."

A negentropic family, by contrast, is one in which each member assumes that, by and large, the others' goals support his or her own. Despite frictions—psychic energy wasted in arguments and fights—a negentropic family, on the whole, reinforces the self system of its members by providing positive feedback to their individual goals. The family functions as a system: There are predictable patterns of activity and shared experience in which the attention of its members is jointly channeled, and, therefore, opportunities exist for members to dissipate energy efficiently in ways that make them feel good.

Of course, every family would "run down" sooner or later without further inputs of psychic energy. The parents have to choose to invest attention in the home and thus forego other attractive activities. The children, as they grow up, must save some of their attention—so strongly attracted by peers—to mind their parents. Families cannot survive unless they are constantly *cultivated*. Like all organic systems, they need nutriment to maintain their shape. In the case of families, the nutriment is attention invested in common goals, which creates a climate of love and mutual support. How this process of cultivation works to produce warm, negentropic families has been studied elsewhere (Csikszentmihalyi and Rochberg-Halton 1981).

Some might argue that negentropic families are valuable because they make our nation strong, or because that is the way Christian, or Japanese, or Jewish families ought to be. Others might endorse them because they will produce better adjusted, more productive adults. These arguments are probably true and have important implications. But negentropic families are important also for a different reason. A child who grows up in such a family is likely to enjoy life more, in a context of mutual support and responsibility for others.

Popular wisdom and expert opinion often seem to imply that as far as the education of children is concerned, the end justifies the means. "Spare the rod and spoil the child," says the old proverb, and the common attitude is that privations in childhood are tolerable as long as one grows up to be a competent adult. But it is questionable whether the principle of postponing gratification really works as well as the so-called Protestant ethic suggests. Quite apart from the fact that children who grow up in entropic families are likely to replicate the conflict in their own lives and spread it through their adult relationships, the question is whether one is justified in producing disorder in another person's experience, no matter how lofty the goal for the sake of which the action is taken.

Thus, perhaps the most important fact one might want to know about a family is, how negentropic is the interaction within it? Does it function harmoniously with the goals of everyone in the family? Although, at present, we lack the methods to answer that question, it is one that needs eventually to be confronted. The paradox is that a family cannot maintain its inner harmony by remaining still. Like all living organisms, it must change in order to survive. The almost symbiotic relationship of the infant with its parents has to gradually weaken, or the infant will not become an individual. By adolescence, the young person must begin to break the predictable patterns that tie him to the rest of the family, for soon he or she will probably leave to become the nucleus of a new family system.

Thus, adolescents inevitably introduce some entropy in their families. The simplest instance concerns the breaking of previously established patterns of physical interaction: The teenager is no longer home for meals, on the weekends, in the evenings. The physical absence of the youth in turn may cause a variety of negative experiences in the parents, ranging from worry to anger, from envy to nostalgia. At least this much disturbance in a previously warm family is unavoidable; it is a price everyone must pay. How much additional conflict there will be beyond this guaranteed minimum depends on the amount of psychic energy the family members are willing to invest in coping with the dislocations growth must cause. It is not necessary for the families of teenagers to be miserable. It is possible to maintain harmony even though all conditions of the system change, provided there is enough attention spent on readjusting individual goals to each other. Of course, this is easier said than done; all too often teenagers and their parents are too busy, too tired, or too discouraged to try to understand what is happening to them, and to find new ways in which they can be happy together. In such cases the system slowly breaks apart. But decay is not inevitable: Potentially everybody has enough psychic energy to keep the system together if he or she so chooses. A family disintegrates because its members agree to let it fall apart; there is no outside force, not even death, that can do it by itself.

Chapter 8

The Companionship of Friends

EVERYBODY knows that teenagers love being with each other—that they crave conversation with friends, in person or on the phone, almost more than they crave food. What we know less about is why friends are so important at this stage of life, what the benefits of their company are in immediate experience and over the years, and what the psychic costs are that a teenager pays from overindulging in this necessity.

As the importance of the family in an adolescent's life wanes, friends move to the forefront. From childhood onward, the role friends play expands to encompass wider domains of experience and serves more important personal functions. It is in junior high school that adolescents begin naming friends as more significant to them than parents (Bowerman and Kinch 1959). In high school, for most teenagers, relations with the opposite sex begin to take up increasing amounts of psychic energy. Flirting, dating, and love become a part of their daily experience.

Compared to the family, friends have everything going for them, at least from the point of view of the adolescent. Teenagers cannot choose their families, but they are free to select their friends. If conflicts arise, the relationship can be ended. Age differences do not place the adolescent at an automatic disadvantage, forcing him to comply with societal norms. Friends do not have to fight over chores, or the bathroom, or other issues that come up in sharing a household. Because of these characteristics, friendships are the most spontaneous relationships in a teenager's life.

Friends are usually peers, that is, people of the same age, with similar backgrounds and interests. Just to sit around talking with them becomes great fun. Because they know the same teachers, are aware of the idiosyncrasies of schoolmates, and have watched the same TV shows, they have enough in common to share and validate each other's reality. Family members usually live in a different world, exposed to different experiences. Friends share the teenager's skills in basketball, music, or art; they know the songs of the same rock stars and are going through similar problems with teachers, parents, or boy friends.

There is no question, then, that friends can induce psychic negentropy—intrinsic motivation, feelings of freedom, happiness, and excitement—at least in the immediate present. But is friendship a good climate for future growth? Many parents and educators fear it as a cause of social entropy. They worry that unsocialized individuals will generate random, deviant behavior—delinquency, drug use, or pregnancy. Writing on the education of youth, a turn-of-the-century French rector placed companionship, along with indolence and sensuality, as "enemies to combat" (Payot 1904). It draws the young into a life of languor, banal conversation, tyrannical obligations, and degraded moral vigor. More recent commentators repeat similar accusations. They caution that ties to friends can retard development, lead to "uniformism" (Blos 1962) and "identity foreclosure" (Erikson 1968). They hold peer associations responsible for drug use (Kandel et al. 1978), delinquency (Sutherland and Cressey 1974), and socialization into a life-style of conformity (Coleman 1961) and consumerism (Henry 1965). The YMCA, the Boy

Scouts, 4-H, and numerous other adult-supervised organizations were founded because of concerns about the negative influence of peers. Adults suspect, and their suspicion is supported by some evidence, that teenagers left to themselves will be up to no good, that both in terms of their growth and society's interest, peer relations are disruptive. It has been said that the peer group has achieved an "obsessive importance" in Western societies, leading to a breakdown of traditional values (for example, Kitwood 1980).

But if friendship leads to deviance, it can also provide opportunities for growth that are not available in other contexts. Harry Stack Sullivan (1953), the psychiatrist, has observed that only peers can give a growing person the kind of unbiased feedback needed to develop a realistic sense of self. In a similar way, Piaget has argued that an autonomous sense of morality evolves by negotiating conflict with peers (Piaget 1965). Indeed, one could argue that egalitarian social relations are learned only through give-and-take with equals (Youniss 1980). Learning to respond to peer pressure could facilitate a person's commitment to group norms, and thus help integrate the adolescent into the fabric of society.

Clearly, friends present opportunities for either growth or disruption. They decrease entropy in immediate consciousness. But the long-term effect might be to induce conformity, thus increasing entropy in the long run. An ideal friendship is one that contributes to order at both the personal and social levels in the short run, and at the same time helps a person find a meaningful place in the world over the years. How reality fits this ideal is the topic we take up in this chapter.

Experience with Friends

Self-reports in the category of friendship include a wide variety of occasions. There are times with bosom buddies and casual acquaintances, with lovers and with competitors. They happen at school and at home, in church groups and at parties, and often by telephone.

Most of the time with friends involves leisure, particularly socializing—talking, joking, hanging out (see Figure 8.1). Free time with the family is often spent in front of the TV, but most of the leisure with friends is active and interactive. Only in 25 out of the 749 occasions with friends were teenagers studying. Most of what they do together is spontaneous, unrelated to the external requirements of adult institutions. It is hardly surprising that they feel extremely free, intrinsically motivated, open, involved, excited, friendly, and sociable (Figure 8.2). In fact, almost every dimension of experience is significantly more positive than it is on the average. Only three variables show a more negative state with friends: concentration, control, and self-consciousness. In other words, the only thing lacking from a perfectly negentropic

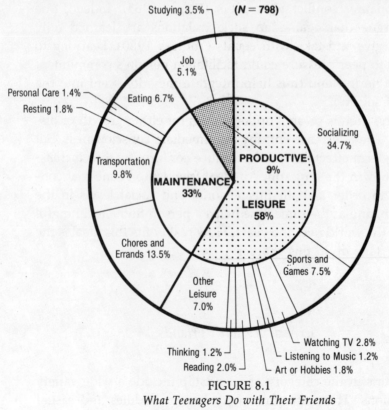

FIGURE 8.1
What Teenagers Do with Their Friends

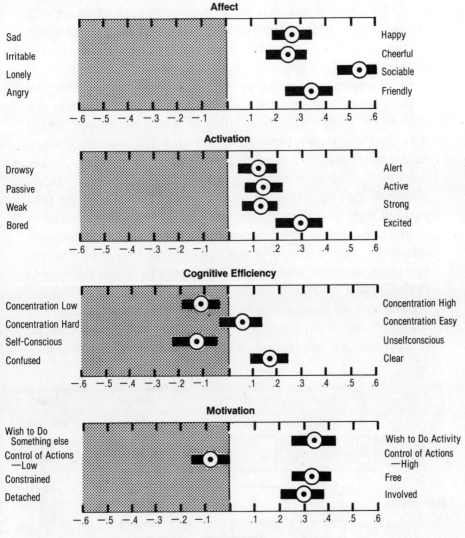

FIGURE 8.2
Quality of Experience with Friends

experience with friends is cognitive efficiency. The significance of these few shadows in the generally sunny picture will be discussed later.

The pattern is similar for boys and girls, upper-middle-class and lower-middle-class adolescents. Across all these groupings, friends are a context of leisure and talk, enjoyment and freedom. Boys were somewhat more likely to engage in sports with friends, but otherwise, differences were not substantial either in time allocation or subjective state (Larson, Mayers, and Csikszentmihalyi 1977).

From freshman to senior year, there is an increase in the total percentage of time spent with peers and within this, there is a shift in the gender and the number of their companions (Figure 8.3). Freshmen spend more of their time in same-sex groups. Sophomores typically come together in same-sex dyads. Juniors meet most often in mixed-sex groups, while seniors prefer being with only one person of the opposite sex. Throughout the four years of high school, each year shows a characteristic movement away from large groups and same-sex friends, toward intimate interaction with a friend of the opposite sex; there is a movement from unisex cliques in the early years to mixed-sex crowds in the middle years and finally to heterosexual couples, following the normative sequence identified by Dunphey (1963).

The quality of emotions reflects a parallel shift from same-sex to opposite-sex companions (Appendix D.11). Freshmen feel

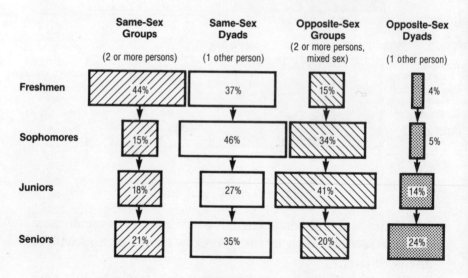

FIGURE 8.3

The Shift from Same-Sex to Opposite-Sex Friends

The diagram shows the percentage of time with friends that students in each grade spent with different types of friends (Chi square = 55.6 p <0.0001).

160

quite a bit happier with friends of the same sex than with the other sex. Sophomores feel about equally happy with both and juniors feel the best with the other sex. Thus, in the first three years of high school, the target of friendship shifts dramatically toward the heterosexual interests ushered in at puberty.

Sexual behavior, as one might suspect, was not strongly represented in our sample of self-reports. Even where a teenager would have been willing to share the experience, his or her partner typically objected to being beeped during sex; hence the pager got turned off. Nonetheless, there are a handful of examples that confirm its pleasurable nature. A senior boy in a very pleasant mood reports that he is lying "on the grass in a park, kissing my girlfriend." A sophomore, also in an ethereal state, reports that he is "getting down," and adds, "You pick some bad time to beep." There was also a girl friend–boy friend pair, each carrying the pager, who report sexual intercourse at the time of one signal. She indicates being absorbed and experiencing a very happy and excited state; he, however, is worried about finding a job, is distracted, and indicates only average levels of mood. Whether these instances are representative or not, of course, we don't know. What the data confirm is that time with the opposite sex, in general, is a very positive experience, especially beyond the freshmen year.

Time with friends is the best part of adolescents' daily lives. It is noteworthy that the adults we studied also reported feeling best with their friends, not with their spouses, children, or colleagues (Donner et al. 1981). The difference is that adolescents are able to spend considerably more time with friends than typical adults—from our estimates, about twice as much.

What part friends play in the lives of teenagers is best illustrated by examining the fluctuations in one teenager's life. The example below comes from a girl who experienced a major frustration during her week of ESM reporting. As the pattern of her moods unfolds over the week, it shows the power which friends have in influencing the quality of her subjective state.

Lorraine's Week

Lorraine Monawski had invested much energy arranging to spend her first year after high school studying abroad. On the Wednesday during the Experience Sampling period, she found out that these arrangements had fallen through. Because of regulations not revealed until the last moment (it was now May), she would not be allowed to go. To make matters worse, Lorraine had turned down an invitation to go camping with friends in order to attend an exchange program meeting that weekend. Now she would be attending neither.

Throughout the week her moods fluctuate tremendously as she attempts to cope with these events (Figure 8.3). Monday and Tuesday are relatively positive—this is before she receives the bad news. Her best times are when she is having lunch with friends at school. It is between 12:15 and 1:30 on Wednesday that she finds out her goals are frustrated, and the effect on her state is quite apparent. At 1:30, she reports watching a movie in psychology class and being very sad, very irritable, very angry, and very closed. Afterward she said, "I wasn't talking to anybody. I was *very* mad." Her mood is still extremely low at 2:55.

From this point on, there is a clear pattern. When she is with friends she doesn't feel bad, and even reports being happy and cheerful. But when she is by herself or in class, her mood drops precipitously. Even classes which she ordinarily finds interesting are boring and cannot hold her attention. She is obsessed with the events in her life. She explains, "When I was alone, I would just think about it." However, the presence of friends takes her mind off the failure of her goals. Even on Thursday when she is watching two girl friends fight (Merri had kissed Danny in the parking lot to Penny's great displeasure), the dark mood is temporarily lifted. Their jokes, their engaging conversation, their troubles absorb her attention and temporarily reduce entropy in her consciousness. The interaction requires her psychic energy, thus she cannot use it to brood over her disappointments.

The week ends with a series of events that begin to restore

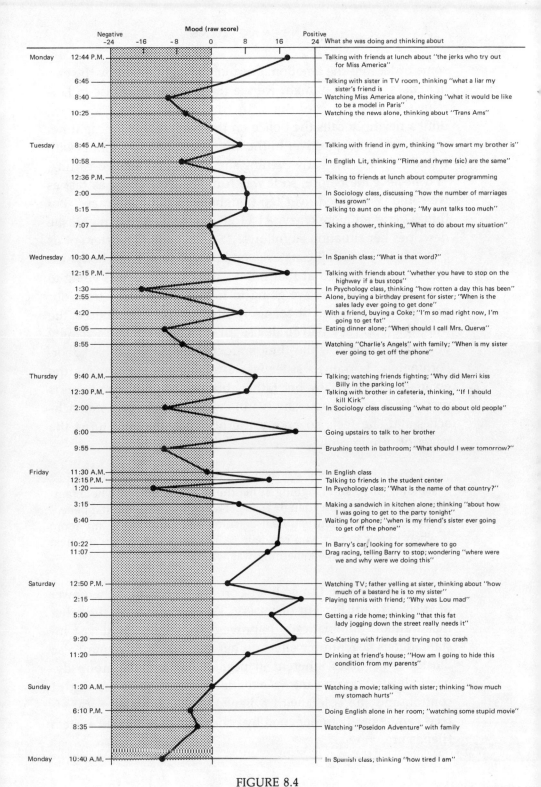

FIGURE 8.4

The Week of Lorraine Monawski

Chart shows Lorraine's mood score for each of her self-reports.

some order into the emotional turmoil brought about by the earlier crises. On Friday night we see the first enduring rise in Lorraine's mood. She goes out with friends and has a good time, until a neighbor calls the police on the party. Saturday night her moods stay quite positive. In the afternoon she plays tennis with friends, then in the early evening she has a good time go-carting. "I'd never gone before, so it was fun. We were going as fast as we could. We tipped over too (laughs). God, it was crazy." But things get even more crazy. At 11:20 P.M. on Saturday night, she describes her situation as follows: "See, my friend's sister got us a little bit too much [hesitates], you know, booze. Everybody was mostly real plastered at that point. And my friend was going to sleep over; how were we going to hide our condition from our parents?" Her father, it seems, waited up for Lorraine by the front door, so they had to devise an elaborate scheme whereby he was distracted while they snuck in through the backdoor. Fortunately, Lorraine's sister was available to help manage the escapade. They get by her father, but her physical condition is pretty bad. At 1:30 A.M. she is still awake because of a stomachache, and she feels so poorly the next day that she turns the pager off until evening.

> I spent most of the day in bed just dying, with my sister just standing there and laughing at me the whole time. The whole family comes in and they laugh at me. They all know what happened. You could tell; when you hear crashing and smashing in my room when I went to bed, you can tell. . . . With bloodshot eyes the next morning, they knew something was wrong."

The most striking thing about Lorraine's account is the power of friends to lift her out of misery. When she is with them her mood almost automatically improves. They have an almost instantaneous negentropic effect on her state. But this account also illustrates liabilities inherent in peer interaction: the group dynamic leads Lorraine into a situation where things are out of control, and she is left with a hangover. These paradoxical effects can be partly understood by considering the type of system friends are.

The Companionship of Friends

Friendship as an Interactive System

Friendship groups stand out as having characteristics particularly suited to a pleasant interaction. The quality of experience in social systems depends on positive feedback, the harmony and clarity of goals, the sense of freedom and openness that prevails in them. The more these are present, the more adolescents will enjoy being in the group, and the more they will want to take part in it.

If we compare family and friends in terms of these positive characteristics of groups, we find striking differences (Appendix D.12). With friends, feedback is more positive, goals are more likely to be shared, and teenagers feel more clear, open, and free. They also report that talk is more likely to be joking with their friends, a quality certain to facilitate negentropic experiences (Larson 1983). These differences hold for boys and girls, with same-sex and opposite-sex friends. Peers in general provide richer opportunities for interaction.

Returning to Lorraine's case, it is clear that the systemic parameters of the peer group raise her spirits in spite of her continuing problems. With friends she not only experiences more positive affect, but also reports the presence of positive feedback and shared goals—as well as feeling clearer, freer, and more open. Alone, in class, with her family, the interactive system is less supportive—hence her mind drifts back to her troubles, and her mood deteriorates. But with friends the world becomes ordered and meaningful again—and full of possibilities for enjoyment. The clearest effects are shown when she is go-carting and, later, drinking on Saturday night.

Across the entire sample of ESM reports with friends, there are strong correlations between positive systems properties and emotional states (Appendix D.13). Affect and activation are most strongly correlated with how free, clear, and open the interaction appears to the respondent. These properties appear to serve as a catalyst for personal negentropy, which in turn has a posi-

165

tive influence on the group. These correlations suggest that systemic and individual negentropy are dependent on each other.

Often the "system" is deliberately set up. One girl described how to have a good time as follows:

> Ideally you are in one spot, a place where you feel comfortable, like your house with your parents not there; several of your closest friends are there and no one is about to come or leave, you're just there, and you get into whatever you are doing, just having a good time. . . . Just yesterday I went to a friend's house for lunch. We were loud and rowdy—I can't describe it—you know, obnoxious . . . because we were out of school. If anyone saw us doing it, they'd think we're gossipy and giggly freshmen. But we were having a great time.

A pair of boys described some verbal routines they played together. They called them "gibberish words," "fringe of obscenity," and "the non sequitur." The game was to catch the other off guard, or to one-up the other. The game took on most excitement when there was a naïve third person, or preferably, a larger audience. They continued even in school, playing the boundaries between rationality and craziness, between being allowed to stay in class and getting thrown out.

For some, being with friends meant long phone conversations in which they shared everything that had occurred during the day, for others it meant shooting baskets in the backyard together, being with a new beau, or playing guitar for the church youth group. The common element was positive feedback—the encouragement of friends allowed the interaction to be carried a step further.

Requirements imposed by the adult world disrupt the smooth running of the peer group. Doing homework with friends, playing in organized sports, and participating in organizations all show fewer negentropic characteristics; feedback becomes less positive, talk becomes more serious. The students report feeling less open and free. The influence of adults appears to add an instant constraint to the system. Negentropic potentialities are strongest in activities independent of adult intervention, such as listening to music, playing informal sports, and talking out of the earshot of grownups.

Perhaps the difference is best seen in contrasting the way teens feel when playing adult-organized sports and informal sports. Informal sports (playing tennis with a friend, playing softball in the park) are described as having some extreme characteristics of a negentropic group; openness, freedom, joking, and positive feelings are at their peak. However, concentration is low and identification with the team is not high; that is, they do not report their goals to be the same as that of others. In sports supervised by adults, they report little openness, freedom, joking, and positive affect; but concentration is high and they identify more strongly with the group goals (Chalip, Csikszentmihalyi, Kleiber, and Larson 1984). Therefore, informal sports seem to contribute most to personal negentropy in the present, whereas sports supervised by adults provide an interactive system that might develop future negentropic experiences by "forcing" teenagers to grow. This difference represents quite clearly the conflict of socialization, the tension between internal and external goals.

Rowdiness and Control

When students were asked when they enjoy themselves most, many chose to talk about times when they were having fun with a group of friends, apart from adults. Again and again, they described these occasions in terms of "being rowdy," being loud, crazy, and wild. Why is this wildness such an important part of good times spent with friends? It is not enough to say that the "animal spirits" of youth are responsible for it. There is something about the group interaction of peers that makes rowdiness happen, even if the individual teenagers involved are not inclined to it. To see how this effect works, we should look more closely at what happens when friendship groups move into high gear.

Teenagers reported being rowdy most often on Friday and Saturday nights when they had long stretches of time free of adult supervision. For some it occurred in conjunction with alcohol or drugs; for others it did not. It was described as a state of letting go, of being swept away by the group mood. Some teenagers who were asked to say what *rowdy* meant defined it as follows:

"Doing *crazy* things, having a fantastic time"

"Being totally insane and feeling excellent"

"Being free"

"Getting stoned to the max"

"Being crazy, partying, singing songs, goofing around, and having one hell of a time"

"Being obnoxious-loud-fun-trouble"

"Going nuts with *Spirit*"

It appears to be a situation in which you are free to say anything, to do everything—friends will support your words and actions, they will come back with something even more crazy and bizarre, something that builds on the inverted reality you are creating. Teens told of trying to drive an automobile from the back seat and of hanging from railroad trestles while a train passed over. Rowdy activities included driving around yelling, throwing cans on people's yards, and having fights in school. They also included less obnoxious behavior: simply acting silly or "spastic," and other deviations from common, everyday norms.

That such a state of uncontrollable glee is the pinnacle of group interactions is consistent with the systemic properties of openness, freedom, and positive feedback (Larson 1983). In the extreme, these are precisely the conditions that make for what cyberneticists call a runaway positive feedback loop, the state of a machine that has only "go" commands, that lacks the homeostatic, "deviation-reducing" effects of negative feedback (Buckley 1967; Bateson 1972). Friendship interactions are "deviation-

The Companionship of Friends

amplifying," and thus have a tendency to get "overheated," to get out of control.

This process is clearly illustrated by reports on Friday and Saturday nights when students are with friends (Figure 8.5). While affect remains relatively constant throughout the evening, it is maintained at the cost of more and more extreme actions: as the night wears on, adolescents report being progressively more excited and less in control. After a peak in excitement between 8:00 and 10:00 P.M., they hit a low during the next two hours of 1.0 standard deviation below normal in the feeling of control. By midnight most of our subjects either went to bed or turned their pagers off, but for those who kept responding, level of control drops to 1.5 standard deviations below the mean. Excitement, alcohol, positive feedback has led them into a helpless stupor.

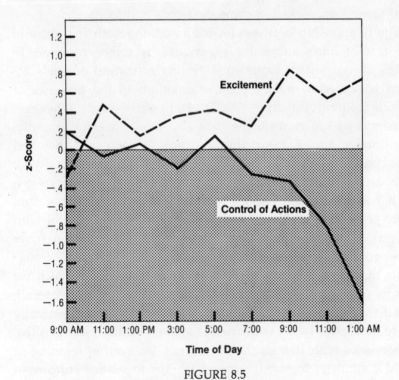

FIGURE 8.5
Losing Control on Weekend Nights
Figure shows average excitement and control of actions reports across the day on weekends when teenagers were with friends

As in the case of Lorraine, regaining control may often require adult intervention.

This is the process that makes teenagers so volatile and prone to many of the extreme behaviors they are known for. Freud (1921) and others who have described states of group excitement (Blumer 1939; Turner and Killian 1957), characterize them by the disappearance of personal control. Individuals regress to an unsocialized, primitive group identity. Some teenagers may be able to maintain control when deprived of negative feedback, but many cannot and are at the mercy of their passions and the leadership of the most impulsive member of the group (Polansky, Lippitt, and Redl 1950). Depending on whom he is with and the mood of the group, a teenager may find himself toilet papering a coach's house or necking with someone he does not know. She may find herself in a long conversation recounting her childhood or throwing up, locked in some stranger's bathroom.

The relationship between feeling in control with friends, and the rest of one's subjective experience, is rather complex. In terms of momentary experience, feeling in control of one's actions is related to mildly positive emotions in the presence of friends (column A in Appendix D.14). In other words, whenever teenagers feel in control, they are also more cheerful, friendly, alert, active, strong, clear; they concentrate more and they feel that concentration is easier. On the other hand, teenagers who, compared to other teenagers, typically feel more in control when with friends are *less* happy, friendly, excited, open, free, and more self-conscious than teenagers whose average control with friends is lower (column B in Appendix D.14). Therefore, over time, control increases entropy with friends. This paradox suggests that if we compare two experiences, the one in which we felt more in control will generally be the more positive overall. But if we compare two individuals, then the one who is generally more in control when with friends is likely to have less positive experiences with friends. In this case, it seems that learning to yield control (at least with friends) helps to reduce entropy in consciousness in the long run, even though it might increase it momentarily.

The Companionship of Friends

Yielding control to rowdiness might result in dangerous liminal experiences. It can easily lead to deviance, by stilling the social controls which ordinarily hold us back if we stray from normative behavior. In this sense, rowdiness is liberating, because we feel free of social constraints, free to do "our own thing." Most of the time, however, this feeling is illustory because it turns out that the apparently free behavior is actually controlled by instinctual urges, habits, or by the norms of the peer group. In some circumstances, yielding control may have a positive long-term effect. Dipboye (1977), for instance, has argued that the deindividuation of collective excitement can renew one's sense of commitment to the social whole. In fact, numerous cultures provide structured occasions of group liminality—like the carnival, which was originally a religious orgy—precisely to serve this purpose (V. Turner 1969). The difference is that American adolescents enter this state without the assistance of cultural structures. Ritualized rowdiness has clear limits and specified outcomes. Without such ground rules the experience may be favorable, but the result is unpredictable. The positive feedback dynamics of adolescent friendship make the outcome of the interaction highly uncertain.

Friendship and Entropy

It would be a mistake to leave the impression that friends are always fun to be with. This is not so at all. Reported thoughts with friends include: "If I should kill Ken," "Why don't this silly boy shut up," "How slow Chas is going," and "How much I hate explaining this survey over and over and over." It is the nature of positive feedback systems to eventually run into crises, and friends generate their share of cataclysmic occurrences. Furthermore, being with friends is also related to higher-than-average self-consciousness, a self-consciousness that is sometimes very self-critical.

Yet, on the whole, there is much less conflict with friends than there is with others. For example, the percentage of negative thoughts is less than half that with the family. On the whole, time with friends is a highly positive experience.

The nagging question remains: Peers are great, but do they help a person grow? Ceding control is related to higher average moods, but what about more objective criteria of socialization? It is not clear, for example, whether friends actually helped Lorraine cope with her disappointments or whether they just drove unpleasant reality away from her mind temporarily. That rowdiness should be the hallmark of good times with peers surely raises questions about implications for growth.

One way to evaluate the long-term impact of friendships is to see how time spent with friends relates to other characteristics. As Appendix D.15 shows, the results are mixed, but they suggest that adolescents who spend more time with friends will have difficulties later on. For instance, while time with friends correlates positively with overall affect, it correlates negatively with school performance and positively with how often students are absent from school. Most notably, students who spend more time with friends report wide swings in moods. These three variables show opposite correlations with time spent at home. To allocate time to friends instead of the family appears to be quite a consequential life choice. The first leads to negentropic experience in the present, but makes later participation in the social system more problematic. The second involves teens in more entropic experiences, but leads toward the acquisition of skills and attentional structures that might make adaptation to the social system more harmonious.

Thus there seems to be support for the notion that the influence of friends may be corrupting. There is no need to assume that this is due to intentional malice. It is simply a result of the fact that an adolescent peer group is made up of individuals who are not yet socialized into adult roles; hence there is no one to provide negative feedback when a person starts acting in ways that conflict with the requirements of adult systems. Without negative feedback, the teen group can quickly develop deviant

172

behaviors. Precisely because psychic entropy is *not* a part of their immediate state, the growth of long-term entropy becomes a possibility.

The Transaction with Friends

For American adolescents, the extent to which friends come to be a central part of daily experience is exceptional. In the Soviet Union and Japan, teenagers reported spending two to three hours per week with friends; for our sample, this figure was approximately twenty hours. Among modern societies, American youth have a special freedom to enjoy time among themselves. It is no wonder that symbols of their life-style (rock music and blue jeans) have become cherished badges of identity by young people throughout the world. The question is, what does this freedom mean for their later lives?

First we should note that the opportunity to spend time together is not particularly new in American culture (Katz and Davey 1978). Also, in many "primitive" societies, adolescents spend much time together in work groups, hunting parties, or play. Partying and escapades are certainly not unique to affluent American youth; in groups as diverse as the Tahitians and Winnebagos, teenage boys organize furtive, late-night raids of sexual conquest (Levy 1973; Radin 1920). Tahitians call adolescence the "age of enjoyment," referring to the group revelry that takes place among friends. However, comparisons to these traditional societies do not explain the liberties granted by modern American society, where the continuity between generations is much more fragile.

All this free time together allows adolescents to form a shared view of the world that differs from that of their elders. They spend much of this time talking among themselves; they talk with each other more than they talk with adults. They discuss school, parents, world affairs; but mostly they discuss themselves and what kind of people they are. By so doing, they forge social identities—of themselves as individuals, but also of themselves as a group. Out of the creative flux among peers, for better or worse, come the new values, the new rebellions, the new music and art forms that will characterize the next generation.

In traditional cultures, this interaction is constrained within canonical forms. Adolescents gossip about elders but do so knowing that some day they will be in precisely the same position their elders are now. They carry out pranks, but these are the same pranks their parents once pulled. In American society, however, the continuity of experience between generations is much looser; goals for future adulthood are ill-defined; and hence boundaries of behavior, models for negative feedback, are lacking. Whereas Sioux youth got together to practice endurance (Neihardt 1932), American teenagers are more likely to celebrate impulses.

It is a mistake, however, to portray teenage society as entirely normless. Numerous studies have shown that even "delinquent" gangs have status systems, strong rules, and normative ways of interaction (for example, Coleman 1961; Henry 1965; Larkin 1979). We found these patterns to be sometimes quite subtle: A friendship dyad might have its own private language, a group might have a "joke of the week," or the norms simply might relate to intimate sensitivity to each others' needs. Sometimes these structures facilitate rowdy behavior (for example, norms regarding partying each weekend), but often they involved sharing comfort and support. When adolescents were angry, unhappy, or in trouble, it was friends more often than family who came to their aid. It is thus that adolescent friendship offers an environment for growth and self-knowledge that the family cannot provide (Douvan and Adelson 1966).

One way or another, most adolescents succeeded in having a better time with their friends than they had anywhere else. This is a tremendous contribution because it sets standards for the kind of life each person will want to lead. It nurtures dreams and aspirations for a kind of experience worth struggling for. Within the context of dating, for example, this produces the experiential foundation for marriage.

Friendship, like anything else, can be cultivated or handled ineptly. In all probability, the runaway, normless behavior sometimes resulting from peer interactions reflects a lack of skills, an inability to deal creatively with its openness. Teens who cannot enjoy playing basketball turn to breaking windows; teens who can't cope with losses turn to cocaine; teens who have nothing to say to a friend turn to more risky sexual involvement. The skills of friendship require more than the courage to provide the group with deviation-limiting negative feedback; they are skills of mutually defining a set of boundaries, staying within them—and simultaneously having a good time. If the amount of time American adolescents spend among themselves provides a lasting benefit, it is the opportunity to learn this competence.

Chapter 9

The Self in Solitude: Perils and Possibilities

AMILY and friends provide a great variety of intense experience, both good and bad. With their limited knowledge of people, adolescents must learn how to handle the pressures in their social environment. The one quarter of waking time they spend alone seems to allow an ideal opportunity to release and restore their inner equilibrium. Yet in terms of the quality of experience, being alone is the opposite of being with friends: of all the contexts in which they found themselves, this is the one in which they felt worst.

This large chunk of life deserves close inspection, for solitude is a paradoxical condition about which little is known. Great works of art or scientific discoveries are usually made by a person struggling on alone. The personal insights that give life meaning often blossom in solitude. Yet most people are terrified by loneliness, and will go to any length to avoid being left alone. One of the major opportunities for growth in adolescence is to learn how to use solitude as a way to reach one's goals, rather than as something to escape at all costs. Before reporting what teenagers did and how they felt when they were alone, it might be useful to review briefly what is known about the place of solitude in human experience and thus provide a context for the results to be reported later. Reflecting on the peculiar opportunities and limitations imposed by this setting will make it possible to interpret the findings more clearly.

Why Solitude Is Dangerous

Being alone is, for humans, a very unusual state. In most preliterate societies, solitude is considered to be unnatural—fit only for witches or madmen. In many African cultures "to be alone in the bush" means to be dead, and no one leaves the company of others if he or she can help it (Bowen 1954). Among the Dobu of the Western Pacific, the fear of solitude is equally strong. "Theoretically a person alone is in danger of witchcraft. Hence there must always be an escort, if only a child escort, for men as well as women . . . even at home it is rare for anyone to be alone except on an adultery or stealing bent" (Fortune 1932, pp. 77, 153). Even for the Romans, solitude was a condition to be feared. To be banished from the company of one's peers to a rural retreat was the worst punishment a citizen could get, short of being hurled to his death from the Tarpeian rock. In fact, a Roman expression for being alive was *inter homines esse,* or "to be among men," whereas the synonym for being dead was "to cease to be among men," or *inter homines esse desinere* (Arendt 1958, p. 7). Given the universal loathing of solitude, it is not so strange that our teenagers shared in it. But what could be the origin of this fear?

In the earliest stages of human evolution, there was certainly a clear survival advantage in keeping close to one's kin. In the jungle or the savannah, a person who spent much time alone had a greater chance of being hurt. For this same reason, mountaineers even in our own days do not venture on a climb alone unless they are very experienced—or foolhardy. So-called social primates, such as baboons, do not survive long in their natural habitat if they keep straying from the troop (Altmann 1980); and the early conditions of human existence must have been rather similar. This may explain why solitude is feared more among people in hostile climes (for example, among African groups) than among people living in relatively benign environments (such as American Indians).

But this simple reason for the avoidance of solitude cannot be the whole story. In many cultures, being alone is feared, not because of physical dangers, but for more mysterious psychic threats that hatch and fester in solitude. The man who keeps to himself is suspected of sorcery. The woman who prefers to be alone is surely a witch. And the poor innocents who against their will find themselves alone, are naked prey to magical powers. It is not just being alone that is dangerous, but any attempt to separate oneself, in thought as well as in body, from one's kin. The notion of individuation, the effort to differentiate oneself from the group, which is so central to the Western idea of personal identity, has been viewed with distrust in most human cultures. What Kenyatta said about his own people could be repeated by almost any person outside contemporary Western nations: "According to Gikuyu ways of thinking, nobody is an isolated individual. . . . his personal needs, physical and psychological, are satisfied incidentally while he plays his part as member of a family group, and cannot be fully satisfied in any other way. . . . in Gikuyu language, individualism is associated with black magic" (Kenyatta 1962, 297–98).

This profound fear of individuation is a splendid example of the symbiotic interdependence between the person and the community, an interdependence characteristic of nearly all people except those imbued with the tenets of Western individualism. Without the group, the person does not exist; and without the person, there is no group. The separation of an individual who has goals that may in principle come into conflict with group goals is seen as a socially entropic process to be avoided at all costs. Even in our culture, remnants of this attitude are still strong. A reclusive teenager makes peers uneasy; they make fun of him; they suspect him of being a weirdo, a maladjusted outcast. Parents wonder if they have done something wrong. Teenagers who internalize this attitude will apply it to themselves, too—so, when they are alone, they will feel uneasy about themselves.

The patterns of attention that define a culture—habits, language, norms, and values—are passed on through interaction between already socialized individuals and those whose attention is still random. Order depends on the continued accessibility of each person's behavior to the inspection of others. The attention of the "group"—whether it is family, friends, or the anonymous mass of the modern city—keeps pulling the person back into the pattern of order when he or she deviates from expectation. Everything that makes the culture stand out from chaos, from table manners to the deepest religious beliefs, is kept in the focus of attention through the psychic energy that each person invests in monitoring the states of the other members of the collectivity. A social system, then, is held together by the mutual attention of the people in it, each expending energy in making the others adhere to the order that is characteristic of the system.

Solitude is a threat to the existence of social systems. Perhaps the concept of witchcraft is nothing more than a label for this latent danger; the man or woman who pulls away from socializing influences is *ipso facto* involved in black magic, because he threatens to increase entropy in the system. Those who do not follow the order of the culture are, by that very fact, helping to destroy it. The solitary person escapes from the attention of the group, and this makes the growth of random thoughts and actions possible; if this pattern were to spread, it eventually would destroy society.

So it is in the interest of every person, as a member of the community, to instill the fear of solitude in himself and in others. What makes this task quite easy is that the same person, as an individual, is already predisposed to shun solitude. Possibly the pleasure we take in each others' company is the mechanism that keeps humans living together in groups, allowing us to benefit from the survival advantages of a social existence. Among recent writers, Elizabeth Noelle-Neumann (1984) has summarized most eloquently the pressures individuals experience in their social milieu. Some of these are based on the positive desire to be with others and to be like others; but equally important is the fear of being excluded from the group. These pressures keep the social system functioning and contribute to the power of public opinion, which evolves to express the goals of the collectivity.

The objective condition of solitude tends to cause the subjective condition of loneliness, and the latter is painful to most people, especially in adolescence. Loneliness resembles hunger both as an experience and as a motivational force: It calls attention to a painful deficit, and it spurs one to put an end to it (Shaver and Rubenstein 1980). Hunger is reduced by taking in caloric energy that keeps the body operating; loneliness is reduced by the psychic energy of others that keeps the self in an ordered state. Without it, we begin to doubt our very existence, and entropy in consciousness increases. Strictly speaking, the physical presence of others is not necessary to relieve loneliness. What counts is getting information that there are people who pay some attention to us; and this can be accomplished by contact on the telephone, by letter, or other forms of mediated communication. Thus, social interaction is indispensible both to the community and to the individual. Neither could maintain its particular form of order without it. As far as dreading solitude is concerned, the interests of the person and of the social system tend to coincide.

The Advantages of Solitude

If this were all there is to it, we could end the story right here and forget about solitude, because no one would ever want to be alone by choice. The fact is that even in preliterate cultures a few persons resist social ostracism and the pain of loneliness in order to live by themselves. Apparently solitude, despite all its draw-backs, is an ecological niche that has some advantages of its own. And the main advantage is simply the other side of the coin of witchcraft; the great personal power that accrues to the sorcerer. It is as if people drew the conclusion that anyone who was able to pull away from the gravitation of the group must possess superhuman powers, and this belief, in itself, is the sorcerer's power. Society attributes power to those who defy it even in our days, as exemplified by so-called charismatic leaders. Charismatic authority, as Weber suggested, derives from a person's ability to disregard the rules of the system: "Pure charisma does not know any 'legitimacy' other than that flowing from personal strength" (Weber 1924, p. 22). The point Weber did not make is that people pay attention to a charismatic leader, not in spite of his rebelliousness, but *because of it.* Anyone who presumes to hold authority independently of the social order will be thought of either as a madman or as someone with superhuman strength, because only such would dare to defy public opinion, the concentrated psychic energy of the collectivity. The act of defiant individuality attracts attention; it might eventually attract a following, and therefore gain actual power. Students who are loners in high school partake of the same ambivalent image. They are often ridiculed and ignored, but sometimes they are secretly respected and envied.

Thus, despite its drawbacks, in each culture there evolves a solitary life-style because of the peculiar advantages that role offers. Few people at any one time are attracted to it. In many preliterate societies, only persons who already differ physiologically from the rest of the tribe become involved with magic; they might be epileptics, albinoes, or bearers of some other mark that sets them apart. Transition to the life of the hermit—feared and respected, but isolated—is easier for those who fail to fit the system in the first place.

The early suspicion in which solitude was held is still with us, but greatly diminished. Perhaps this is due to the fact that in Western cultures the parameters of the social order have become increasingly internalized A rather thorough and overpowering

socialization has resulted in the development of a strong conscience, or superego, which makes it possible for a person to
withdraw from the company of others and still be controlled by
the standards of the group (Whiting and Whiting 1975). At the
same time—and perhaps more importantly—the social order
has been gradually extended to embrace all the physical space in
which a person could move. Whereas an African hunter's village
was a tiny enclave of order in the chaos of the forest, our world
is covered by an invisible network of laws and regulations that
leave not a square inch unprotected and free—at least in principle. No matter how far one goes within the country, the laws of
the land, the value of money, the ways of speech and thought,
the commercial advertising, and the fast food are essentially the
same. Thus solitude is no longer so dangerous; we know that
there is no way to really hide from the system.

In our days, solitude is feared not so much because it is a
threat to the community, but rather because it causes personal
entropy. To be with others is a strong human need, as many
psychologists have pointed out (for example, Murray 1938; Sullivan 1953; Schachter 1959). When this need is not satisfied, one
usually feels lonely, just as when one cannot satisfy the need for
food one feels hungry. Loneliness is probably the worst experience one can have while still remaining relatively sane (Sullivan
1953; R. Weiss 1973); it is a feeling of "frozen isolation," "empty
silence," and "naked horror" (Hobson 1974).

Yet, while solitude is still generally feared because it can easily
lead to loneliness, in recent years others have pointed out its
potential advantages (Suedfeld, Grissom, and Vernon 1964; Larson 1979). These are, in part, linked to the very success of that
process of socialization just described. As the social order becomes more ubiquitous, the attraction of escaping it grows
stronger in proportion. Thus privacy becomes increasingly valued, and people are willing to spend large sums of money for
experiencing temporary solitude. At least in the West, few persons are satisfied to think of themselves simply as the carriers of
cultural patterns. We need to feel that we can structure our own
attention, that we can choose how to invest our psychic energy
regardless of cultural blueprints. To achieve this kind of individ-

uality, a certain amount of solitude seems essential. For "who can know what he thinks and feels, if he never has the opportunity to be alone with his thoughts and feelings?" (Young 1966). Another reason for the necessity of freedom from systemic constraints is expressed by Jourard (1966, p. 312):

> Other people can chain one to one's present ontological status by their very modes of relating. A parent, spouse, friend, or authority-figure can exert a pressure to keep on behaving, and even experiencing, in ritualistic modes. Freedom from the experienced impact of others' physical or psychological presence is the first step in the fulfillment of the freedom to grow.

The quotation above stresses a point that is especially relevant in adolescence, namely, the developmental necessity of solitude. To grow, one must break out from the role expectations that bind persons to their previous status. An adolescent is no longer a child, except to his parents, who cannot break the habit of thinking of him as "their baby." If he wants to stop feeling like a child, the adolescent will have to spend less time in relationships that treat him as one, and more time by himself, figuring out who he is and where he is headed.

Solitude illustrates well the paradoxical condition of being human. On the one hand, we fear it because of its potential for social entropy; on the other hand, we secretly admire those who are able to endure it. Solitude is painful, the cause of the most entropic subjective experiences; yet we need it to separate ourselves from the social matrix and to achieve that individuality on which the outstanding achievement of our civilization are based.

The Ongoing Experience of Solitude

The pool of solitude self-reports is comprised of all the times students marked that they were "alone." (See Figure 9.1) It includes time when they had the house all to themselves, as well as time other people were in the next room. It includes times

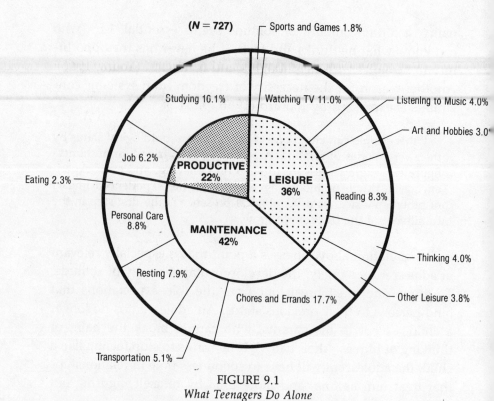

FIGURE 9.1
What Teenagers Do Alone

alone in public, in the presence of strangers, as well as occasions in the sanctuary of their bedrooms. When teenagers were talking on the phone, however, they were coded as if they had been with friends even though they were physically alone.

Earlier chapters have already shown that teenagers report the lowest feelings when they are alone. For instance, in Chapter 5 we have seen that their affect and activation are significantly lower alone than when they are in school with other students, when they are with their families, or when they are with friends. Providing fuller details, Figure 9.2 shows the same pattern, confirming the entropic quality of the experience. The most extreme characteristics of solitude are feelings of loneliness and detachment. However, the remaining variables that measure emotional order and energy activation show significant decrements as well.[1]

1. Boys and girls reported closely similar experiences when alone (Larson, Mayers, and Csikszentmihalyi 1977).

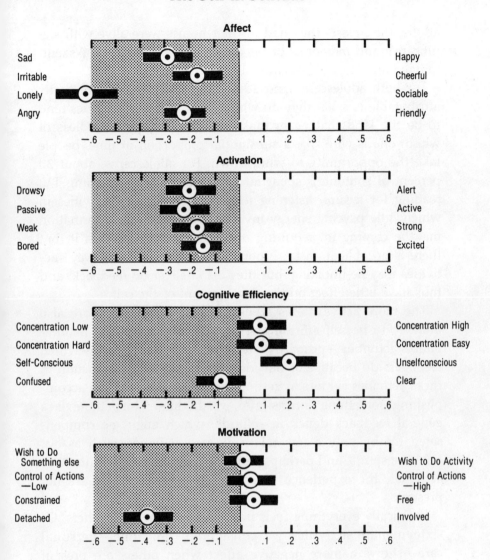

FIGURE 9.2
Quality of Experience Alone

We should mention that the adults we studied also reported feeling significantly worse in solitude, although not as much as adolescents (Larson, Csikszentmihalyi, and Graef 1982). Apparently, when teenagers are alone, they are *more* alone. This makes sense in terms of the findings of another study where adults were more sensitive to the presence of other people in the inanimate environment around them. Particularly among older adults, the objects they had in their homes were alive with significance and memories of persons living and dead (Csikszentmihalyi and Rochberg-Halton 1981).

For both adolescents and adults, the lower moods are partly attributable to what they do when alone. Solitary activities tend to be the kind that never make one very happy regardless of whom one is with. For a substantial proportion of time, people take the opportunity to wind down. For adolescents, about 30 percent of solitude is spent in passive activities—watching TV, reading for leisure, listening to music, or resting—activities in which little psychic energy investment is required. Information may be coming in, requiring one's attention to process it, but there is no obligation to respond. These passive "one-way" activities may be untaxing, but they also deliver no feedback, and thus have little effect on the development of the self.

The more active things adolescents do when alone are also unlikely to be self-affirming. They are productive and maintenance activities—primarily studying and housework—which teenagers do because of outside constraints. The satisfaction in these activities is more in getting them over with than in accomplishing something intrinsically worthwhile. Thus, there is a general feedback deficit in solitude, which might be compensated for by only a few relatively rare activities, such as art, hobbies, sports, and perhaps eating. However, even within these activities, the experience is less positive when others are not present.

Practically everything feels better when done with others. Of sixteen main activities we considered, only one—personal care—shows a more negative affect when others are present (Larson and Csikszentmihalyi 1980). Teenagers do not appreciate company when they have to attend to their appearance and bodily needs. But in the remaining fifteen activities, having someone else around improves the affective side of the experience quite remarkably. The same is true of the activation dimension, with one exception: When eating, teenagers report being more active and strong alone.

It seems clear, however, that the effects of company on one's feelings are greater in leisure and in some maintenance activities than they are in productive activities. The most impressive gains in mood when others are present are in arts and hobbies, sports, listening to music, watching TV, and chores. There is little or no effect on classwork, homework, and job. In these structured productive activities, the company of other people has little chance to improve one's feelings.

Is being alone a worse experience in all respects than being with others? A glance back at Figure 9.2 suggests that this is not entirely true (see also Larson and Csikszentmihalyi 1978). Cognitive efficiency appears to function more smoothly in solitude. Adolescents feel less self-conscious alone; they concentrate more and with less effort. At the same time, they feel relatively free, in control, and intrinsically motivated. It is as if psychic energy was more easily available, more under the control of the self. When others are present, where attention goes is influenced by the goals of other people; alone, it can be deployed more in terms of the person's own intentions.

The conflicting nature of the solitary state reflects the paradox of solitude itself. People need to be alone to develop their individuality, but they dread to be cut off from interaction with others. The self needs constant attention from others, as a plant needs light. To remain in an ordered state, the self requires others to confirm its existence. Unless others recognize me and my goals, I begin to doubt that there is such a thing as "I." These doubts demand turning increasing amounts of attention inward to bolster the sagging self, leaving less attention to deal with other information. It is thus that the experience of loneliness takes hold, increasing emotional entropy in consciousness. At the same time—provided loneliness is kept within bounds—the absence of others makes it possible to order our thoughts, to concentrate better, and thus to achieve cognitive negentropy. Loneliness is the price to pay for individuation, for refusing to be determined entirely by the social context. In adolescence this price appears to be higher, yet the psychological tasks of this period—resisting conformity and developing identity—make it more essential than ever to pay it.

Thoughts When Alone

It is easy to stereotype solitude, to imagine it as a nebulous part of teenagers' lives—when the public person disappears and unknown forces take over. Like members of traditional cultures, we are tempted to infer that some kind of witchcraft must be taking place.

The Experience Sampling reports, however, indicate that for much of adolescents' solitude this is not an accurate picture. A representative sample of their thoughts when by themselves includes the following:

"If I should water the plants"

"How I was going to do my homework and rehearse tonight"

"The omelet I was making"

"My future college roommate"

"What this blooming story was about"

"What it would be like to be a model in Paris"

"Doing this bong of hash"

"Finishing my math"

"Getting a beat on the drums to sound like a drummer in Hendrix"

One can see that they are often actively engaged in evaluating, planning, and doing things. Consciousness has not been overwhelmed by emotional entropy. The topics of thought cover a broad range of areas, from world affairs to one's looks; they include instances of humor and fantasy, deliberation and labor.

Katherine Tennison, the musician described earlier, certainly used her solitude effectively. For example, the pager once found her alone at home, playing jazz. This is something she could not do in front of an audience that might evaluate what she expressed in her playing. To improvise, to let her feelings come into the music, she needed complete freedom from external feedback; she wanted the chance to judge herself on her own terms. In this instance she was having a great time. In addition, Kathy also reported that she valued being alone on the porch after school. She would come home exhausted and seek the chance to "unwind," looking through catalogues or magazines.

There are many examples of solitude being put to good use: a boy who shot baskets in order to think by himself; a girl who spoke fondly of the silence she had discovered at the bottom of a lake while scuba diving; a boy who was devoted to photography; a girl who sometimes closed the curtains when her parents weren't home and acted out her fantasy to be a cabaret dancer. Many students used solitude to study—cognitive efficiency is easily better when studying alone (Figure 9.2). Time alone was used to fantasize and experiment, to relax and recover, or just to be free from distraction.

The skill to use solitude is the ability to keep oneself engaged, to find opportunities for action even in the absence of social demands and a structured activity. Adolescents who used solitude constructively were still lonely alone, but they had found ways to keep themselves going without social reinforcement, at least for an hour or two. They were developing skills to function autonomously. Perhaps in the future they will be able to use these same skills to also be independent of the need for continuous social reinforcement when they are with others. Thus it seems that a valuable developmental achievement is the ability to pursue one's goals independently of either the presence or the absence of people.

However, the kinds of thoughts reported when alone also suggest that in solitude teenagers often play out worrisome experiences in their mind. Here are some examples:

"My car accident a week ago"

"How tired I am"

"About how much I weigh"

"My back problem"

"All the homework due tomorrow"

There are several instances of girls doing nothing but waiting for their boy friends to call. Worry, self-criticism, and distress are common subcurrents. If irritation with others was a frequent theme of thoughts with the family, doubts about self are a recurring theme of time alone.

A number of adolescents said they did not like to be alone. "Why?" they were asked. "Because I start to think," was a common response. Lorraine Monawski was one person who said this. When alone, the information she processed was almost exclusively negative; worry took over her thoughts, leaving her weak. For Lorraine, particularly in a crisis, solitude was a state of psychic entropy.

There are many other examples of this passive, vulnerable solitude. Quite often "nothing" was what teenagers were thinking about. Gregory Stone recounted deliberately "blanking out" his mind when alone at work. A girl described spending hours in her room, worrying and rocking in a rocking chair. Perhaps the most startling examples of helpless solitude come from our study of bulimia (Johnson and Larson 1982). This Experience Sampling study was conducted with fifteen young women, aged 19 to 32, who had been clinically identified as having a syndrome characterized by episodes of compulsive eating followed by purging via heavy doses of laxatives or vomiting. We discovered that being alone, particularly at home, was an extremely negative experience. Yet these women spent an inordinate amount of time in this state, not because they lacked friends or lacked social skills, but because a combination of anxiety, shame, and self-doubt held them there. Solitude was the context in which they did their binge eating, and food was sought as a means to escape negative feelings. Eating provided a simple goal that temporarily blanked out other concerns; purging afterward provided a means to regain control. One might consider this cycle of behavior as an "active" means for coping with solitude; except that, in addition to the damage it did to the body, it also didn't work very well. It left the women feeling no better on the self-reports following the binge, and added on an extra burden of shame.

Among men, comparable compulsive patterns of dealing with

solitude can be seen: gambling, drinking, whoring, and violence. People unable to deal with themselves alone seek out drastic means to confirm—or to escape—their existence. It is the context of Hamlet's brooding soliloquy in which the disorder around him takes hold of his thoughts. It is the context in which Dostoyevski's Raskolnikov is possessed, first by the idea of murder, then by guilt, as ways to create direction for his purposeless life. For people lacking the skills to bring rational structure to solitude, being alone *is* a dangerous context and certain types of witchcraft *do* occur in it.

Long-Term Effects of Solitude

To evaluate the solitary condition, one must consider not only the momentary experience it provides, but also its long-term effects. Solitude might be like a medicine, bitter to swallow but beneficial in the long run. To begin unraveling the immediate from the delayed correlates of aloneness, teenagers' moods were compared at four different points: just before they entered solitude, the first time afterward, when they were alone, the next time when they were still by themselves, and finally when they returned to the company of others. The pattern of feelings reported at these points resembles closely the one reported in Figure 9.3.

The figure shows that, prior to being alone, adolescents say they are just as "alert" as they usually are in company. But as soon as they are alone, they report being significantly more drowsy. While they stay alone, their level of alertness does not change appreciably. But when they rejoin the company of other people, they report feeling much more alert, in fact *very significantly more than they usually report while with others*. The same thing happens for cheerfulness and feeling strong; and the improvement in state appears to occur irrespective of how lonely a person feels.

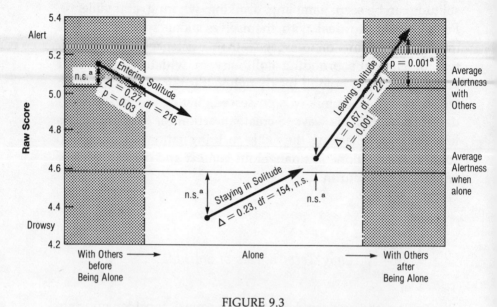

FIGURE 9.3

Changes in Alertness when Entering and Leaving Solitude

The figure is based on times when students filled out two self-reports within 120 minutes. It shows the changes in ratings of alertness from the first to the second self-report. (Adapted from: Larson and Csikszentmihalyi 1980)

Figure 9.3 suggests two things: first, that solitude *causes* the change in moods, rather than vice versa. It might have been argued that deteriorating moods precede withdrawal from company: First one feels more drowsy, then one decides to be alone for a while. If this explanation had been true, the level of alertness should have been lower than average before solitude, and it should have been higher just before leaving it. The pattern in the figure is more compatible with the original explanation: That, in general, it is the state of being alone that depresses moods.

The second message conveyed by Figure 9.3 is that being alone improves one's appreciation of other people. Psychological states improve after solitude; in addition to being more alert, teenagers report being significantly more cheerful and strong right after solitude than they usually are when with others. We found the same pattern to hold true for adults as well (Larson, Csikszentmihalyi, and Graef 1982). Of course, this rebound is not a long-range effect, but it suggests that in the dialectic of everyday life the ability to withdraw occasionally improves the

192

experience of social interaction, if only through the excitement of being freed from loneliness.

The real long-term consequences of being alone can only be assessed through a longitudinal study; but even then it would be difficult to know exactly what causes what. Suppose one finds that young adults, who as teenagers spent a lot of time alone, have more trouble getting adjusted socially than those who spent less time alone as teenagers. Would that prove that solitude in adolescence made later adjustment difficult? Unfortunately it would not. It might be that the solitary teenagers had adjustment difficulties to begin with; thus, their being alone was a symptom rather than a cause of social maladjustment.

Among the students in our group, teenagers differed widely in terms of how much time they spent by themselves. One person reported being alone half the time she was paged, another only once. The proportion of time spent alone seems to be a stable aspect of the teenagers' life-style; some are consistent loners while others tend to be generally gregarious (Larson 1979; Larson and Csikszentmihalyi 1980). Neither Socio-Economic Status (SES), sex, nor age correlated with the proportion of time alone. Loners did not get better grades in school, nor were they more creative (as measured by Guilford's Unusual Uses test) than gregarious students. There was, however, a slight correlation between amount of time spent alone and intelligence as measured by the SCAT (School and College Ability Test). Of the two components of this test, the quantitative and the verbal, only the latter correlated significantly with solitude.

Loners spend more of their time at home, and especially in their bedrooms. They spend less time with friends, they study more, read more, and also spend more time thinking. The content of their thought is also different. Amount of time spent alone correlates negatively with percent of thoughts about sports and the opposite sex; it correlates positively with proportion of thought devoted to school subjects and to national and cultural issues. All of these relationships point to the conclusion that solitude in adolescence is not an occasion for escaping the socializing influences of the adult world. Modern print and communication media allow us to be together while we are apart. In general, those who spend more time alone appear to be introverted young people who have already internalized societal goals. They pursue Camus's image of a world in which "millions of solitary individuals work hand in hand; every man, on the foundation of his own sufferings and joys, builds for all" (Camus 1960, p. 272). Again, we do not know whether the sober life-style of the loner is caused by the amount of time spent alone, or whether an introverted personality trait is responsible both for the amount of solitude and for the life-style. Those who spend more time alone, however, seem to have adopted more personalized, internal life goals (McCormack 1984).

In terms of their overall quality of experience, teenagers who spend more time alone rate themselves significantly less friendly, sociable, open, and self-conscious. They are *not* less happy and cheerful, however, and neither is their level of activation and motivation less. On the whole, then, loners are not suffering as a result of their life-style; they are more introverted, but not unhappy. They appear to have adjusted to solitude as a way of life.

Actually, the relationship between how much time a teenager spends in solitude, and how happy and well socialized he is, is much more intriguing than the above generalization would suggest. A closer look at the data reveals nonlinear trends; those who spend intermediate amounts of their time alone, 25 to 30 percent, have the highest average affect and do better in school. It is those who use solitude in moderation who appear to benefit most (see also Larson and Csikszentmihalyi 1978). However, this was not true for all groups in the sample. Younger teenagers, those from a lower SES (Socio-Economic Status) background, and those with low SCAT (School and College Ability Test) scores, show no benefit from solitude. Among the older, higher SES and more "intelligent" students, several quadratic relations appeared. Within these groups, the advantages associated with intermediate solitude were clear and apparent (Larson 1979, pp. 183, 185). The pattern is illustrated in Figure 9.4.

These findings suggest that certain skills, or a certain maturity, are required before a person can learn to make use of solitude. Age helps to develop these skills, and so does intelligence. Middle-class culture provides tools that are useful to tame loneliness;

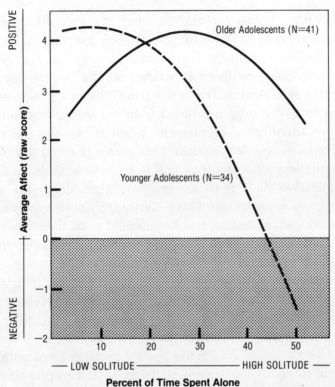

FIGURE 9.4
The Relationship of Average Affect to Amount of Solitude
The amount of time an adolescent spends alone (%) (From: Larson and Csikszentmihalyi 1980)

perhaps habits of introspection and autonomous activity are encouraged more in such families. The capacity to use solitude is the capacity to structure one's own attention, to set one's own goals, and to provide oneself with meaningful feedback. If one lacks such skills, solitude is nothing more than a frightening vacuum.

The Uses of Psychic Energy in Solitude

So, a favorite argument of many philosophers, Is solitude good or bad? hinges on a spurious alternative. It is clearly both. Being alone is painful; compared to being in the company of others, emotional states deteriorate on practically every dimension. Psy-

195

chic negentropy is easier to achieve when there are other people paying attention to us, validating with their psychic energy our own existence. Loneliness literally drains psychic energy by making it necessary to divert attention from the outside world to the starving self. And as we look inward, the image we see reflected is that of a person isolated from the world, impotent to attract the attention of others. The result is that we feel even worse. For most people it is paradoxically true that the self grows stronger the less attention they pay to it. Action produces feedback, reflection does not. Bowling, drinking, carousing with friends proves we exist; thinking—Descartes notwithstanding—does not. Unless, of course, one has learned to produce feedback with one's thinking, as a philosopher or an artist can. But that is a difficult skill few teenagers have mastered yet.

While solitude can be depressing, it also is necessary for breaking free from the constraint of others. For teenagers, this means a partial withdrawal from the company of family and peers. An adolescent who spent all his free time with the family or with friends would forfeit the chance to experiment with independent thoughts and activities. To grow in a culture such as ours, where individuation is a requirement of selfhood, one must alternate between integration with, and differentiation from, social systems. One must learn to give oneself feedback, as well as to use feedback from others.

Thus, solitude is generally an entropic experience, but has the potential for increasing negentropy in the future. However, even moderate amounts of solitude are worthless to those who have not developed skills to interact with themselves when alone. Teenagers need to learn how to use the potential benefits of solitude. These seem to be generally of a symbolic nature: reading, thinking, studying, or working within the discipline of a craft, art, or science. They provide feedback to the self by making things happen in line with the person's intentions. This feedback is not as concrete as that provided by other people; but it is potentially more objective and honest. Those who learn to use it avoid the worst consequences of loneliness and strengthen their selves in the process.

The Self in Solitude

Most people—not just teenagers—are unable to fill solitude with a productive activity, presumably because they have not learned the necessary skills. Even daydreaming must be cultivated; most people do not have a natural gift for shaping their thoughts in ways that are constructive or enjoyable, but it is a skill that can be learned (Singer 1975). As we saw in Chapter 5, teenagers don't like thinking, because it usually takes the form of worry. The most dramatic instance of inability to structure solitude was shown by the bulimics we studied. They could not stand being alone, and eating—the most basic, the most thoroughly programmed activity of the human organism—provided a means of escape. Only by gorging and then purging could they regain some sense of control. People who do not know what to do when they are alone cannot get feedback to their intentions. To the extent that they cannot *do* anything, the existence of their self becomes questionable, resulting in the specter of loneliness.

Apparently, to *be* one must *do*. To know that we exist and that we matter in the world, we must act in ways that prove that existence. This is relatively easy to accomplish in the company of others: a bare minimum of social skills guarantees that those around will acknowledge us. Friends usually provide positive feedback indiscriminately. Alone, it is more difficult; we must convince ourselves that we exist and that we matter, by making things happen that would not happen by themselves.

Those who cannot act alone may escape loneliness, at least temporarily, by diverting their attention to a passive involvement with music or television, activities that keep them plugged into the world vicariously. This strategy is probably better than crying, worrying, taking drugs—or "thinking about going insane," which is what one teenager said he did when alone. But evading solitude does not seem to be a good solution in the long run. The conditions of modern life force a certain amount of time alone on us, whether we like it or not. To control our destinies we must have some calm, untroubled time to reflect on the available choices. It is better to feel alive alone with ourselves than, for lack of knowing what to do, to drug our consciousness as a way to avoid the terror of nonbeing.

Chapter 10

Coping with Classes

IN the lives of teenagers, the school vies with family as the most prominent adult institution. Part jail, part temple of learning, it takes up one full third of an adolescent's waking time. What happens during those long hours? Experts can tell how much English and math students learn in schools, how their IQ scores affect their performance, even how socially involved they are while in school. But this is only the tip of the iceberg. Reading and math scores are important, but more important yet are the psychological strengths and weaknesses nurtured or weeded out by formal learning. As more than one observer has noted, and most of us suspect from direct experience, "What is learned in high school, or for that matter anywhere at all, depends far less on what is taught than on what one actually experiences in the place" (Friedenberg 1966, p. 89).

If students felt, on the whole, that being in school advanced their goals, if they enjoyed the academic challenges, their selves would glow stronger as they learned. But schools are essentially machines for providing negative feedback. They are supposed to reduce deviance, to constrain the behavior and the minds of adolescents within straight and narrow channels. Thus it is difficult for many young people to feel that schools provide negentropic experiences. In this chapter we shall see how different subject matters and different classroom activities are related to the quality of experience and see the effects of moving back and forth between classes and other settings. In addition, we shall explore the relationship between how students feel in class and what grades they get at the end of the term. It is important to begin finding out what the educational process does to the self as a whole, not just to its cognitive dimensions.

A community needs people who are self-confident, motivated to achieve yet respectful of others, who are adaptable, original, and at peace with their own selves, more than it needs students who score high on tests. Yet the former traits are difficult to measure while academic performance is easy; therefore, schools are evaluated in terms of what can be measured, while the rest is ignored. It is impossible to tell how much harm or good schools do until the total impact of formal education can be assessed, not only its most obvious cognitive results.

The lack of clear measures for evaluating psychological effects of formal education has not deterred scholars and laymen alike from passing judgment on what happens in schools. Some of the studies of high school life present a rather dismal picture (see, for example, Bowles and Gintis 1976; Coleman 1961; Friedenberg 1966; Havighurst 1948; Henry 1965; Hollingshead 1949; Holt 1967; Goodman 1964; Illich 1971). Based on sensitive observation, empathy, and common sense, they carry conviction— at least for those who share the observer's assumptions. Unfortunately, their divergent conclusions are often difficult to reconcile. Although most commentators agree that schooling is a powerful source of alienation among youth, the reasons proposed for this state of affairs are often diametrically opposed to one another (see Larkin 1979; Wynne 1980).

The Historical Mandate of High Schools

In the roughly five centuries of their existence, Western public schools have performed a variety of functions. In Europe, they first served to pass on the all but lost learning of classical antiquity and the lore of the Church. In the turmoil of the Middle Ages, the cathedral schools tried to maintain the symbolic patterns of a culture threatened by constant barbaric invasions. More specifically, they served to recruit and train the clergy, whose power depended on its access to an esoteric knowledge derived from the past. How important this purpose was is shown by the fact that the earliest schools of the West were often taught personally by a bishop, who in those times occupied one of the most powerful positions in society (Ariès 1962, p. 139).

With the decline of the Church and the emergence of strongly centralized nation-states, schools began to respond to different needs. Especially in France and England, the demands of a bureaucratic civil service dictated common standards of literacy and accounting procedures; thus school curricula began including such topics as modern grammar, arithmetic, and bookkeeping, to serve requirements of a broader segment of people.

Schools also began responding to emerging notions of personal development. The medieval belief had been that human character was a fixed, immutable entity, but enlightenment thought began to acknowledge the role of experience in molding adult personality. Jean Jacques Rousseau propounded a theory that the natural inclinations of the child had to be gently nurtured and protected from the corrupting influence of society, while others saw a need for schooling to subdue and domesticate the child's unruly instinctual tendencies. In both cases the implication was the same—an expanded role for schooling in the lives of young people.

In no place was this expanded role given more credence than in the newly founded United States, where dreams of a utopian social democracy were based upon a belief that education could cultivate the best in human nature. Through universal schooling, America was to rise above the despotic patterns of life in the old world. Horace Mann, the fervent head of the Massachusetts school system, declared that society would be "cleared from the harpies, the wild beasts, and the foul creeping things which now dwell therein!" (1891, p. 215). Schools were to nurture desirable personal traits such as industry, obedience, and cleanliness, and to propagate the values of equality and cooperation.

In the early years of the nineteenth century, Mann and other reformers heralded universal *elementary* education as the key to the development of "the new race." But in the later part of the century, a succeeding generation of reformers turned to *secondary* education to realize the dream. The "comprehensive high school" was conceived as a miniature version of society that would refine civic responsibility and provide finishing touches on older students. Run as an ideal democratic community, it would play an embryonic role in promoting social evolution within the wider society (Krug 1964). Frightened by massive waves of immigrants not yet socialized to the system, other experts called bluntly for the use of the schools as a means of "social control," an instrument to tame these uncivilized newcomers, suppress their excessive "individualism," and teach conformity to American society (Ross 1901). In later years, in the 1930s and 1960s, high schools would again become the focus of major campaigns for societal reconstruction and reform.

Since these beginnings, schools have been conceived as a means to a social end. Whether that end involved passing on the classics, providing vocational training, taming the masses, or founding a social utopia, the role of schooling has been to prepare youth for a productive role in adult society. The objective was to reduce randomness within individuals so as to synchronize their goals with the social order, whether that was the existing one or an idealized social order envisioned for the future. Carrying out these social goals, however, presupposed that the school could engage the students' cooperation.

From the adolescents' point of view, the ends of schooling are clearly external to their immediate interests. Schooling is not designed to appeal to what is familiar and instinctually interesting; rather it deals with the abstract, the complex, the unknown—with materials that are inherently difficult and alien: French, mathematics, literature, ancient history. In other contexts—with family, with friends, and in solitude—the activities and topics of thought are at least partially negotiable; there is some latitude to change the situation according to personal interests. But the activities of schoolwork are fixed by social purpose into a rigid institutional structure. Assignments and tests follow upon each other regardless of whether the students are ready or not. Hence, of all parts of an adolescent's life, this is the least responsive to spontaneous inclinations.

Put in these terms, the task of education is one of socializing through seduction. The success of the school depends on how effectively it can engage the students' minds toward its objectives. Can it generate interest, motivation, and focused attention directed toward the goal of creating conformity to its conception of an "educated" adult? The school in this study was one of the best in the Chicago area. The students' reports suggest how effectively a very good high school succeeds in achieving this goal.

The Pattern of Adolescents' Attention in School

In the 1950s a blue-ribbon commission recommended that the high school day be divided into at least seven class periods (Conant 1959); the school in this study had nine. An important result of this subdivision is that much of the time spent in school has nothing to do with learning, but is taken up by walking to and from classes, open periods, and lunchtime, most of which is spent with friends. Thus, in its very conception, the school day is set up as an emotional tug-of-war between classwork and friends. It is important to consider this noncurricular time to understand the school experience, but first we will focus on what happens during formal classes.

Coping with Classes

The domain of class self-reports is comprised of all times the students reported being in a school class. It includes shop classes, art classes, and gym, as well as mathematics, science, and English classes; it excludes study halls, passing between classes, and hanging out in the student center. It also does not include studying at home, which falls in the domain of either family or solitude.

During class, the students reported their main activity to be related to some form of academic activity for a remarkable 78 percent of the self-reports. Listening to the teacher, studying, and taking tests accounted for a much larger portion of time than did diversions like socializing, passing notes, or sleeping (Figure 10.1). However, the fact that students listed schoolwork as the activity they were doing does not mean they were giving it their undivided attention. In fact, they indicated schoolwork as their topic of thought for only 40 percent of all occasions in

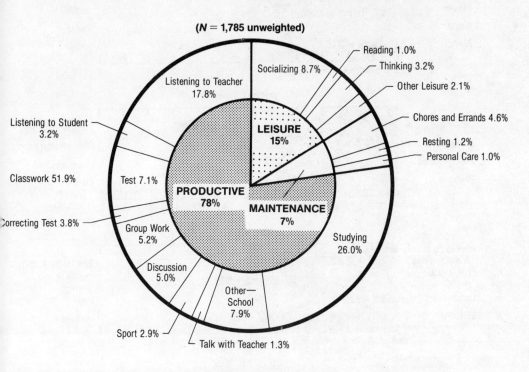

FIGURE 10.1
What Teenagers Do in Class

class. More important is the rather abysmal pattern of activation, cognitive efficiency, and intrinsic motivation shown in Figure 10.2.

Compared to other contexts in their lives, time in class is associated with lower-than-average states on nearly every self-report dimension. Most notably, students report feeling sad, irritable,

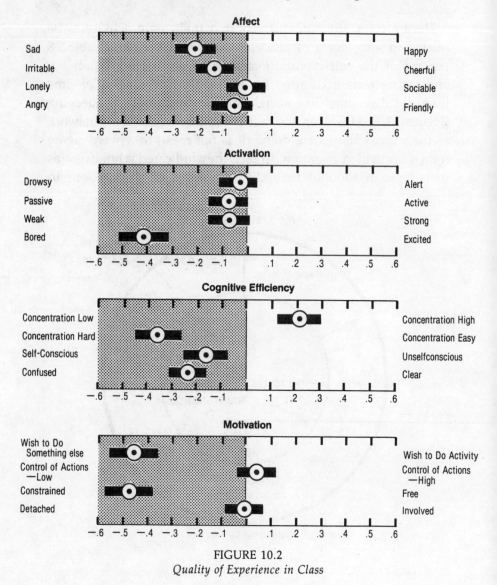

FIGURE 10.2
Quality of Experience in Class

and bored; concentration is difficult; they feel self-conscious and strongly wish they were doing something else. The only encouragement in this profile is their higher-than-average concentration. In spite of negative feelings and motivation, it appears they are able to tune into class for at least some of the time. Perhaps because school can motivate students extrinsically with immediate punishments and long-term rewards, it wins at least a portion of students' attention, although in conjunction with negative affective and motivational states.

That the profile of average states in class is a strained, uneasy compromise of elements is evident when we look at the correlations among these various dimensions of consciousness. Concentration in class is both deeper and easier to achieve when students are in a favorable emotional and motivational state (Chapter 5). Feeling strong, active, and motivated is related to a more efficient cognitive state, suggesting that it is when students are intrinsically motivated that the school is successful in capturing their attention. Yet motivation in class is rarely intrinsic, hence concentration in class is achieved at the price of great effort and often results in feelings of confusion rather than clarity.

A number of researchers have come to similar conclusions using one-time assessments of experience (Moos 1979; Ugurolglu and Walberg 1979). Good moods and good grades go together in school; clearly, negentropic states of consciousness provide better conditions for learning. It is unfortunate, therefore, that the average student is usually bored, apathetic, and unfriendly to the situation.

The founders of the American high school undoubtedly envisioned rows of attentive students happily absorbing lesson after lesson. One hundred years later the reality is far from this vision. Even in a very good high school, such as the one studied here, students are neither attentive nor happy, and they are probably absorbing only a fraction of the information being presented. This picture varies somewhat, however, for different parts of the curriculum. Some academic subjects and some ways of learning appear to produce less psychic entropy than others.

How Class Content Relates to Attention

Do students tend to be as happy—or rather, as unhappy—in algebra as in gym? We looked at reported states according to type of class to see how students fared with different parts of the curriculum. Classic academic subjects such as mathematics, foreign language, and English showed the lowest levels of intrinsic motivation, coupled with low affect and activation (Appendix D. 16). These classes, which deal with highly structured abstract symbolic systems, appeared to produce the greatest entropy in students' consciousness. In comparison, classes that provide more concrete goals and require more than intellectual skills, such as industrial arts, physical education, and particularly music, were associated with more favorable motivation and with positive affect. These classes involve students in some form of physical and sensory participatory activity, whereas math, English, and languages are entirely cognitive.

The difference is particularly evident in the pattern for the item "ease of concentration." In English, foreign language, and history, the students report that it is substantially harder to concentrate ($z = -.36$ on the average) than in physical education, home economics, or music ($z = -.05$ on the average). Clearly, they experience the more academic topics as more difficult. To order complex symbolic systems requires more psychic energy. Many students may not have enough to cope with these challenges. It is tempting to attribute the low motivation of students in academic classes to some deficit in their moral fiber: "Kids today are spoiled and unwilling to take work seriously." However, it is also possible that many lack involvement, not because they will not work diligently, but because they cannot.

There is another factor to be taken into account. The quality of consciousness in class is also related to the type of learning activity that is taking place. Appendix D.17 shows that intrinsic motivation is relatively high in informal activities like group work and discussions. This is also when students are most happy and active. Passive activities like listening to the teacher or to other students are much less pleasant. Ironically, while listening to other students might be "democratic," it is one of the least successful activities in getting students involved, except—as we will see in a moment—for the student who happens to be talking.

There is one activity that is a curious anomaly from the general pattern. When taking a test or doing a quiz, students report extremely low motivation and affect, but also extremely high concentration. This combination stands in marked contrast to the correlations between affect and cognition we discussed earlier. While it is generally more likely for concentration to occur in conjunction with positive affect and motivation, tests represent an opposite situation. The great majority of classroom involvement conforms to the paradigm of the carrot, but this is the stick: this is concentration inspired by the fear of an external punishment. And it seems likely that the coercive influence of tests accounts for at least some of the low states reported at other times.

The classroom provides largely negative feedback. It is opposite from the situation with friends where a wide range of novel, random, and crazy actions may be reinforced. The ratio of thirty to one provides the teacher with little opportunity to respond to each student in a supportive or personal way. His or her job is to see that students conform their behaviors to accepted definitions of being educated. This may be done through punishment, threat, or reward, but the basic thrust involves "deviation reduction," which is the technical definition of negative feedback. From the students' point of view it is easy to see why the experience is often unpleasant. Conforming requires more than simply being good, it requires attending to and learning complex information with which one is unfamiliar.

However, the purpose of schooling is not immediate gratification, but rather psychic change toward adult goals—thus the justification for coercive techniques to capture and restructure the students' attention. Unfortunately, the result is that the average student pays little attention to the goals of the classroom, and does so without enthusiasm or pleasure.

A Case Study: Freud, Marx, and Darwin versus Boy Friends and Fire Drills

There is another story to be told, represented not by *average* states in class, but by the *variability* in consciousness that takes place therein. Eight adolescents from the study happened to be in the same world history class, all responding to pagers during the same week. The sequence of their self-reports provides a good illustration of how the subjective picture of a classroom fluctuates.

It was an advanced level course for freshmen and sophomores, a class students generally liked. It was small, with only seventeen students, and the teacher lived in the neighborhood, and thus was well known. The students also knew each other pretty well and apparently got into lively discussions. "Everyone has a good sense of humor," we were told. The presence of pagers, therefore, was cause for some joking, but the students appear to have been quite candid nonetheless.

The week was one in which the students themselves were running the class. Each had prepared a report on a major nineteenth-century personality and had to present it to the group. What happens in such circumstances is particularly interesting, given that the situation combines peer interactions, normally fun, with the usually unenjoyable, task-oriented goals of the class.

Monday's report is one on the theories of Freud, by a bright and sensitive student we shall call Andrea (see Figure 10.3). She is successful in motivating the class: All four students who are carrying pagers are paying attention, and they report high activation. Andrea's activation is the highest; as she leads the discussion, she is very excited, alert, and strong. Perhaps it is her involvement that keeps the other students attentive.

The story is different on Tuesday. Now seven students are carrying pagers and their self-reports show a wide range of moods, and only four are paying attention. Either Darwin is not

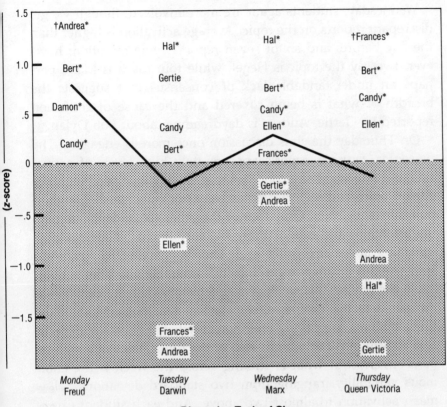

FIGURE 10.3
A Profile of Activation Levels in Four History Classes
The dark line shows the average for each class session.
† Indicates student who is giving the presentation
* Students who report paying attention

as interesting as Freud or the presenter is doing a poorer job. Bert feels the latter is true and is arguing with the presenter about what he is saying. Gertie and Candy are talking to each other, and one comments sarcastically that the speaker is making a fool of himself. Andrea, having given her report already, has her mind on other matters. Preoccupied with a boy she has a crush on but does not know, she is watching her hands shake and tries to calm herself down. She also comments that, "the guy next to me is drawing the neatest airplane," and attempts to duplicate it on the pager sheet.

Wednesday, students again are more involved, though we get discrepant reports on the topic. Average activation is higher than the day before, and six of seven report paying attention; however, two say the topic is Hegel, while four say it is Marx, perhaps an understandable lack of consensus that suggests the breadth of what is being covered and the cause of confusion reported by Gertie. Andrea is daydreaming about Bob Dylan.

On Thursday the class discussion once more is engaging. The presenter, Frances, reports appropriately high levels of activation, but afterward she concedes that she is dissatisfied with her performance and feels her notes were not quite good enough to pull things together. Only four of the other six students are paying attention, and one of these is "very bored." Gertie is daydreaming about fire drills, and Andrea is trying to figure out how she can arrange to run into this adorable guy after school.

On the whole, this week of world history class is positive—as compared to the profile of average states in class. Most of the time, students are paying attention to what the teacher expects, and activation is fairly high. Two of the four classes rate high on involvement. But what is striking across the week is the enormous variability, ranging from two standard deviations below mean activation to almost two above. And each student except Bert and Candy show substantial variations within their own reports. Numerous explained and unexplained fluctuations in state occur.

Even within each day, these students underwent dramatic changes in state before, during, and after world history class. For example, on Tuesday, Frances's activation level increases by four units following her torpor in class. At 3:15 P.M., listening to the Darwin presentation, she is extremely bored, passive, and weak, but at 5:15 P.M., she is at home playing a Beethoven sonata and is in top form. Meanwhile, Gertie, who was inspired by the Darwin presentation, registers a drop of three units between 3:15 and 5:15 P.M.

Perhaps what is most significant about school is not that the typical states are so entropic, but that the general pattern is so chaotic. To someone observing this class, it might have appeared an orderly epitome of good, democratic, high-school education:

students engaged in lively discussion about four of the great figures of the last century. Yet what was taking place in the students' minds was clearly a different story. Competing goals often directed the students to focus on information that was completely irrelevant to the stated goals of the course. Emotions derived from the ups and downs of their personal concerns kept disrupting their precarious concentration on the teacher's agenda.

Emotional variability has a great impact on the process of schooling. The cognitive activity required by class must find its place in a kaleidoscope of changing emotional states. Thus the success of class in catching students' attention is a highly uncertain matter. This uncertainty defines the amount of social entropy present in the class, which must be reckoned with in addition to the psychic entropy caused in the consciousness of students.

Mood Fluctuations in the Typical School Day

Following students' moods across a school day shows how they experience the variability. It also allows us to examine the competition between class and friends for their attention. The constant switching back and forth between classes and hallways, gyms, and lunchrooms keeps scrambling their moods—concentration dissipates as they leave class, but positive affect improves. The opposite happens as they walk back into the classroom. It is amid this alternation of emotions that learning is supposed to take place. The sequence of excitement versus boredom each day is presented in Figure 10.4.

Not unlike adults, adolescents get up in the morning with little excitement. In the preschool hours between 7:00 A.M. and 8:20 A.M., few of them are enthusiastic about facing the day. On the full range of mood items from excited-bored to happy-sad, they rate their emotions as negative. It is clear that early morning hours are among those difficult times with family when positive moods are eclipsed by practical maintenance needs. There are conflicts over use of bathrooms and hostility across the breakfast

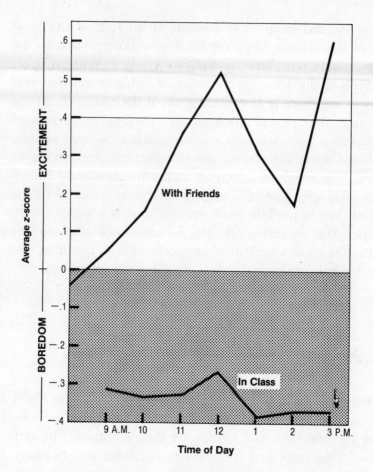

FIGURE 10.4
Excitement and Boredom during the School Day

table. Even with friends at this time of day, moods are relatively negative.

When they get to class, some of their emotions improve, but others remain at the same low level. The average reported state is boredom and wishing to be doing something else. Only around noontime, when students take lunch with friends, does excitement rise considerably. In fact, some of the best interactions with friends are reported during noonhour conversations and joking around the cafeteria table. After lunch, however, the emotional baseline dips again as students return to class. The average state in class is generally negative, regardless of the

212

hour. Only after school do average moods improve again. In sum, the school day could be pictured as two valleys of negative experience separated by one peak at lunchtime.

Contact with friends occurs most often during lunch hours, but it also takes place between classes and during free periods. The quality of experience when with friends is about the same in school as it is outside of school: Students feel happy and motivated.[1] Thus, when they shift from being in class to being with friends, their moods register a dramatic improvement, as can be seen in Appendix D.18. Average moods improve by one half a standard deviation or more. Conversely, when they return to class, when they make the transition back from friends to schoolwork, their moods show an equally drastic decline. Class appears to have an almost instantaneous entropic effect on consciousness. The two halves of Appendix D.18 are almost a mirror image of each other. The greatest changes occur in two of the intrinsic motivation variables: The experience of freedom and the wish to be doing the activity are the most severely affected.

Clearly, one source of variability in the school experience is due to the repeated contact with friends. Whether this variability helps or hinders the educational process is not clear.

To begin answering this question, we looked at the moment-to-moment continuity of states within the two contexts of class and friends, and in the transition from one to the other. Appendix D.19 shows the correlations of contiguous self-reports on the various dimensions of experience.

When staying in the same class or when going from one class to another, moods remain stable. Almost every variable is correlated from one time to the next. There is also a similar, if less pronounced, stability when the two consecutive self-reports are filled out in the company of friends in school. But when crossing between the two contexts, psychological states are completely discontinuous. In statistical terms, there is no predictability from one time to the next. In other words, friends disrupt the pattern of consciousness from the previous class. Thus, if a student be-

1. Research of Kelly and associates (1979) suggests that there may be a great deal of variability from school to school in the kinds of experience students have while they are outside of class but still inside the building.

comes deeply involved in a class, the interactions with friends are almost sure to disturb that concentration. Repeated contacts with friends during the school day appear to prevent engrossment in serious scholarship.

At the same time, however, friends bring order to the entropic states an adolescent might encounter in class. While they erase positive involvement, they also bring an end to negative states. In fact, this latter effect could be the more important one because there is a tendency for concentration to wane the longer a student is in class. When filling out reports in class two times in a row, concentration drops significantly, and the wish to be doing something else increases (Appendix D.18). Contact with friends appears to check these losses in cognitive efficiency and motivation. Friends apparently revitalize a student and increase his or her capacity to concentrate on class work.

Thus, contacts with friends play both a negative and positive role, disrupting positive attention, but also reviving students whose attention has waned. On the one hand, they stand in the way of serious, prolonged concentration, but on the other hand, without them concentration might be even more rare. The effect of peer interaction in school is that of a randomizer—it scrambles a student's attention. It provides a dose of positive, deviation-amplifying feedback to counter the negative, deviation-reducing feedback of the class. After being with friends, an adolescent will be in a different state, possibly one more receptive to learning, possibly one less receptive. On the average, there seems to be a slight relative gain. But the really significant impact of friends is probably not this slight gain, but the variability that is introduced into the school day.

Teacher's Dilemma

The great fluctuation in their students' consciousness presents a serious predicament to the teachers. They are confronted with twenty or more teenagers whose minds are usually elsewhere.

Their job is to engage the students' attention with information that is not about sex or violence, that is not related to the students' immediate personal lives, and, furthermore, may be difficult for them to learn. They have before them a group of highly moody, distractable teenagers, generally unaccustomed to concentrating on anything for more than 15 minutes. How can they step into the flux of their lives and reshape their attentional processes?

The example of the world history class reported earlier shows that how the class is conducted does make a difference. Some of the students who took the teacher's role were effective in engaging their peers. During the Darwin presentation, five of the seven students showed a drop in emotional states compared to their prior self-reports. In contrast, the discussion of Marx and dialectics was associated with an elevation in mood for six of the seven students. It is clear that there are ways of presenting information that are more effective in attracting students' attention (Csikszentmihalyi 1982b; Plihal 1982).

Teachers in the high school we studied had developed many different styles and strategies to insure that students paid attention to them. Often these were dramatic theatrical devices. One teacher had been known to pull a dead fish out of his desk drawer in the middle of a lesson. Another was notorious for tongue-lashing students who were even two seconds late to class. Some flamboyant teachers were greatly loved and basked in almost magical awe. Others, perhaps not as skillful, were seen as crazy or unreliable, especially when their unpredictability extended to the way they graded students.

Some teachers made their classes like a TV show, full of entertainment. One teacher did this quite literally; if he had three points he wanted to get across, for example, he would switch an imaginary channel between each one so that each was its own separate show. And to provide relief he would make up advertisements appropriate to the topic of the moment, or improvise comical monologues on "the misunderstood comma," or a new book.

The most impressive approaches were ones that directly pulled students into the subject matter itself. A sociology teacher teaching sexual relations had discovered in *Seventeen* magazine a series of "lines" guys often give girls in trying to coax them into sexual involvement. Skillfully he confronted the class with each one, pressing the girls to generate an array of clever responses, and shaming the boys lest they ever try making advances with this kind of manipulative rhetoric.

High school teachers are rarely given credit for their cleverness in generating interest in the subject, yet this is a prerequisite for any kind of learning. It is true that even more effective than clever stunts borrowed from the world of entertainment is the teacher's genuine interest in the subject he or she is supposed to teach (McCormack 1984). When a person is intrinsically motivated in what he does, chances are that the curiosity of others will be aroused. They will want to know, why is this person so interested in this boring subject. Once curiosity is caught, the teacher's job is made much more easy.

What is unfortunate is that all of this seduction must be done at a group level—with each student participating remotely as another face in an audience. Within a year a teacher rarely gets a chance to learn more than a student's name. Boys and girls advance through the grades, having never experienced education in a personal way. Teachers can offset the pain of their negative feedback with group classroom techniques, but rarely does a student reap the rewards of personal attention and support. Schools are designed to maximize students' acquisition of knowledge as a cold and anonymous affair.

School in the Economy of Adolescents' Lives

The rallying cry of reformers at the turn of the century was education for "social efficiency" (Krug 1964), a term that suggests schools should operate with the utilitarian calculus of Henry Ford's assembly lines. William Bagley, the education professor who first used the term, wrote:

Coping with Classes

Social efficiency is the standard by which all forces of education must select the experiences that are impressed upon the individual. Each subject of instruction, every item of knowledge, every form of reaction, every detail of habit, must be measured by this yardstick [1905, p. 60].

Almost eighty years later, after decades of classroom research, we have little realistic conception of what efficient education might entail. It is apparent from the data just considered that students are less malleable than most educational theorists suspected. It is quite a difficult task to "impress" experiences on their consciousness against their will. But perhaps learning to tolerate the boredom, the variability, and the emotional disorder experienced in class is actually part of the "social curriculum" of the school. Through sitting in class they may learn to endure the complexities of life and the challenge of emotional growth in a hostile and competitive society. Conversely, the abrupt shifts in emotional states, the impersonality, the internal chaos might constitute an obstruction to serious learning. Efficient preparation for adulthood might require long periods of stable, patient attention focused on structured topics.

These are questions to which there are as yet no answers. Educational research provides no wisdom as to what balance of booklearning versus emotional experience, structured attention versus spontaneous curiosity, extrinsically versus intrinsically motivated work, is related to adult negentropic outcomes.

With friends the most important task adolescents have to master is learning how to build behavioral boundaries, and how to generate negative feedback while continuing to have a good time. In class the requirement is opposite: to learn how to deal with external boundaries and negative feedback without feeling overwhelmed by them. In an adolescent's life, friends represent enjoyment, school represents preparation for the future, and family and solitude lie somewhere between these poles. Growth, as we shall discuss in the final part of the book, involves learning to synthesize the opposition presented by these extremes.

PART IV

TRANSFORMATIONS

Chapter 11

Conflict and Chaos in Daily Life

IN an ideal conception of development, an adolescent moves through the various domains of life while gaining new skills in each. From family, perhaps, one learns trust and personal discipline; from friends, comradery and democratic ideals; from solitude, reflection and self-understanding; and from school, the cognitive skills to function in a productive, adult career. Each day, each hour is a new lesson. Through an accumulation of meaningful experiences, the young person establishes a more complex, better-ordered self, and a more integrated relationship with the world.

There can be little doubt from what we have seen that the reality is far from the ideal. With their families, teenagers report feeling closed and detached; conflicts with parents and siblings stand in the way of attention to growth. In solitude, loneliness drains their energy; while concentration usually improves, happiness and strength tend to fade. We might have expected adolescents to be alive and attentive during school, where they are

221

confronted by a variety of intellectual challenges. Instead, they are unmotivated and able to pay attention for less than half the time. The context in which adolescents come closest to the optimal conditions for growth is that of friends; here they are happy, active, and inspired. Yet peer pressures and a lack of discriminating feedback limit what can be learned; with friends immediate pleasure tends to take precedence over everything else.

In this chapter we attempt to unravel the underlying causes of entropy in adolescents' lives. What prevents adolescents from making better use of their experiences? Why does so much go wrong? For young people to develop sturdy selves, they must find order and stability in their lives. What causes their consciousness repeatedly to be jolted into disorder?

The answer to this question lies in understanding how adolescents negotiate the hard realities of their everyday world. First, we will consider the forms entropy takes in each of the basic experience settings—the adult-structured domains of family and school and the adolescent-controlled domains of solitude and friends. Then, we will present a case study to illustrate how these problems follow each other, one after another. Lastly, we will evaluate what is common to all these occurrences of entropy: What are the underlying threads in teenagers' difficulties? Understanding the repeated problems and the limits they set will provide the framework for us to go on to examine where the potentials for adolescent growth lie.

Family and School

The family, for many teenagers, is a major source of discord. Conflicts occur over rolling the toothpaste, doing the laundry, and the hours a teenager keeps. While the topic of fights may be mundane, the underlying issues are often much deeper. They reflect basic issues in an adolescent's interactions with parents and siblings.

Conflict and Chaos in Daily Life

The main issue is autonomy. A young man who feels that most of his psychic energy is controlled by his parents, that he can't pursue his own goals because he must do what others ask of him, is threatened at the very roots of his identity. How can he be a person if all he does is follow instructions? He might as well be a robot. If he wants to feel like a person he must rebel, either by directly confronting his parents, or behind their backs, by blowing off steam with peers.

Rebellious youths are typically in pursuit of freedom, attempting to wrest control of their own psychic energy. The problem is that teenagers' freedom is always tied up with that of their parents, often in complex ways. Marge wants to go out to a movie with friends, and she cannot understand why her mother is refusing to let her go. Why can't she be in control of her own time? The mother's objection may stem from the fact that she is tired of doing all the housework without any help. *Her* psychic energy is being controlled by Marge, whose clothes she washes, whose meals she cooks, and whose board she pays by working full-time. This particular movie may not be the issue for her as much as her own bitterness that Marge will not do her fair share. She will not take responsibility for the vital maintenance tasks that are a part of sustaining her life.

In innumerable subtle ways, we always exploit the psychic energy of those close to us, and are exploited in return. In a family we expect to make sacrifices, that is, sometimes to give more than we take. What makes a warm family so special is the trust among its members, the implicit knowledge that, in need, one will always be helped. But not even the warmest family can survive long if one member expects the others always to be sacrificing for his or her sake. A balance has to be found, an equitable exchange that allows each member to realize personal goals.

Most adolescents learn to strike this balance the hard way, after much trial and error. In some cases they are the exploited ones, taken advantage of by siblings or by parents who insist on controlling their children's destiny. In such cases the conflict revolves around the teenager's struggle to carry out an age-appropriate personal task—the development of an autonomous self. In other cases it is clearly the adolescent who exploits the parents, expecting with the egocentric insistence of youth that they allow him to reach his goals without concern for the costs to themselves. Most often, perhaps, both processes are going on at the same time, and sorting out the competing claims and counterclaims becomes an exceedingly complex matter than can lead to escalating conflict.

Whatever the situation, the family is inevitably a context in which negative feedback must be administered and endured. All parties set limits, make demands, and impose sanctions, creating inevitable entropy. The family is a cauldron of competing forces, and a teenager must learn the rudiments of give-and-take that make communal life possible: habits of cooperation, self-sacrifice, and mutual responsibility. It is a naïve fantasy that family life should be always idyllic. In fact, one must cultivate difficult skills in order to reduce the entropy caused by the conflict between divergent goals.

School, like the family, is an institution that tries to bend adolescents' goals in directions that they often resent. Forcing the attention of students into preset channels, it deprives them of control over their psychic energy. It is true that, taking the long view, one can see how the school experience will eventually *increase* the students' control over their psychic energy and help them to achieve goals they choose to have. But for many teenagers, it is difficult to take this long view, and even when they do understand its value, they still may resent the imposition of schooling here and now.

We should recognize that the claim that schools are for the good of children is a bit specious. Strictly speaking, schooling is only good for the adults that the children will one day become. And even this only because the society we have evolved requires the kind of education that school provides. It is no good pretending otherwise, and ignoring the inevitable conflicts created by a system that forces young people to confine their bodies and their minds to mechanical restrictions that are a bane to their freedom.

The entropy school creates promises to be a greater and greater problem for adolescents. Schools spread in Europe during the seventeenth century, when the demands of an increasingly mercantilistic and bureaucratic culture required literacy. To function within the current world, adolescents now have to master an expanding array of information. The definition of literacy is extending to include computer programming, calculus, statistics, chemistry, and consumer skills.

Advances in technology represent only a part of the increasing complexity of the world that adolescents must enter. It has been said that the greatest achievement of the Apollo program was not the hardware that carried astronauts to the moon, but the extraordinary managerial and administrative systems by which tens of thousands of scientists and engineers were able to bring this hardware together (Brooks 1980). Material technology has brought with it an increasingly differentiated and intricate social order, taking the form of large, more complex, and more interdependent organizations like IBM, GM, and the federal government. Whereas daily life used to depend on maintaining good relations with a handful of influential people, it now requires skilled manipulation of complex social and bureaucratic organizations. The purchase of a car, a virtual necessity of modern life, inducts the consumer into a web of complex systems including road, energy supply, parts distribution, maintenance, registration, insurance, police, and legal systems (Hannay and McGuinn 1980). The extent of complexity in the social order underlying daily life is particularly evident in the legal sphere, where laws and the threat of lawsuits have come to govern ever-expanding aspects of daily intercourse, from muffler design to consultations with doctors to parental behavior. The number of lawsuits mediating this increasingly intricate social order is now doubling every 12 years (Lieberman 1981).

It is clear that knowledge of rules, techniques, and information has an increasing importance for members of our culture. The task of absorbing this mushrooming volume of knowledge falls directly on the young, and it is the job of schools to teach it to them. The National Commission on Excellence in Education (1983) suggests that, if American adolescents are to grow up being competitive with their peers in other technological nations, they will have to spend more days a year in school and more hours doing homework, and they will have to tackle much more complex information. But the survival of the world as a whole requires that people not simply compete, but also be able to invest constructive attention into its continuance. The Club of Rome has voiced concern that there is an increasing gap between the complexity of the world and people's understanding of it (Botkin, Elmandjra, and Malitza 1979). For society to remain viable, it is argued, people must have the mastery to identify emerging problems in the social order and to shape creative solutions before they get out of control. Adolescents will not grow to be adults in the present; they will have to live their adulthood sometime in the future.

It is easy to see why school is such a frequent cause of entropy for teenagers. They just want to be kids, but the weight of an unknown future rides on their shoulders. They bear the load of mastering an enormous amount of cultural information, information which is necessary, whether they like it or not, for their survival as adults and for the survival of society. Thus, many show the kind of high-strung anxiety exhibited by Katherine Tennison, whose experience was discussed in Chapter 6. The tension, frustration, anger, and disorganization these adolescents report in school, is in part terror of the vast amount they need to learn to become adults. No matter how much they acquire, there will always be more; no matter how well they do on a test, there will always be another test that is harder and more challenging.

Solitude and Friends

When adolescents are alone, nobody tries to force them to do things they dislike. They do not have to load the dishwasher or study for exams. Yet, surprisingly, solitude brings more emotional entropy than school or the family; loneliness and passivity are an almost inevitable part of the experience. This is a clear indication that teenagers' problems do not all result from conflicts with adults. When they are given their freedom, whether in the privacy of their bedroom or in the outside world, entropy intrudes on their consciousness more than ever.

A person is vulnerable to a different set of threats when alone than when with people. In the family or in school the battle lines are drawn, and the adolescent fights concrete infringements on his freedom. But in solitude he or she is facing a much more intangible opponent. All the problems encountered in the rest of life gang up on the solitary person, making him feel helpless and insignificant. When Lorraine's plans to study abroad fell through, the failure assumed threatening proportions in her mind; it was not just this particular plan that went awry, but that all her hopes seemed destined to come to nothing for the rest of her life. When with others, she could avoid these thoughts; but when she was alone, it all came tumbling back into her mind.

Most people can tolerate working alone or watching a movie alone, because their attention is taken up by the job or the vicarious life enacted on the screen. Anxiety does not have a chance to gain a foothold in consciousness. But few people feel comfortable when by themselves unless they have something definite to do. Whether watching TV, reading the newspaper, or just killing time, teenagers feel much worse when they are alone. The reason is that they are unable to structure the situation to make up for the absence of others. They cannot as easily set goals or provide themselves the pats on the back that friends or family members usually provide. Hence, reality tends to crumble around them, and they watch helplessly as they become victims of worry, passivity, and uncontrolled longing for others.

Entropy in solitude takes the form of aimlessness resulting from inability to structure one's activity. Those who have learned to function autonomously will fill their solitude with hobbies and constructive activities, even with learning, meditation, and reflective thought. Those who don't have the personal skills to shape their attention this way will flee from the anxiety of solitude artificially, through alcohol, drugs, or numbing entertainment.

The dangers of solitude to society must also be recognized.

Some teenagers become good at structuring their activities alone, but at the expense of goals shared with others. Autonomy is a virtue within our culture, but if taken too far it can turn into social deviance. Teenagers often go through a period of despising everyone else—parents, friends, "society." This stage can be useful because it helps an adolescent to become independent and self-reliant. But the young person who keeps up this attitude year after year may cause trouble; cut off from the checks and balances of one's peers, one's genius might flourish, but so might alienation and madness. Thus, solitude carries threats of entropy, both to the individual and the collective.

The entropy related to friends is in some ways the most difficult to deal with—partly because it is so difficult to detect. Most teenagers are so relieved to be with friends that they gladly lower their guard, and refuse to exercise any criticism. After all, compared to family, school, and solitude, friends provide an optimal context of experience. Unlike the first two, friends don't force us to do things we don't like; unlike solitude, friends provide amusement and diversion that keeps attention occupied. Most teenagers will tell you that friends represent the best and most meaningful part of their lives.

The companionship of peers is indeed seductive. It nurtures the self discreetly. Friends seem sensitive to one's own unique individuality—they are understanding, supportive, even affectionate, and they know how to have a good time. With friends an adolescent can unburden his soul, knowing he or she will be accepted. More than parents, siblings, or teachers, friends are responsive to the self and willing to support it unconditionally.

The problem is that, of the many potential friends, few actually turn out to be such, particularly in early adolescence. Most "friends" are just peers, competing for the same goals as we are. Thus, teenagers forever rewrite their list of friends and enemies, depending on the latest events. Greg Stone, for example, drops his old girl friend without thinking about it twice. Whereas friends can be very supportive, they can also turn on you, and the anonymous crowd of peers becomes a critical, sometimes frightening mass. To avoid ridicule, many teenagers are willing to resort to the most abject conformity. Young people who resist adult rules with great determination submit meekly to the opinion of other adolescents. Adolescents who become overly dependent on feedback from peers end up falling from the skillet into the fire. No sooner do they win emancipation from their families than they lose their independence again by letting peer values determine their goals.

As with solitude, entropy with friends can be both personal and social. The root of the problem is the absence of reliable, reality-based feedback. Friends set goals, define rules, and define feedback, but only in the service of present enjoyment. Even the most sensitive and affectionate friendship is likely to be founded on a short-term framework of goals. Some of the worst feelings come from being abandoned by a buddy, scorned by one's own gang, or left by a boy friend or girl friend. With friends there is also a danger that interactions will lead further and further away from the norms of society into rowdy and delinquent behavior. The runaway positive feedback of friendship groups can easily career out of control. Entropy with friends results from the lack of homeostatic mechanisms.

Entropy as a Constant Companion—The Week of Jerzy Madigan

The typical day of an adolescent does not unfold like a well-organized pageant. Their experience of life is more like a turbulent sporting event in which hopes and frustrations, elation and disappointment follow each other in no particular sequence. With the family, warm feelings are disrupted by the irritations of living together; in class, a sharp word from a teacher can destroy feelings of well-being. In solitude they are besieged by internal feelings of disorder and emptiness; and friends are an unpredictable source of entropic experiences, potentially as bitter as any other.

To appreciate the cumulative effect of entropy in adolescents' lives we need to look at how it adds up in the daily experience of individuals. Jerzy Madigan, aged 17, was a football star at Belmont High and an average student. As his week unfolds, we see him continually stumbling into difficulties in every part of his life (Figure 11.1). His spirits recover each time, but then he gets himself into another mess.

He started carrying the pager on a Monday afternoon and was feeling pretty good. During the first signal he is playing basketball in gym class and writes, "What the hell am I doing on such a lousy basketball team!" In spite of this predicament, he is cheerful, friendly, and is glad to be doing what he is doing.

At home that evening he has a good time joking with his sisters, but then they turn on the Miss America pageant, which depresses his mood. Television, as we have seen, has a consistently negative effect on teenagers' states. Nonetheless, Jerzy watches, even though he wishes he were doing something else. A call to his girl friend later that night gets him away from the TV and revives his good cheer.

The next morning at 8:40, we find him in a blue funk again, while taking the shower. A school dean has called him into his office that day, and he is worrying about what might be on the dean's mind. What has he done wrong now? Unfortunately, we don't find out much about this event, because Jerzy does not respond to two signals during the morning. His next report is at 2:58 P.M. when his moods are up again—he has sneaked out of school, the weather is beautiful, and he is having a pleasant conversation with a friend about being stoned. Apparently nothing terrible happened with the dean.

Just an hour later he reports another instance of entropy. He is playing basketball in the alley while talking with his sister and a friend of hers. In an attempt at prowess he tries to dunk the ball in the hoop. The ball goes in, but he comes down on some newspapers, falling on a garbage can and banging his arm and knee. He is in pain ("I almost killed myself," he writes) although the presence of the girls keeps him from feeling as bad as he might, had no one been there to witness his heroic crash.

Wednesday, we finally get him in class, and it is another low point. He is bored, detached, confused; time is passing slowly and he greatly wishes to be doing something else. In the interview he reported, "It's one of those classes where you just go and listen; there's not much to do." The students try to argue with the teacher, but his attitude is, "I'm right. Just take it from me." Jerzy's mood is low, but only until the class is over. Later in the day, he reports high moods, except when he is hassled by neighborhood kids while sitting on the porch with his sister. They had just spit at him, and he is angry, threatening them with violence.

On Thursday morning Jerzy receives a signal while walking to school alone. He reports feeling passive, detached, unmotivated, and bored—the entropic pattern we know to be associated with most teenagers' solitude. The same profile occurs at 10:00 P.M. that night when he is again alone. He is lying on his bed, reading *Sports Illustrated*, and listening to a "great" concert on his stereo. But in spite of all this sensory input, he still feels weak, passive, and unmotivated. Entropy is a repeated and persistent part of his life.

Friday morning he gets upset with his "bitchy mom" when she makes him take out the garbage. This makes him irritable, angry, and lonely. But fighting with his mother is not as entropic as being in class. At 1:20 P.M., he is sitting in etymology class and is very bored, constrained, and unmotivated. Unable to concentrate on the teacher's lecture, he thinks about his girl and about the drinking he is going to do after school.

At last, after a week of stress and taking orders from others, Jerzy is free to do what he pleases. Friday night he has a good time drinking and driving around with his friends. There is one hitch, however. They have a little too good a time, are a little too free and easy, and their rowdiness leads the police to suspect them of stealing warm-up jackets at the racquetball club. Whether they did so or not we do not know. But it is clear that the mutual stimulation of this group of friends has led to a situation where they were in trouble with adult authorities. "Police suck!" he writes in a drunken scrawl on the back of the beeper sheet.

The next day, Jerzy is very tired from lack of sleep. This makes

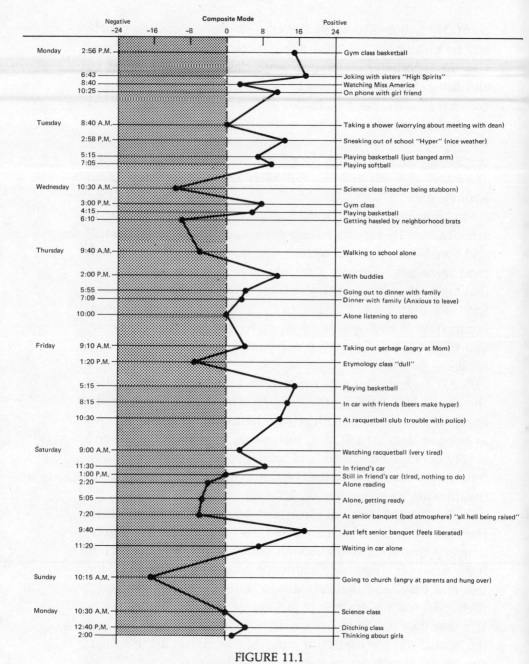

FIGURE 11.1
The Week of Jerzy Madigan
(From: Larson, Csikszentmihalyi, and Graef 1980)

him detached and irritable. In the evening he goes to the senior banquet, and the signal comes right after Greg Stone and his toga-wearing friends have turned the affair into pandemonium. Food has been flying between the Heads and the Jocks, and the principal is now lecturing everyone over the loudspeaker. For Greg Stone, you may recall, this incident was great fun. But for Jerzy and others who were not a part of either faction, it spoiled the event.

Jerzy's lowest mood comes the next morning when he is riding to church with his parents. He is irritable, angry, and hung over. He feels it a tremendous injustice to be dragged out of bed just for church, and, on top of it all, his parents are playing opera music on the car radio. His acrid comments on the situation were quoted in Chapter 7.

In sum, every time Jerzy turns around it seems as if he runs into something that will stand in the way of his goals. Encounters with entropy follow one after another. While Jerzy's character is unique, his rate of reported problems is by no means unusual. We saw similar patterns with Greg Stone, with Katherine Tennison, with Lorraine Monawski, and with all the others. Consciousness was continually being disrupted. There were few occasions when focused involvement in anything was maintained for long.

Why Things Go Wrong

Entropy takes many forms in adolescents' lives: from interpersonal conflicts with family and friends to internal strain faced in solitude. It includes stupid mistakes caused by lack of experience, disappointments from wild risk-taking, disillusion after high expectations, and pain in the endurance of mundane daily life, in sum, the agony of confronting raw reality. Teenagers constantly face the discrepancy between the way they want the world to be and the way the world actually is.

Of course, adults are hardly immune to encounters with entropy. They stub their toes, burn their tongues on their coffee, and accidentally drop china. Their disasters can be more momentous than those of their children—loss of a job, marital separation, financial ruin. But adolescents seem more prone to daily frustrations, and when things do go wrong their sense of order is more likely to be disrupted.

What is important is to understand the patterns of entropy particularly common to teenagers. Is there a pattern in the ways in which things go wrong?

The most frequent scenarios seem to involve becoming overwhelmed. Again and again, adolescents are overpowered by situations: the demands of school, the intransigence of a parent, high expectations they impose on themselves. The result is anxiety, worry, agitation, panic, anger, and fear. A girl described sitting in chemistry, "Listening to Mr. Molitor and going 'insane'; I just don't understand why H+ is +." A boy described "going out of my mind" because he couldn't solve an algebra equation. A major paper required in English classes made many students distraught long before it was even assigned.

The experience of being overwhelmed is frequently caused by goals set by school, family, or peers. But a major component is often the teenagers' own expectations. We saw the high goals Katherine Tennison set for herself. In a sense, Greg Stone was no less ambitious in his attempt to juggle two girl friends at once, and Jerzy was no less foolish in attempting to dunk the basketball. Adolescents have extraordinary hopes for the future, wildly idealistic notions of love and good times, and great expectations about what is possible.

The problem is perhaps not the size of the expectations— adults also load pressure upon themselves. The problem is that teenagers lack the experienced sense of their skills to carry them out. There is no accurate matching between persons' abilities and what they take on. Often absent is any realistic sense of what these limitations are—for example, the simple fact that their bodies have only so much energy, and that they tire after being awake so long. Thus Jerzy stays up all night with little regard for how he will feel the next day. Teenagers' vague and unstable self-concepts prevent them from accurately rationing their abilities. The result is that they often become overwhelmed, like Katherine, who panics over a homework assignment that ends up taking only 20 minutes.

The opposite of being overwhelmed is being unchallenged. This occurs when people are uninterested in the opportunities available, when life holds no challenge or intrigue in what it asks. It can apply to life generally or can be focused within specific contexts. Jerzy and many of his peers greatly enjoyed their friends but were uninterested in helping around the house. In contrast was Chandra, a gaunt, cheerless girl who had no interest in anything but schoolwork.

Boredom is endemic to adolescents because there is much in their life that they do not control. They have not had a chance to internalize the richness of possibilities that are available. Perhaps also, they have not had the opportunity to numb themselves to the simple, mindless tasks that are a requirement of everyday living. School is boring because they are not invested in its goals. And a simple task such as feeding the dog becomes acutely painful because it is so relentless and unavoidable.

This situation is manifested as boredom, lethargy, and sometimes self-hate. Students like Jerzy reported watching television even though they despised it. The result was that afterward they despised themselves. Likewise, several had friendships that were dull and empty but they kept them up because they had no better choice. Again, the effect was to instill in them a sense of cynicism and bad faith.

A classic example of boredom is teenagers who spend hours in front of electronic games. While these can be stimulating and meaningful for a while, they often disintegrate into little more than a mind-filling routine. Surprisingly, many don't actually "play" the game, they simply follow memorized routines for winning.

The problem is that adolescents often have no meaningful goals. They have not had the time to attach themselves to anything they consider worthwhile. As a result, nothing is challenging to them, and their skills fall into disuse. Entropy takes the form of a meaningless waste of time.

Being overwhelmed and being unchallenged have common elements. They both represent states of imbalance between a person and the world. In one case the world offers too much, in the other too little. Underlying them both is a breakdown in a person's ability to control his or her actions—to set meaningful goals, define limits, and provide and receive feedback.

Of course, it is possible for experiences of entropy to serve as negative feedback. Katherine seemed to learn from her mistakes; she recognized that her bad moods were a sign that something was wrong and she needed to change it. But for many, this realization is slow. Others confront challenges by denying their existence, or by adopting cynical responses. One student, for example, mentioned cheating in school as a way he had come to use to deal with the overwhelming demands. Others found alternative ways to cope with or shut off the requirements of the adult world.

The Adolescent Predicament

Originally we considered entitling this book "Catching Teenagers' Attention," a name we quickly abandoned lest it be perceived as a manual that tells parents and teachers how to manipulate young people to their ends. Nonetheless, the basic issue remains the same. How is it possible for adolescents' attention to be engaged by the challenges of adulthood? Under what conditions will their spontaneous interests be transformed toward constructive purposes? This cannot be accomplished by adult manipulative tactics; it must involve a process of reciprocal exchange between growing persons and their environments. If there is a process of "catching," it is as much the teenager as the adult who must do it.

What we have seen in this chapter is that entropy repeatedly stands in the way. In fact, the whole book has shown that adolescents' daily lives are a minefield of things that go wrong. Family, friends, teachers, and strangers are inevitable sources of conflict. The predicament of modern adolescents is that they must face these realities in addition to expanding cultural and technological requirements for adulthood.

It is not safe to assume that they will automatically join society, that they will turn into adults who order their lives according to the goals provided by the culture. Adolescent delinquency, suicide, and drug use indicate that many may be choosing not to grow up to fit the social order. In the late 70s, significant numbers of youth responded to adult society by becoming "punks," a movement in which coldness toward others was a hallmark and sticking safety pins in one's cheek was a sign of membership (Hebdige 1979). As is often the case, when confronted by an intolerable external order, adolescents are unable to restructure it harmoniously: they lash out instead, preferring to destroy the alien patterns and reconstitute their lives along goals that they can control and understand, even if these are primitive and ultimately destructive.

Trying to avoid entropy in experience is not a feasible goal. There is no way to escape conflict while still living a purposive life. Rather, disorder sets the conditions of growth. It establishes boundaries and sets challenges to attention. The question is, how can adolescents grow within these constraints? Is it possible for them to keep experience fresh, to enjoy living in the present while investing attention in future development?

Of course, there is no simple answer to this kind of question. We can only report what is suggested by the adolescents studied here. With this concern in mind, we interviewed them about the times they mastered the threats of immediate entropy, when they emerged from the struggle refreshed and enjoyed what they were doing. Their stories provide the material for the next chapter.

Chapter 12

Converting Challenges to Enjoyment: The Flow Experience

I F bad moods occur when there is conflicting information in consciousness, the opposite is true of positive experience. When we feel good, what passes through awareness is like music: sensations, thoughts, and feelings flow without effort and build into a common theme that fits with our goals.

How do teenagers get to feel this way? Partly by doing things that are designed to make them feel good. In the course of history, mankind has invented a variety of methods for creating and restoring order in consciousness. They vary all the way from the sublime to the frivolous; from religion and art to sports and entertainment. These activities provide a sense of excitement and elation that is rare in everyday life. They are not necessary for the survival of the body, but they do help maintain harmony in consciousness and provide a framework of order in experience.

To borrow a parallel from the physical sciences, we will call those institutions that help people feel better, psychic "dissipative structures." This is a term made popular by Ilya Prigogine (1976, 1980), the Nobel Prize–winning chemist who has grappled with the question of how it was possible for ordered complexity to evolve in nature, given the second law of thermodynamics, which essentially says that everything is continually falling apart. What he concluded was that living systems have a special ability to use bits of energy, while they are dispersing, to create and store order. Plants, for instance, are very good at transforming light, the waste product of the sun's combustion, and various organic materials, also waste products, into complex material patterns and processes. Prigogine coined the term "dissipative structure" to describe this ability to exploit chaos, to make use of available scraps of energy that otherwise would be lost or would add to the disorder of the universe. All energy and order decays and dissipates with time. But dissipative structures are able to turn this eternal loss into at least a temporary gain. Psychic dissipative structures, therefore, are those attentional habits that can exploit random, conflicting information to create order in experience.

We can distinguish two major types of such structures: those that make adolescents feel good in the present, and those that might help them feel good later, as they grow into adulthood. The two types are not mutually exclusive, but it is useful to look at them separately. In this chapter we shall examine the first type, those activities that provide teenagers with negentropic experiences in their current lives. These might be looked at as short-range dissipative structures, ways of acting that restore order in consciousness. In the next chapter we shall consider long-term dissipative structures, those that contribute to enduring personal and societal harmony.

Converting Challenges to Enjoyment

Emergent Experiences

To identify the kind of activities adolescents find most positive, the ones that correspond to short-term psychic dissipative structures, we asked each student one question: "What are the things in your life you enjoy doing most?" Out of the answers to this question we hoped to construct a picture of the perfect experience as teenagers see it.

The answers we got were many and diverse; some students described as few as three things they "enjoyed most," some went as far as listing fifteen. The median number was eight activities. To get a clearer picture, we focused the questioning on the activity each person mentioned as number one, or on two top choices, when the student could not decide which was most enjoyable.

These activities are listed in Table 12.1. The seventy-five students mentioned 51 *different* activities as being most enjoyable. One thing is immediately apparent. Practically all the items listed in the table are leisure activities: talk, sports, hobbies, or recreation. This is not really surprising; it simply confirms that, for adolescents at least, leisure activities act as dissipative structures that transform conflict and randomness into order in consciousness. But the second striking thing about the table is the great variety of different activities listed. This diversity of favorite activities poses a problem: Is there a pattern in all the individual uniqueness? What is there about enjoyable experience except to say that some kids like scuba diving, others like to play the guitar, or be with their friends, or go to bars? What can be the common elements in such different activities that provide negentropic experiences?

Even combining the fifty-one different activities in some appropriate groupings barely helps. In Table 12.1, there are seven groups. The largest is sports, followed by interpersonal interaction: being with friends, or with a particular friend. In some ways, these two large groups represent opposite experiences:

TABLE 12.1
Survey of Most Enjoyable Activities

		N	Totals
Interpersonal	Friends	18	
	Boyfriend/Girlfriend	6	
	Family	2	
	Talking over Phone, Parties, Bars	4	
			30
Sports: (team)	Baseball, Softball	5	
	Basketball	6	
	Soccer, Volleyball, Hockey	3	
(individual)	Tennis	5	
	Sailing	3	
	Track	3	
	Skating	2	
	Water Skiing	2	
	Scuba Diving	2	
	Flying, Golf, Swimming, Wrestling, Skiing, Horseback Riding	7	
			38
Outdoors	Camping	2	
	Nature, Travel, Fishing	3	
			5
Art	Singing	4	
	Dancing	4	
	Music	3	
	Ballet	2	
	Piano	2	
	Guitar	2	
	Acting, Photography, Jewelry	3	
			20
Automotive	Cars, Racing, Motorcycles	4	
			4
Passive	TV	8	
	Being Alone, Cards, Getting High	3	
			11
Productive	Work	2	
	Shopping	2	
	Baking	2	
	Using Brain, Reading, Mowing Lawn	3	
			9 117*

*Note: 33 teenagers mentioned one and 42 teenagers mentioned two activities as being most enjoyable, for a total of 117.

Sports, especially individual ones, are based on competition and peak performance; friendship, by contrast, depends on cooperation and relaxed, informal interaction. The next largest cluster after sports and friends is art. Most of these activities, seventeen out of twenty, involve music. Neither the visual arts nor writing are mentioned even once among the top two favorite activities, although they appear further down the individual lists.

Groups of almost equal size mentioned passive leisure and productive activities. Passive leisure is mostly TV watching, which no one ever mentioned as a favorite activity by itself.

As interesting as what is included in the list is what is not. For example, despite the open and relaxed nature of the interview, not one of the respondents gave sex as the most enjoyable activity (it was mentioned a few times, but never first), and only one said "getting high" was what he liked to do best. This omission could mean one of several things. It could mean that our adolescents are so repressed that they cannot admit, even to themselves, where their main enjoyment comes from. Or it could mean that while they know, they feel embarrassed to admit it, and prefer to place socially legitimate activities at the top of the list. Finally, it could also mean that the teenagers reported accurately what they actually experienced, and that, contrary to popular beliefs, sex and drugs are indeed not the most enjoyable activities teenagers experience. They might be the most *pleasurable*, but they are not necessarily the most *enjoyable*; the distinction between these will be explored later, after we get around to defining the nature of enjoyment.

The list presents an embarassment of riches. Its variety suggests that almost any activity—even work, shopping, or baking a cake—can provide the height of emotional harmony which will dispel, at least temporarily, entropy in consciousness. When one looks at the reasons for enjoyment, an even more bewildering variety appears. Not only are the things teenagers claim to favor different, but the reasons for favoring one activity over another also appear to be extremely idiosyncratic.

To give a sense for this variety, let us look at four typical adolescents, two girls, two boys, and see how they explain why their favorite activities are so enjoyable.

Ronny, a tough young man with a lower-than-average scholastic record, said that what he most enjoys doing is spending time with his grandmother in Wisconsin, then football, basketball, baseball, being with friends, hunting with his dad, and street hockey, in that order. What he definitely does not like is "being bugged." His life is full of disorder, and he has a low tolerance for any additional hassles. Thus, it is perhaps not surprising that he characterized most of his favorite activities as "rough sports." The foremost among these is football. Ronny plays defense—end or linebacker—and has been on the school team for two years. He says he likes "mauling people, and hurting 'em so they're afraid to come again." It is important, he says, because "I want others to know about me." This aggressive acting out suggests that Ronny needs clear, unambiguous feedback about his existence, which can be easily gotten in competitive settings, especially those involving aggression. If you hurt someone, or shoot an animal in hunting, you know you are somebody, it creates a certain kind of order out of the chaos. The pain on the face of the adversary or the lifeless carcass are witness to your awful power. As is all too often the case, personal negentropy for Ronny is achieved at the price of denying the goals of other beings. The order in his consciousness is achieved at the expense of disorder elsewhere. Because of this, the psychic dissipative structures Ronny uses are far from efficient—the total amount of disorder in his environment is not reduced.

But Ronny's story is not so simple and clear-cut. The first activity he mentioned was living with his grandmother in Wisconsin. He had lived in that small town until he was three years old, and he looks back on that period with nostalgia. Ronny returns almost every month, for several days, to visit his grandmother. He describes his stays in the country as occasions for total gratification: "If I want something—I just ask my relatives." As soon as he gets there, the word spreads around to the girls that he has arrived, and "the phone calls start coming in." Grandmother takes Ronny to bars, and he takes girls roller skating, to the movies, and parking in the woods. While grandmother indulges him, Ronny doesn't mind reciprocating somewhat.

244

He does work around the yard, or on the cars: "I don't mind doing it for her." This set of activities appears to be as enjoyable to Ronny as the first, yet in contrast to football or hunting, it does not create disorder in the environment.

So it is not only that almost every teenager in our sample prefers a different activity, and for a different reason. Even the same person, on closer inspection, shows preferences for seemingly incompatible experiences. Ronny, the macho sportsman, reveals a soft underbelly, a hankering for being spoiled by grandma.

Joan is a pretty and fairly average student. She lists going to concerts as her favorite activity, followed by tennis, football, cooking, shopping, and softball. The concerts she speaks of are by two groups with teenage appeal, Chicago and The Beachboys. Going to a concert is not something to get into and out of casually. "You work yourself into it by listening to their music over and over again before the concert," Joan explains. Afterward, the effect may last for over two weeks while Joan keeps reliving the experience as she fantasizes about it and talks it over again and again with her friends. One wonders how many subscribers to the Chicago Symphony, or how many concertgoers the world over, invest so much psychic energy in and gain so much emotional order from their musical experiences.

The center of the experience is "the natural high" of the concert itself. As the musical numbers follow each other, Joan starts to concentrate on the rhythm of the performance, on the response of the audience to the sound. She begins to be caught up in the pounding beat of the music that unites the crowd into an organism that breathes, screams, and moves together. To the observer, the heaving mass might seem pure chaos, but the way Joan describes it, the insider experiences belonging to a uniquely negentropic system. This feeling is accomplished by "thinking what they [the musicians] are thinking." Joan concentrates on the sounds, words, expressions, and movements of the singers, until she feels exactly the way she is supposed to feel. Presumably all the other teenagers in the audience are experiencing the same feeling at the same time. The result is a harmony of hundreds of consciousnesses tuned in on the same wavelength: feelings, images, fears, and longing alternate in unison, each person's consciousness magnified and reflected a hundredfold.

No wonder Joan, and so many young people around her, call this sort of experience a "natural high." Emile Durkheim, the great sociologist, believed that religion and culture (the earliest psychic dissipative structures) began in such orgiastic settings around the campfires of our ancestors. Durkheim (1912) called the feeling of unity induced by the beat of drums, the dance, and drugs "collective effervescence"—a state of being leading to "collective consciousness" and eventually to a belief in the reality of a social organism transcending the individual. Others have pointed out that in an already organized society, mass frenzy of this kind helps to destroy the existing roles and rules, and redirects the attention of audiences away from existing goals (Dipboye 1977). The passionate lyrics of rock music, combined with its repetitive, stable beat, create order out of the chaotic psychological variability that we have seen characterizing adolescents' lives. It uses their daily cast of feelings, their longings and impulses, to shape a powerful emotional experience, generating awareness of class solidarity among the young (Frith 1981). It gives girls like Joan the feeling that they belong to something huge, powerful, lively—an emotional "high" that one simply cannot get in everyday life. Compared to it, the other things Joan enjoys, like cooking and shopping, appear pale and mundane. Tennis and the other sports she likes, although they give her a sense of power and aliveness, fail to provide the excitement of being part of a great crowd, of being a small speck of sensation merged with the pulse of the group consciousness.

Bruce's way of enjoying himself is similar to Joan's, but is much more diffused and relaxed. He mentions twelve activities he enjoys most, including horse and floor exercises in gymnastics, swimming, and bike riding. But he says that being with friends is the all-around favorite. He describes this as being sort of a smooth, easygoing, negentropic system. Bruce says he "likes to have things kind of set so I don't have to worry about anything." With friends he doesn't have to worry because "you can be yourself and say what you want—talk about anything you want. If you're in a bad mood, they know," whereas "if you're with people you don't know, you have to think about what to say. With friends it comes automatically, you can say anything." Apparently Bruce enjoys being in a group where interaction moves by itself, so to speak, without needing attention devoted to checking and monitoring the system.

The goal of the group is simply to "have a good time. But you don't think of it as a goal, it just happens." It happens when one of the guys starts a routine, perhaps saying, "Boy, are we having a good time." Each friend has a somewhat different routine that the others know and know how to respond to. Thus the "system" is made up of well-integrated, but differentiated units that smoothly trigger off set sequences of mood and behavior in each other. When a routine starts, it tends to snowball: "lots of gossiping, giggling, laughing." Soon they might become loud and rowdy, or even obnoxious. The action lasts as long as "everyone stays in the same mood. Any change, if it starts to rain, if someone leaves, may stop it."

What Bruce describes is an interaction system in which each person's psychic energy is focused inward on the other members, with the goal of providing positive feedback to each other. Habit has taught them what to expect from each other; they know how to produce a good mood and how to stay there. What they do sounds similar to the performance of a chamber orchestra, or, more accurately, of a jazz ensemble. Instead of modulating sound, they harmonize mood through sequences of jokes and physical movements. In the random flux of everyday life, they create a familiar pattern of negentropic interaction.

Joan and her cohorts achieve a merging of consciousness through the mediation of the rock group and its sounds; Bruce achieves it through the "routines" he and his friends have developed to focus attention on the good times they are having. Although they are using different means, both teenagers help to create a concentration of psychic energy by focusing their attention on the same moods and feelings. Then, when all this concentrated energy takes shape and begins to exist, as if on its own, each teenager can feel a part of this pattern of order that transcends his or her individuality, and can forget how small and fragile the self is.

By contrast, Lynn emphasizes control, precision, and skill as her conditions for enjoying what she does. She mentions twelve activities, half of them social, half musical. Her favorite activity is dancing: ballet, modern, and jazz. On and off, she has been dancing since she was four years old. At the time of the interview she practiced 2 or 3 hours a day, and was always on the move between a downtown studio, a local club, and the school gym. Outside of studying, there is nothing else Lynn devotes as much psychic energy to as dancing. She says, "It's the only thing I can really do that my mind really concentrates on." By now, involvement in the dance starts very easily: She is "into" the activity "as soon as I put on my leotards." For Lynn, dance provides a psychic dissipative structure because the activity makes it possible for her to concentrate her attention. Whereas in normal life her attention is often wasted in random patterns— she is as emotionally variable as anyone else—when dancing she focuses her attention and uses it efficiently.

Lynn has learned a way of interacting with space through her own body, a way of expressing herself through disciplined movement. This kinetic language allows her to become part of a very special system of communication. In it she finds an "outlet for my energy, an escape." But escape does not mean relaxation; quite the contrary. To escape into the world of dance one needs constant discipline and effort. Dancing "is like putting a machine together and making it work," a matter of precise, skilled performance; "You have to get the technique before you can work on the art." But it is worth putting up with it all because "I like being in control. That's why I like to dance."

Characteristics of the Flow Experience

The differences between how Lynn, Bruce, Joan, and Ronny describe their favorite activities are, at first sight, very noticeable. There does not seem to be much in common among any of them. And if one were to add the stories of the remaining seventy-one students, the variety of explanations would increase in a linear fashion.

Yet, there are certain underlying similarities in these accounts. By looking at how these teenagers describe enjoyable experiences, a pattern does emerge. For instance, all four said their favorite activity provided challenges that required *concentration* on some aspect of the environment. For Ronny it is the football opposition, for Joan the sound and expression of the rock band, in Bruce's case it is the friends' routines, in Lynn's, the sequence of movements in the dance. In each case, one had to learn first a set of *rules of interaction* (call it football, music, dance, or just "goofing around" with friends). Then, by shaping consciousness and behavior in accordance with the rules, each teenager became able to participate in the activity. As they did so, their actions produced *feedback.* That is, each person was able to tell how well he or she was doing in terms of the rules. For Ronny the feedback was provided by the adversaries he left lying on the field. Joan read it from the expressions of the faces of the audience and musicians, telling her that her feelings were shared. Bruce could tell it from the interplay of comic routines, and Lynn from the mirror in the studio, the reactions of her teacher, the audience, and ultimately her internalized standards of excellence in conjunction with kinesthetic sensations.

As adolescents get involved in their own thing, they begin to exist in a special environment set apart from everyday life. Football, music, friends, and dance—each is a little world of its own, providing unique experiences: sensations, feelings, and thoughts that are ordered, predictable, yet very different from the mundane occasions of normal existence. By restructuring consciousness according to the rules of the activity, the person loses track of his or her usual self. One becomes *less self-conscious* because there is less attention left to focus inward. Whenever the self is noticed at all, one sees it interacting with a larger system—the team, the music, friends, the pattern of the dance—so that one actually experiences a sense of *self-transcendence,* or of belonging to a more powerful system.

The spontaneous choice of challenges that require concentration, a set of rules to guide one's psychic energy, clear goals and feedback, loss of self-consciousness—these are the main elements of those experiences people find most enjoyable. They are the conditions for the state of psychic negentropy that we have called the "flow experience" (Csikszentmihalyi 1975, 1980). Of course, these conditions are present, to a certain extent, in everything we do—in doing homework, riding the subway, or eating dinner. But in everyday life, rules are often contradictory, goals are unclear, and feedback lacking. Everyday experience is often confusing and unsatisfactory. Therefore, we search out or create activities where rules, goals, challenges, and feedback are sharp and well-ordered. Flow activities tend to produce flow experiences in those who participate in them. Football, music, dance, friends—and the many other activities listed in Table 12.1—are psychic dissipative structures, or flow activities, designed to provide negentropic experiences.

This cluster of conditions that trigger flow is not limited to adolescence. In fact, we first discovered it in adults (Csikszentmihalyi 1975). When we asked chess masters, rock climbers, composers of music, and even surgeons to tell how it felt to be involved in what they liked to do, they described their experiences along these same dimensions. In all of these activities, the experience of enjoyment was characterized above all by a deep, spontaneous involvement with the task at hand. In flow, one is carried away by the interaction between the self and the activity: the climber and the rock, the painter and the canvas, the surgeon and the operation. To the extent that one feels immersed in the activity, the distinction between *I* and *it* becomes irrelevant. As a teenage rock dancer describes her experience, "when I'm dancing, I don't use my awareness of myself to control or direct my body. It seems to just exist. It's tuned in mostly to the music or the environment and less to controlling or directing my actions."

Attention is focused on whatever needs to be done, and there is not enough left over to worry or get bored or distracted. The sense of time becomes distorted; hours pass by in minutes, even though afterward it might seem that an eternity has elapsed. This is how the rock dancer talks about it:

> Two things happen. One is that it seems to pass really fast in one sense. After it's passed, it seems to have passed really fast. I see that it's one in the morning, and I say, 'Ah, ha, just a few minutes ago it was only eight.' But then while I'm dancing . . . it seems like it's been much longer than maybe it really was.

The ego that surveys and evaluates our actions disappears in the flow of experience; one is freed of the confines of the social self and may feel an exhilarating sense of transcendence, of belonging to a larger whole. One mountaineer describes the experience of climbing: "It's . . . almost like an egoless thing in a way—somehow the right thing is done without . . . thinking about it or doing anything at all. . . . It just happens . . . and yet you're more concentrated." And another says: "You become a robot—no, more like an animal. It's pleasant. There is a feeling of total involvement. . . . You feel like a panther powering up the rock."

These qualities describe how people feel when they enjoy what they are doing. Surgeons in the operating room or laborers on the assembly line use the same words to describe their work when it is enjoyable and rewarding. Flow differs from "pleasure" in requiring active participation, whether mental, physical, or both. Psychologically it includes all four dimensions of psychic negentropy—activation and cognitive efficiency as well as motivation and positive affect. Despite the huge differences among the things teenagers said they enjoyed, the underlying reason for enjoying them was the same: When involved with the activity, they experienced psychic negentropy. Playing football and playing the violin are certainly very different, but in both cases what motivates the player to play is the ordered state the activities create in consciousness. But what makes an activity capable of producing a flow experience?

Whether an activity is enjoyable or not depends a great deal on the balance of challenges it provides, in relation to the actor's skills. When an activity presents too many opportunities for action, or challenges, and these overwhelm our skills, we feel anxious. When skills outweigh the challenges available we feel bored. Flow occurs when we come close to matching the two. Football, music, dance, interaction among friends, and the hundred other activities our teenagers mentioned as being the most enjoyable, all offer a certain range of challenges against which teens match their skills. It is important to note that challenges and skills are partly objective features of the activity or situation, partly the results of one's subjective attitude. The two are related, and both are important in producing the experience. For instance, Joan presumably can enter flow more easily in a rock concert than in a dentist's waiting room, because the concert presents her with a manageable task appropriate to her skills. But even at the dentist's, she could experience flow if she restructured the situation to optimize its potential challenges—by playing out a song in her head, by focusing her attention on a challenging article in a magazine, by joking with the receptionist, or by making critical observations to herself about the decorative scheme in the waiting room.

An essential feature of this structure of challenges and skills is that their balance is not static. If the complexity of challenge does not increase with time, flow gives way to boredom. As we practice an activity, our skills in it increase until they outweigh the challenges. Hence, to maintain flow, there must be provisions made to find new things to engage our attention and skill, lest what used to be fun drift into tedium. For a dancer like Lynn, this means new moves to learn, more difficult sequences to master, or perhaps it means developing an interest in teaching others to dance, or in the esthetic, historical, or biomechanical dimensions of the medium. Pleasure can be repeated again and again, as instinctual tensions build up and demand to be released; enjoyment, however, must grow in order to survive. Unless the experience becomes more complex, it stops providing enjoyment (Csikszentmihalyi 1982a, b). This fact has very important implications for adolescent development. While pleasure does not lead anywhere, enjoyment stimulates the acquisition of new skills, and thus promotes growth. And what is more, it does so without increasing entropy in adolescent consciousness.

Measuring Flow in Different Activities

To see how well this theoretical model works when applied to teenagers' experiences, Mayers (1978) asked the seventy-five students in this study to rank their favorite activity, and then the courses they were taking in school, on ten items, each of which was supposed to measure one dimension of the flow experience. For example, one item said, "I would do it even if I didn't have to," which was supposed to tap the autotelic, or intrinsically motivating aspect of the activity. Table 12.2 shows how the four students described earlier in the chapter ranked their favorite activities and courses on this dimension.

All four teenagers said that they would do "a great deal" of their favorite activity even if they didn't have to; they gave a 9, the highest score, to it every time. By contrast, school classes were rated, on the average, 3.2 by Ronny, 7 by Joan, 2.6 by Bruce, and 6.2 by Lynn. Clearly the two boys would be unlikely to study if they didn't have to; for them school is quite uniformly exogenous. For the two girls, some classes are as endogenous as their favorite activity is: gym for both, science for Joan, and French for Lynn. This fact, that *some* classes could be intrinsically motivating, is a very important point to which we shall return later; it suggests that even productive activities can be enjoyable.

There were nine items in the scale, in addition to the one shown in Table 12.2. Eight of the ten items were highly correlated, showing that they are tapping related elements of experience. The sum of scores on the full ten-item scale was used to assess how close to an ideal flow experience the most enjoyable activities were rated, and then to compare these ratings with the way various school classes were rated.

Most of the enjoyable activities were rated an average of 7.5 over the ten items of the 9-point scale. The average for those classes each student ranked most enjoyable was 7.2. In other words, although favorite activities were rated as providing more flow than favorite classes, the difference was rather small, although significant. Other classes, however, were rated much

TABLE 12.2

Students' Rankings of Favorite Activities and Classes

"I Would Do It Even If I Didn't Have To":		Student's Name			
		Ronny	Joan	Bruce	Lynn
A Great Deal	9	Football*	Rock Concert* Science Gym	Friends*	Dancing* French Gym
	8				
Quite a Bit	7	Math	English Humanities		Sociology
	6				American History
A Fair Amount	5				English
	4	Gym			
Sometimes	3	World History	Astronomy	Sociology Earth Science American Literature Child Development	
	2				Computer Programming
Almost Never	1	English Spanish		Gym	
Rating of Favorite Activity:		9	9	9	9
Mean Rating of Classes:		3.2	7.0	2.6	6.2

*Favorite activities

lower in flow; the average for the second-ranked class was 6.3, for the third-ranked, 5.5, for the fourth- and fifth-ranked, 4.7 and 4.4; each was lower than the preceding one by a value significant at the one-in-a-thousand probability level.

In other words, the theoretical dimensions of the flow model, when operationalized in the ten-item scale, bear out the claim that enjoyment consists of a particular cluster of experiences that can occur in playful leisure activities or in formal school classes—experiences that cut across the superficial diversity of such things as football, dancing, working, skating, or being with friends.

Work, Study, and Enjoyment

Common to the things we enjoy doing is this feeling of being totally alive. Unfortunately, in our culture at least, people usually experience flow only in nonproductive activities like sports and games. Most people never get to to enjoy doing the things they need to in order to survive and be accepted in contemporary society—things like study or work. Required activities become sources of psychic entropy. We know from the previous chapters that teenagers experience productive activities—homework, classwork, work—as entropic, and the same is true of most maintenance tasks. Adults are not that much better off; the typical worker finds his or her job constraining and alienating (Csikszentmihalyi and Graef 1980; Rubinstein, Csikszentmihalyi and Graef 1980).

Most teenagers, like most adults, feel free and involved only in leisure settings, when they listen to music, go out to a movie, drink with buddies, fiddle with a hobby, or become involved in a game of cards or touch football. Thus, we have developed a dichotomy in our culture between things we must do against our will and things we want to do but which need not be done; between unpleasant necessities and pleasant frivolities. This distinction is so engrained that by now it appears to be a fact, a law of nature. Many people take it for granted that study, work—the serious business of life must be boring and meaningless.

Splitting life by such a dichotomy is neither natural nor inevitable. In societies that existed prior to ours, people lacked clear distinctions between work and leisure. What they did for a living often merged into what we would call art, religion, sports, or sociability (Dumazedier 1974; Gunter and Gunter 1980). In less developed societies, singing, dancing, drinking, and partying are so much a part of productive hunting or gathering activities that one simply cannot tell where one starts and the other stops (Firth 1929; Sahlins 1972).

The enjoyable quality of work does not stop with simple hunting societies. In the technologically sophisticated manufacturing districts of eighteenth-century England, for example, weavers and other craftsmen worked at home, surrounded by their family and friends, setting their own plans, schedules, and pace. Work at the looms was intertwined with songs, riddles, and talk (Thompson 1963). Just as the workplace was not separated from the living space, the activity of work was all of a piece with the rest of life.

The real separation between production and leisure begins only about two centuries ago, with the advent of factories. In the eighteenth century, factories developed into "dark, satanic mills" not so much because working conditions in them were harsh—they had been harsh all along—but because by specializing *only* in work, they destroyed the psychological integrity of the worker. In the name of efficiency, of standardization, the factory routine makes it practically impossible for the worker to achieve flow.

The segregation of adolescents in schools occurs historically about the same time as the spread of factories, and for similar reasons. Schools apply methods of mass production and industrial efficiency to the socialization of youth. They try to change attentional structures—goals, habits, cognitive skills—by coercing youth to attend to standardized, sequential information. The curriculum is an assembly line that pushes ideas and activities in front of the student at a fixed rate, ready or not. What is manufactured, however, is a great deal of internal discomfort. To save time, schools concentrate on academic subjects to the exclusion of the issues teenagers really care about. No wonder that the goals of schools have become foreign to most students, and that formal learning is a context for severe psychic entropy.

The fiction that people can actually live in the one-dimensional world of the school or the factory is responsible for much of our unhappiness with day-to-day existence. Of course, whenever possible, people do not conform to the constraints of these institutions.

In a typical 50-minute high school classroom lecture, the average student is awake, staring more or less eagerly at the teacher who is passing on the information, yet at least half the time the student is not really thinking about anything even remotely related to the lecture or to the subject matter. Typical thoughts in the classroom cover the weather outside, prospects for the weekend, and the state of one's digestive system. "Nothing like 40 minutes of taking notes to bore a person to death," writes one girl. Another girl, contemplating hassles with her father, is thinking, "how the male ego needs to be fed." Such thoughts are not great indications of psychic negentropy, but they at least indicate to the students that they are in control of their own consciousness, shaping their thoughts with reference to their own goals. This knowledge alone seems enough to prevent the worst effects of psychic entropy.

But is this situation beyond remedy? Does productive work have to be tolerated in suffering, like the Biblical "curse of Adam"? Many people will claim that it is a romantic utopia to believe that work and study can ever be enjoyable. But if we give up that hope, we forfeit the chance of changing the existing conditions in factories, offices and schools. The guiding ideal, however utopian, should be to slowly transform all social institutions, even the productive and the maintenance ones, into dissipative structures that will increase order in consciousness instead of decreasing it.

Making "productive" activities more flowlike is not an unrealistic goal, even in the alienating technological milieu we live in. We already know that professional jobs can provide as much enjoyment as any leisure activity does (Csikszentmihalyi 1975). Even less challenging jobs occasionally produce the conditions for flow experience. And as we mentioned, teenagers ranked at least one class, on the average, as being almost as flow-producing as their favorite leisure activity. It is true that four of the five classes they took were significantly less enjoyable. But the impressive thing is that usually there is at least one class out of the five that produces intense flow experiences in the student, close to the same order he experienced in dancing, listening to rock, or playing football. Through clarifying goals, through balancing challenges and skills, through meaningful feedback, students find enjoyment in doing something directly related to their development. This modest finding has tremendous implications, because it proves that school need not be dull and alienating. Amid the constraints, the negative feedback, and the chaos that often characterize classes, it is possible to cull bits and pieces of order that allow one to turn it into an enjoyable time.

Ironically, enjoyment of a given class is not only intrinsically rewarding, but it gets students better grades as well. Flow in school is more than its own reward; it brings external rewards in its wake. Apparently when a class is enjoyable, one learns more from it. At the end of the semester, after we collected flow ratings of the various classes that each student was taking, and after we obtained the ESM-pager reports from the same classes, we also were able to obtain the semester grades students received in those courses. Thus, it was possible to see whether there was any relationship between how much a student enjoyed a class and how well he or she did in it. As Appendix D.20 shows, the classes students rated as having flow-like attributes (that is, the ones they got involved in, where time passed quickly, where the experience was enjoyable, etc.) were the ones in which they wished to be when they were paged, and they were the classes in which they *received the higher grades when the semester was over.*

It is interesting to note that how happy or how strong and alert a student feels in a class has no bearing on the grade he or she will get in the course. Apparently moods in class are influenced by too many other factors for them to show a clear relationship to performance (Appendix D.20). But how intrinsically motivated a student is, and especially how many dimensions of flow he or she experiences in class, predict performance rather well. In fact, when one does a regression analysis on semester grades, holding Grade-Point Average (GPA) constant, the correlation of the flow scales and semester grades climbs to $r = 0.50$. One fourth of the variance in grades and in the reported flow experiences overlap when the students' scholastic achievement is controlled for. Thus the relationship between flow and grades does not simply mean that the better students enjoy classes more. It means that regardless of a student's ability (GPA), the class he or she enjoys more is the one he or she will get the better grades in. In other words, the enjoyable course is the one in which the student will do best. Hardly a staggering revelation—yet what enormous changes there would be if this obvious finding were heeded!

It would mean that educators might stop worrying about how to transmit information, and concentrate instead on how to make learning enjoyable, because only when going to school becomes a flow activity will students be motivated to learn on their own, and grow in the process. Otherwise, education becomes just another alienating experience that increases entropy in the present while offering the specious promise of increasing future negentropy.

To make education enjoyable (and hence growth-producing), two sets of conditions must obtain: The institution needs to present students with opportunities for action they can cope with, and increase these challenges as the individual skills of the learner develop; the teenager should be prepared to internalize the challenges presented by the institution, and have enough skills to begin acting in the school setting. If both these conditions are fulfilled, learning will take care of itself. Sounds easy? Of course it is not. Mass education, despite the increasingly detailed cognitive and affective profiles it provides of individual students, still cannot match teachers' skills with students' skills well enough to make teaching and learning enjoyable.

Research leaves little doubt that the quality of schools and the dedication teachers bring to their jobs make a great difference (Coleman et al. 1982; Rutter et al. 1979). But there is another side to the coin. Not only are educational institutions unable to meet individual students at the level they need to be met in order to be able to experience flow, but schools are increasingly frustrated by students who are less and less able to recognize an intellectual challenge when they see one. It is very difficult for teachers to make academic learning enjoyable when young people lack even the simplest intellectual skills. Difficult, but not impossible. If paraplegics can learn to enjoy playing basketball, a TV-reared generation can surely learn to enjoy the use of the mind.

The best medium of growth in adolescence is a flow activity; when fully involved with challenging actions that test the limits of one's skills, persons know they are alive. Year after year, flow experiences *realize* a person's existence; they build a self that is conscious of its freedom and its history. Without them, how would you know that you existed? Deprived of flow, the self is a plaything of exterior forces, a powerless shadow.

Critics might claim at this point that too much emphasis on enjoyment smacks of hedonism. The claim that optimal development requires flow seems decadent to some people, because they fear that if young people are permitted to enjoy themselves, nothing will ever get done: How are you going to keep them doing what is necessary once they have learned to enjoy themselves? This fear is based on two misunderstandings: the first, that only leisure provides enjoyment; the second, that enjoyment is a form of pleasure. As we have tried to show, neither one of these assumptions is true. It is now time to give a closer look to this second source of misunderstanding, and examine how flow experiences, rather than producing the passive contentment of pleasure, on the contrary drive the person to increasingly complex states of consciousness. With the help of these experiences, more permanent and stable psychic dissipative structures can be built, thus allowing teenagers to resist successfully the onslaught of chaos in later life.

Chapter 13

The Growth of Complexity: Shaping Meaningful Lives

$\mathbf{F}$LOW experiences provide evidence that life is worth living. When they play football, dance, or do the hundreds of other enjoyable things they do, teenagers *feel* the harmony between dimensions of consciousness: between goals, thoughts, emotions, and activation. Their psychic energy is focused, and their being functions as an efficient whole. But the ability to find enjoyment is not enough to ensure that a person will grow up to make the most of his or her potential. After all, some adolescents learn to enjoy activities that do not build habits of discipline or skills: activities that waste human and material energy. Others grow up enjoying activities that are not only wasteful, but destructive. Therefore, one must conclude that the ability to enjoy everyday experience is necessary, but not sufficient to avoid psychic entropy in the long run. One must also learn to enjoy activities with increasingly complex goals, activities integrated with the goals of others. Optimal conditions for growth are present when a person experiences flow while doing things that are negentropic in the long run—for the self as well as for the social system.

This chapter will explore some of the paths for accomplishing this. First we will show how flow experiences, by their very nature, require gradual increases in the complexity of a person's skill. Flow activities can be just temporary shelters to protect one from entropy, or they can provide life-long patterns of order. Second, we will examine longitudinal data from our adolescents and some retrospective data from adults to show how these processes actually take place.

The kind of psychic dissipative structure we will consider is the capacity to create meaning. This is the ability to relate isolated bits of information to each other, and ultimately to one's goals, for example, the ability to see a passage from Shakespeare as pertinent to one's life. I understand the meaning of a smile on a friend's face when I comprehend the feelings or purposes to which it is related—and when I know how the friend's purposes are related to mine. The meaning of a book is revealed when we understand its goal and we see how it is related to ours.

Events in the world are not ordered by nature to conform with our desires. They occur, rather, in random or threatening sequences. To see this, all we have to do is look at the haphazard struggle among living things that takes place on a forest floor, or at the political relationship among nations. According to Prigogine, the species that can cull fragments of energy from whatever is available, that can pull order out of this chaotic jumble, are those that survive. In a sense, adolescents face a similar situation. What is true of organisms at the biochemical level seems to be also true of persons trying to cope with the world. The key to growth is the ability to make sense of disordered information and energy, to make it serve one's goals.

Teenagers cannot avoid psychic entropy only by playing football or playing the flute. They also must learn to give order to the events that normally produce boredom, rage, or despair.

The Growth of Complexity

When teenagers learn to reinterpret disorder in ways that make sense, when they can turn boredom into useful reflection, when after an argument with their parents they don't just brood but get to see the parents' point of view and how it relates to theirs, then they have learned to use a powerful tool for decreasing entropy: the meaningful interpretation of experience.

Perhaps the ultimate achievement in this effort is the development of a personal *life theme*. This process consists of transforming misfortune in one's life—or in the wider social environment—into a goal that gives direction and meaning to a whole life. For example, a young man whose mother dies of cancer might feel the integrity of his self teetering under the blow; but he might pull himself together, vow to become a doctor, and to help defeat the disease that killed his mother. This story—a true one by the way—is in its main outlines so common as to be almost trivial. It is an example of how a person builds his life around a theme, a meaningful arrangement of goals and of means, out of deepest tragedy. Thus it represents the most permanent and solid dissipative structure that individuals can use against the constant threat of entropy in their existence.

Flow activities and life themes are by no means the only hedges against disorder that it is possible to devise. Political institutions, religious beliefs, feelings of solidarity and love are extremely important systems of order that can act as dissipative structures mediating the impact of random frustrations. If we limit the discussion to enjoyment and the creation of meaning, it is simply because these processes are more directly under the control of teenagers, and because to deal with all the other alternatives would require a separate volume. But enjoyment and meaning promote the whole of experience, and when they are present, it is likely that the rest of life will be ordered, too. Let us begin, then, by considering how flow activities contribute to permanent growth processes.

Complexity and Flow

It is relatively easy to enjoy pleasurable sensations, the kind we are biologically programmed to seek out: food when hungry, sex, the primitive beat of music that mimics states of physiological arousal. It is easy to enjoy power, the ability to spend money and control other people. But pursuit of these spontaneous sources of pleasure does not lead to growth. Experiencing pleasure simply returns the organism to a homeostatic balance; it does not propel it to change toward greater complexity. The man who is motivated only by the pleasure of sex or power might accomplish many impressive things; he might build palaces for his mistresses or start gigantic wars of conquest. However, despite all his accomplishments, he is unlikely to grow as a person because the goal he pursues is as old as the pyramids or the caves of our hairy ancestors. At the end of his efforts, he is the same man he was at the beginning.

Persons who wish to fulfill their potential for growth must learn to invest psychic energy in goals that are not yet given automatically in the genes. Only by superimposing the pursuit of *voluntary* goals on that of *spontaneous* ones does a human being become a *person* who consciously chooses behavior. Only by achieving control over attention does someone transcend the life of a mere organism.

An adolescent who enjoys only what he is biologically programmed to find pleasurable misses many opportunities. He will play out the part handed down to him through his genes but will not experience the negentropic interaction with more complex challenges that cultural evolution has made possible. The runaway positive feedback spiral teenagers experience with friends, the total participation in a rock concert, the oblivion induced by drugs feel good while they last, but afterward one is not very different from what one was before: No muscles, no skills, no mental structures were developed that would allow one to meet future entropy better prepared.

But when one passes from the positive experience of biologically programmed pleasure to enjoyment, which is dependent on the use of skills, it becomes clear that enjoyment and growth are closely related processes. To see the connection, it is useful to represent the conditions that make flow possible by the set of coordinates in Figure 13.1. Enjoyment tends to occur whenever a person feels that his or her capacity to act matches the opportunities for action in a given situation. In short, flow is experienced when personal skills match situational challenges, that is, when a person is in the central channel of the graph.

For instance, a tennis player will not enjoy a game if the opponent is either much more experienced, or much less experienced. Surgeons do not enjoy trivial, routine operations, nor the ones where the patient's odds of survival are slight. But they do get into flow when all their skill is just barely enough to save the

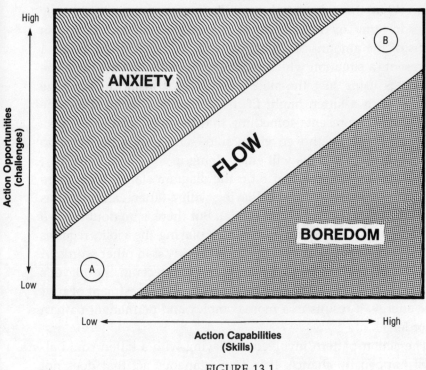

FIGURE 13.1
Model of the Flow Experience

patient's life, and the outcome hangs in the balance. High school students do not enjoy classes in which they are overwhelmed by assignments, nor the ones so easy that they are boring, but the ones where knowledge can be mastered when the student really tries hard (Csikszentmihalyi 1975, 1978b, 1980; Gianinno, Graef, and Csikszentmihalyi 1979; Mayers 1978).

Ordinarily, when people enjoy an activity, it is because of this balanced tension between challenges and skills. If the challenges get to be too high, and a person begins to doubt that he can make it, worry ensues and eventually turns into anxiety. If, on the other hand, a person feels frustrated because there is no way to make use of his or her skills, then boredom follows; when boredom becomes extreme, it yields to anxiety.

With these simple rules in mind, it is easy to see how enjoyment and growth are related. One characteristic of the diagram in Figure 13.1 is that the "flow channel" encloses a diagonal area. What this suggests is that flow experiences differ: they differ in terms of the amount of challenges attended to, and in terms of the amount of skills involved. In the diagram, point A represents a situation which requires few skills and in which the person is using just the skills needed—for instance, someone playing with a kitten might fit the description. Point B, on the other hand, represents something that requires great skill—perhaps playing a Beethoven violin solo—and only a person who has the necessary skills will enjoy doing it.

This does not mean that B on the diagram stands for a more *enjoyable* experience than A. Playing with a kitten can be just as much fun as playing a violin sonata. But there is no doubt that B is a more *complex* experience than A: playing the violin requires greater skills than playing with a cat. To say it in other words, A and B correspond to equally negentropic effects in the player's consciousness. But because B requires a larger investment of psychic energy, it results in a more complex and permanent pattern of order.

The action-pattern involved in playing with a kitten could almost happen by chance. It is a spontaneous act that does not require unusual concentration of attention or previous knowledge. Anybody could do it any time. But a Beethoven violin solo could not happen by chance. Its existence depends on a voluntary focusing of attention, on prolonged practice coordinating sensory-motor pathways, memory, and imagination. Its unlikelihood is a triumphant challenge to entropy. Complex accomplishment is admirable, because it is rare to shape order out of chaos. It is difficult to make things happen that would not happen if left to themselves. And once a complex challenge is mastered, it provides a skill that can be used again and again.

The action pattern indicated by B on the graph is in some sense "better" than the one marked A. The advantage is not given in the experience itself—B does not "feel" better than A—but rather in its consequences. The more complex action represents growth, the actualization of human potential in the face of chaos. If this is true, why doesn't everybody move up the diagonal? Why is so much of what people choose to do banal, and why does so little of it require complexity of any kind?

Growth is the natural condition of life. Action patterns over time tend to become more complex. This process is represented in Figure 13.2. Let A in the figure stand for a boy who has just learned to play the piano; his skills are low, but because he plays very easy pieces, he can get involved with them and enjoys the experience.

If he keeps on playing the same easy pieces, A's skills will increase relative to the stable challenges, and he will become bored (represented by A_1 in the figure). At that point, he is likely to do one of two things. He might stop playing the piano because it is no longer enjoyable. Or he might take on greater challenges by learning more complex pieces; this would return him into the flow channel at point A_3.

Another possibility is that A is forced by his teacher to play pieces that are too difficult in relation to A's skills (A_2 in the figure). This produces a sense of anxiety in A_2, who is overwhelmed by the demands of the situation. To reduce the anxiety, he might do one of three things. He might give up playing altogether. He might return to playing the easy pieces as in A. Or he might practice long enough to develop his skills so he can

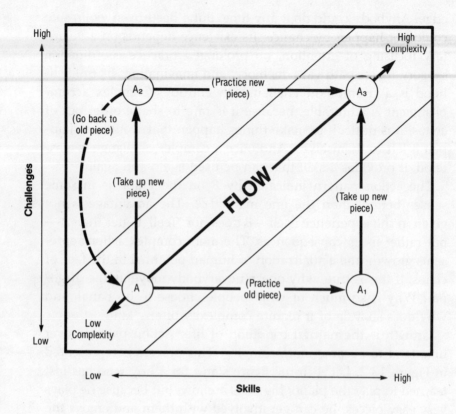

FIGURE 13.2
Alternative Paths for Returning to the Flow Channel When Playing the Piano

master the more complex music, and end up back in the flow channel at A_3.

This means that enjoyment is an unstable state that always drifts into boredom or anxiety. To keep experiencing flow one must try doing new things, and do them better every time. Like the dissipative structures in the physical realm, flow is a precariously balanced state that tends to break down with time, unless it reconstitutes itself into a more unlikely system of interaction. Boredom and anxiety represent the negative feedback that makes us realize we no longer enjoy what we are doing. To recapture that enjoyment, we must formulate increasingly complex goals, face new challenges, and learn new skills.

Thus enjoyment is like a built-in thermostat that indicates whether we are operating at full capacity, at the leading edge of growth. Yet many people resign themselves to lives of boredom, or of constant worry, and give up the opportunity to grow.

Perhaps the main reason adolescents stop growing is because their initial lack of skills is exposed too suddenly to excessive challenges. A child who cannot draw—or thinks he cannot—will keep doodling stick figures; anything more complex is too difficult, and failure might expose him to ridicule. A student who has been confused by long division in elementary school will tend to freeze when confronted with an equation, knowing that its solution is beyond reach. The expectation of failure becomes a self-fulfilling prophecy that precludes further growth. A certain amount of skill is required even to perceive challenges in the environment. If you cannot play, a piano is just a piece of furniture; if you can, it is a source of endless opportunities for action. To a climber, a wall of rock might offer days of challenging experiences that will be treasured all through life. The same wall is just a featureless slab of granite to the nonclimber, barely noticed and immediately forgotten.

Most persons' environment is a potential playground full of exciting things to do. The catch is that, to the naked eye, they are invisible. A person must be already initiated to enter one of the cosmic games. The price of admission is learning to recognize the challenges, making the effort to see what can be done. Complex activities, like mathematics, music, poetry, or rock-climbing, require substantial investment of psychic energy even to be perceived as options. To actually practice them takes continued focusing of attention in ever-more-unlikely patterns. But only by paying this price does one grow, and taste enjoyment.

For some adolescents, growth has been blocked by external obstacles: a harsh environment, an oppressive social system, a depressive childhood. The more attention is required just for physical survival, the less of it is left to discover paths of growth. The Greeks took it for granted that their slaves were not fully human, since they spent all their psychic activity in goals dictated by survival. Not so long ago teenagers had to work in

269

factories from dawn to dusk, six days a week, with hardly a moment's rest. Today they have to work less than half as hard, yet many of them, when they get home in the evenings, have barely enough energy left to turn on the TV and relax in a dazed stupor until it is time to go to bed.

External obstacles can drain away attention, and leave us too exhausted to start on one of the many paths of growth beckoning just outside our range. But the impediments that the physical environment or the social system place across the path often become excuses to rationalize away the unwillingness to make the necessary effort. Hardships can prevent growth, but only if one lets them. Even in the most precarious situations, when most people do give up, some do not. Instead of huddling up under stress and conserving their psychic energy, they use it to find new opportunities for action, develop new skills, and, instead of stagnating, they grow.

It is probable that most workers of the industrial revolution spent the few hours they had free drinking gin and playing cards. The strict routines of the factory left them too exhausted to tackle anything more complex. The sociologist Le Play found that typical French workers of the nineteenth century spent over 10 percent of their income on liquor, and none for the education of their children (Le Play 1879). Although potentially there were thousands of things they could have done, most genuinely felt that they could do nothing but drown their sorrow in drink. But not everybody did this. As the anthropologist Anthony F. C. Wallace shows in his careful reconstruction of life in early industrial Pennsylvania, despite the grueling hours in the mills, some workers found the strength to write or to involve themselves in politics, religion, or even science; many others used their savings to start a business, and to strike out in a new direction (Wallace 1978; Thompson 1963).

The Growth of Complexity

The Ordering of Experience

To know how to take a neutral or adverse situation and redefine it as a challenge that will sharpen one's skills is a tool that makes it much easier to confront adversity in later life. This ability is closely related to another dissipative structure of consciousness, which consists in the interpretive skills teenagers develop to give meaning to their experiences. To see how these skills are learned, we shall report briefy on a reinterview of twenty seven adolescents from the original sample, two years after the first study. These were teens who had been freshmen and sophomores the first time around, and were now juniors and seniors. In addition to repeating the ESM procedure, these students answered questions in interviews directed at uncovering change during this period. Two years is a short period, but we hoped that some of the growth trends would be visible even in such a reduced time span.

The four years of high school are in some respects all part of adolescence, but one does not have to look very carefully to see differences between a freshman and a senior. At fourteen, the young in our culture are still considered children; at eighteen, they are expected to behave like adults. Somewhere in those four years a mature human being is supposed to emerge out of the cocoon of childhood.

In the past chapters we have noticed several differences in the activities and experiences of teens at the beginning and at the end of this period. For instance, seniors spend 10 hours less a week with their families than freshmen, and 10 hours more with their friends. The type of friendship interaction changes from large same-sex groups to opposite dyads, and whereas for freshmen the most favorable experiences are with same-sex chums, for seniors they are with one person of the opposite sex. Solitude, which is strongly entropic for younger teens, becomes tolerable, in mild doses, for older ones. These were some indications of how life experiences change as the crucial years of adolescence pass by.

The first surprising result in comparing ESM data from two years apart was how much similarity there was in the conscious-ness of individual teenagers. Those who usually said they were happy as freshmen also said they were happy as juniors. The correlation of overall affect means was .77, and of overall activa-tion .62, both extremely significant. If one looks at the separate contexts, however, one notices that affect with family and in solitude are not predictable from early to late adolescence, while affect with friends and in school remains consistent (Appendix D.21). Apparently friends and school, the most voluntary and the most involuntary contexts respectively, remain stable over this period in the quality of feedback they provide. Relationship with family and with the self, by contrast, undergo enough change to make some teens who had been happy alone or with their parents now unhappy, or vice versa. But overall it seems that by tenth grade most adolescents have developed a con-sciousness that is either basically ordered, or vulnerable to frus-tration—at least as measured again two years later.

So far we have looked at stability of experiences over time and between persons. This has shown that if John rated himself hap-pier than Jim at fifteen, chances were he would still rate himself happier at seventeen. But one could look at stability in a differ-ent way, and ask: are adolescents on the whole happier at seven-teen than at fifteen? The results suggest that, as far as immediate experience is concerned, the two years seem to make no great difference. Except for a significantly higher level of activation with friends, teens report essentially the same moods across the two-year period. If anything, moods tend to be more negative at the later date, even though the drop is not significant statisti-cally. It would seem, however, that the only reason the overall experience is not more negative is because relationships with friends have improved. This gloomy conclusion is somewhat al-tered, however, by results from a different part of the same study.

Other data indicate that their lives have gotten better. When asked to rate how they felt globally compared to two years ago the majority reported that things had improved. For example, in their relationships with their families, 52 percent said they were happier now, 12 percent that they were less happy, while the remaining 36 percent reported no change. Roughly the same pattern held for friends, alone, and overall. In fact, the majority rated their experiences as having improved in every context, both in terms of affect and activation (Freeman 1982).

How can the results of the pager reports, which show no change in experience, be reconciled with the questionnaire answers showing improvement across the board? To answer this question, we must consider some of the things adolescents said in the interviews. What they describe is a change, not so much in the quality of experience itself, but in the way experience is interpreted, the way it is evaluated and stored for future reference.

What emerges overall is an improved ability to use psychic dissipative structures, that is, to give purposeful meaning to entropic experiences. For instance, here is what one girl says about how her family relationships have changed:

> It used to get on my nerves, the time with my family; like they do something that bugs me it'd make me mad; like I'd be sitting and watching TV and someone would jump in front of me and that would make me real mad; now I still get mad but not that mad; a lot of my friends went off to school, so they're gone; but my family will be there; I think I accept them more; like my grandmother had a stroke a year or two ago, so she was real sick, so we spent a lot of time there, and when she talked to my father it was like he was a boy, and I never thought of him as growing up and being my age, so then I started to think about that and that he must have had a hard life, so I felt less selfish, and I don't get that mad at him when he asks me [to do things] . . ."

She still gets just as mad when the family crosses her, but the anger does not mean the same thing it did earlier. She can accept it better, she can identify with members of her family, and thus be less selfish. The immediate experience of anger is placed in a broader context of information, including values and goals; therefore, the effect of the experience is transformed. How to control and integrate entropic states with the family is well expressed by this advice given by a boy:

Your parents can't completely understand you; you gotta understand where they're coming from. When you have something that goes wrong, getting pressure not just from them but from friends and school, don't take it all out on the family; try to sit down and explain instead of blowing up; try to be more calm. . . . I think that's the best way.

This boy is beginning to assume responsibility for ordering social relations beyond his own selfish goals: "You gotta understand . . . ." Instead of wasting energy in "blowing up," he sees the value of achieving a harmony of goals by sitting down and discussing calmly. By investing a little attention in creating order, he saves a great deal of the psychic energy he formerly spent in brooding about disorder.

The ability to reflect on the broader consequences of action, and thus to tolerate experience that is entropic, applies to relations beyond the family. Solitude, too, changes its meaning, even though the immediate experience is still negative. Here is a typical account from the interviews.

Instead of thinking I'm alone because others aren't with me, it is because I choose to be alone; I don't think 'Oh, no one likes me'; I'm not alone because there aren't things for me to do, I'm just alone because I choose to be alone and I'm not as self-conscious being alone, doing something myself. Sometimes around here I'm just not up to going out, I'll just stay home and read or watch TV and I don't mind shopping alone and running into a bunch of my friends; I used to do a lot of camping, but don't have much time for it this year, but when I go up into the north woods I get really reflective; I like to go for walks by myself, I don't think about being alone, separated, isolated as much as I did 2 years ago.

And another one:

When I was younger like freshman and sophomore year I didn't think you should be spending a lot of time alone or even some time alone; you should be out being social; it used to bother me sometimes being alone. . . . I used to think it wasn't healthy to be alone and now I think it's a lot healthier sometimes just to be alone. . . . I used to sometimes be really bored when I was by myself; now I always find an interesting thing to do, I'm never bored.

The Growth of Complexity

The major change is that earlier these teenagers perceived solitude to be involuntary: They thought they were alone because others were avoiding them. Now, however, they feel they can be alone by choice. With age and experience the threats are less intimidating (Coleman et al. 1974); more importantly, they know how to find interesting things to do by themselves. The experience is still painful, but now it provides opportunities for using skills that were not seen before. The psychic energy spent in solitude is no longer wasted in self-pity, but can be used to pursue the teenagers' goals.

The ability to stand solitude goes hand in hand with emancipation from the peer group. Many older adolescents seem to have developed a strong enough identity to resist the pressures of friends:

> Two years ago if they had bothered me I wouldn't have told them to leave me alone; now if they bug me I tell them to go somewhere; (Why?) 'Cause we just built that relationship; I'd rather be alone than with my friends, cause they always want you to do things and I'd rather do what I want to do.

One teen is willing even to break the sex-role taboo against boys cooking, in his assertion of independence from peers:

> I'm looking at myself more not so much as how other people look at me, I always used to worry about what other people thought and now it doesn't matter because I'm the only one I have to please; I take a new attitude about life; kids in my class might go out and get wild drunk, but that doesn't appeal to me, and I think, heck, if that's what they want to do let them go out and do it, but I'm not gonna do it; whatever I want to do I'm going to do it, like some kids wouldn't get caught dead in the kitchen baking cake, but I enjoy it so I'm gonna do it, who cares?

Liberation from external peer pressure implies that friendships become more meaningful: more freely chosen, more clearly related to the teenagers' goals. The potential for runaway positive feedback becomes checked. They learn to find enjoyment without yielding control. With time, interactions with friends might become more than an opportunity for uncontrolled dissipation of raw energy; intimate friendships might provide a discriminating and constructive dissipative structure in their lives. If immediate experience has not gotten better, it is partly because they are taking on more complex and sophisticated challenges.

These maturational trends have been described by previous researchers. For instance, it has been said that, as they move through the high school years, teenagers learn to recognize their parents' needs and thus become less estranged from them, less ready to engage in "token empty rituals of disaffection" (Douvan and Adelson 1966). Decreasing preoccupation with popularity and peer approval also has been often documented (for example, Looft 1971; Conger 1977; Costanzo 1970; Berndt 1979). Teens still feel angry when parents attempt to socialize them, they still feel lonely when alone. But they are learning to put experience in perspective, to control psychic entropy by ordering information in consciousness. If they can explain a negative emotion, if they can see reasons for a painful subjective state, this very process of interpretation creates order and reduces the entropic effects of the "raw" experience. The obstacles to their goals are still present, but now teenagers accept their necessity, understand the reason for their existence, and begin to see how they can reach their goals despite these obstacles.

These processes of reinterpretation are particularly visible in how people cope with trying experiences. In recent years an increasing number of psychological approaches have come to acknowledge that human development occurs within a context of stress and frustration. The notion of conflict, of course, is central to psychoanalysis. In dialectical psychology, the basic tenet is that growth takes place as a result of the continuous resolution of radical polarities between the self and the environment (Riegel 1976; Rychlak 1976). Existential psychology claims that to live an authentic life one must face up to the unavoidable stress and uncertainty of the future (Kobasa and Maddi 1977).

In turn, psychologists have come to recognize that a powerful means for reducing the negative impact of stressful events lies in how we think about or how we reinterpret experience. Freudian therapy and its offshoots are based on the premise that if one only talks about painful events, there is a chance that they will lose their power over the psyche. Lazarus, Averill, and Opton (1974) single out "reappraisal" as one of the main mechanisms by which the effects of stress are mitigated. Even behaviorists are beginning to use cognitive reinterpretation techniques. Meichenbaum's (1977) stress-innoculation training involves the "relabeling" of painful experiences, a process which increases tolerance of pain and decreases its perceived intensity (Sanders 1979). The same training works when applied to other experiences. If, for instance, an angry person is given a word to label his emotion (for example, "anger"), he might be able to reduce the emotion (Novaco 1975).

By talking and thinking through their problems, adolescents learn to control conflict in everyday life. This process is a powerful tool for creating order out of chaos, for changing the valence of feedback from negative to positive, thereby turning a source of weakness into an input that strengthens the self. Of course, it is a tool that must be used with caution. To deny the reality of something unpleasant is just as bad as to let oneself be overwhelmed by it. Reinterpretation that distorts the actual state of affairs becomes a deceptive defense rather than realistic coping (Lazarus, Averill, and Opton 1974; Kobasa and Maddi 1977).

A boy whose girl friend has left him might feel despair because of the loss of all the psychic energy he had invested in the goal of being with the girl. He can reinterpret the event by denying the importance of the relationship. This is the classical "sour grapes" response. It is a way of coping that distorts the actual state of affairs, however, and thus cannot lead to psychic negentropy, which requires a harmonious order among the contents of consciousness. A more effective way is to recognize the hurt caused by the breakup of the relationship, while at the same time recognizing that the future holds other opportunities for friendship and love, and that from an objective viewpoint the loss cannot be as acute as it is experienced at the moment. In other words, the experience is placed in a more realistic perspective. Its sting is removed, not through denial, but by relating the event to the full range of the person's hierarchy of goals. In the new context, the distressing event acquires a new meaning which is less entropic than it originally was. This solution allows the memory of the past relationship, however painful, to remain in consciousness, and to become integrated with new experiences. The psychic energy invested in the relationship is not lost, but remains at the disposal of the self. This kind of reinterpretation maintains psychic order while preserving the integrity of the self and allowing further growth.

The ability to take disorder and turn it into order is perhaps the major skill adolescents perfect as they grow into adulthood. Learning to use the dissipative structures culture provides to alleviate frustration is the main task of maturity.

The Development of Life Themes

In our research we could not observe how teenagers go through the steps of building a permanent set of goals that would serve to give purpose and meaning to their lives. This is a slow process, with many stops and starts. Only a few adolescents actually develop fully authentic life goals—most are satisfied to pursue the goals society prescribes: a college education, a job, marriage, children, and life within conventional standards of morality. To the extent that these prescribed goals give order to their lives, they will be satisfied adults. But some young people are unable, or unwilling, to shape their attention exclusively according to cultural blueprints. They struggle to define their own goals, to build a custom-made dissipative structure to direct their psychic energy. Only a longitudinal study, in which people are followed from early teens into adulthood, can give a clear picture of how such life themes develop.

A less reliable source of information is a *restrospective* study, where adults are interviewed to find out how the goals by which they order their lives were developed. Some years ago we conducted such a study with Olga Beattie Emory, and a brief summary of it will begin to show how life themes originate and give direction to life. Thirty adult men were interviewed; half were successful intellectuals—professors, physicians, lawyers, and politicians—and the other half blue-collar workers. The childhood environment for all thirty was as similar as it could be: Both groups came from poor immigrant families, both were equally plagued by illness, alcoholism, illiteracy, and poverty. Yet somehow half escaped its entropic background and achieved rare heights of complexity, while the other half led lives that were predictable given the conditions of their childhood. What made one group able to reshape its life conditions?

There might have been many reasons that we have not begun to fathom. But one clear difference was that practically all the men who broke away from the constraints in which they were born had developed in adolescence goals that were to focus their energies for the rest of their lives. Each constructed for himself a *life theme*, a set of challenges that kept him struggling, and that forced him to develop skills of a rare complexity. The men whose lives were predictable did not create such a scheme. At most, they gave order to their lives by adopting a ready-made goal suggested to them by their parents—like honesty or thrift—and let that goal shape their psychic energy (Csikszentmihalyi and Beattie 1979).

For both groups the goals that gave direction to their lives emerged out of entropic experiences: poverty, loneliness, helplessness. And both groups survived by focusing their attention on goals that acted as dissipative structures by restoring order in their consciousness. The difference was that the men who overcame their handicaps saw their plight as part of a broader human problem, and so were able to attack it at a more general level than the others. For example, Henry and Julian, two typical respondents in the study, were both poor as children. But Henry got to see his deprivations as caused by the social exploitation of illiterate immigrants, while Julian learned to ascribe his family's poverty to his father's lack of thrift. Henry attributed the cause of poverty to laws and institutions that could be changed, whereas Julian blamed human nature. As a teenager, Henry decided to learn the law in order to help other poor immigrants in situations like those his family had encountered. Julian decided to save every cent he earned so that he would not end up poor, as his father had.

The two adolescents found different meanings in poverty; that is, they related it to different causes, which in turn suggested different strategies of solution, different life goals. Henry became a lawyer, achieved a high position in President Truman's cabinet, and helped to implement legislation that made the lot of the destitute easier. Julian worked hard, bought up a number of apartment buildings, and was able to save several hundred thousand dollars by the time he was sixty. He never got married, and lived in a small room all his life, fixing the buildings he owned and being as thrifty as was humanly possible.

Why were the lives of Henry and Julian, and the two groups they represent, so different when the environment they grew up in was the same? The answer seems to be that while the environment was the same in terms of material obstacles and opportunities, it was not the same in terms of meaning and information. Despite poverty, illness, and family strife, Henry's parents trusted that the culture held solutions to their difficulties, and they encouraged him to find them. They believed that education could provide knowledge to improve life. So from the earliest years Henry remembers his parents reading stories to him, and he remembers himself reading voraciously. As a teenager he drew from books examples of people who had been able to cope with problems similar to his own. It was from these successful solutions preserved in the cultural heritage that Henry, and other men who escaped the deterministic forces of their childhood, fashioned their life goals (Beattie Emory and Csikszentmihalyi 1981).

Those who spent their lives in their parents' footsteps do not remember being read to, nor did they read on their own as children. They do not seem to have realized that the predicaments they faced occasionally had been surmounted by strong-willed individuals; they lacked cultural models whose example might have helped them to formulate more complex goals.

The Growth of Complexity

Thus, growth in adolescence depends in large part on the amount of meaning one is able to extract from the culture. Culture is made up of patterns of information shaped by the psychic energy of previous generations. It constitutes a potential resource because it can increase the efficiency of the psychic energy of those who use it. For instance, arithmetic evolved over thousands of years as a system for ordering numerical quantities. Untold individuals spent their lives refining the four basic operations. Nowadays a child can learn them in a few weeks, spending a minute fraction of his psychic energy in doing so. The same is true of almost any complex pattern—from making music to building bridges, from growing grain to understanding the causes of disease.

Growth in complexity involves extracting as much order as possible from the information stored in the culture. Some of this is done automatically; every child learns a language spontaneously in a few years, whereas it took his ancestors tens of thousands of years to invent it. But much of the information requires voluntary effort to decode and reconstitute it as a useful pattern of psychic energy. Those who have enough free energy to invest in these patterns learn to integrate the power of past generations into their own consciousness. This is how a person grows beyond the limits of individuality. Among teenagers of this study there were some who were learning to draw on the skills of past generations, and in so doing were increasing the complexity of their own consciousness—Katherine Tennison and Andy Gridwell, for example. Others seemed to face life almost alone, relying only on their native skills to achieve their goals. This is a pattern he saw in Greg Stone and Jerzy Madigan, who were caught up in the early search for good times.

The paradox is that those who absorb skills from the culture—like Katherine and Andy—do not automatically accept cultural goals to direct their lives; whereas people who do not benefit much from the cultural heritage—like Greg and Jerzy—tend to spend their life chasing the traditional rewards their society has to offer. As long as everything goes well, as long as health and prosperity reign, the two solutions work equally; they both keep consciousness in an ordered state. But where entropy enters the system—as it usually does, sooner or later—persons equipped with broad cultural skills and a self-forged approach to life have a chance to weather the storm. They can take negative feedback and change it around in such a way that positive adaptation can be brought about. They can make meaning from disordered experience. The order in consciousness, instead of being destroyed by the stressful event, gets reconstituted around a more complex goal.

A life theme may not increase the net enjoyment in people's existence. But it seems clear that it affects *where* they find it, and whether that enjoyment contributes to their ultimate goals and the well-being of society. Julian found pleasure in a simple and repetitive way of making money; he could enjoy nothing more challenging. Henry, in contrast, learned to gain pleasure in tackling the demanding and difficult challenges of the legal profession. His life theme provided the structure to teach him to cull satisfactions from the more complex struggles faced by a lawyer and politician.

None of the teenagers we studied revealed a fully developed life theme. All were trying and testing different channels in which to invest their attention. Greg and Jerzy pursued good times with friends relentlessly, a direction not likely to lead toward greater complexity. Katherine and Andy, in contrast, were learning to direct their attention to more challenging opportunities. They were learning to find enjoyment in more complex systems of order. Progressively, such lives might coalesce into the overall pattern of a life theme.

Being Adolescent, Becoming Adult

To grow means to learn to interact with more and more complex dimensions of reality. A child knows the world in which its body moves, a world of simple sense impressions and basic emotions.

The Growth of Complexity

Around this concrete world are discovered concentric envelopes of meaning, increasingly difficult to understand and increasingly hard to master. These deal with physical, technical, and mathematical concepts, with morality and responsibility, with beauty, with love, and with the stuff of the galaxies.

In this book we have learned how this process of growth is encountered in teenagers' everyday life, how it threatens and invigorates them as it unfolds in daily experience. Every experience can be either a challenge that stimulates growth, or an obstacle that retards it. What happens in adolescence depends on the order a person is able to impose upon the complex opportunities of daily life.

In negotiating the path to adulthood, adolescents can draw upon many sources of aid. Most parents try hard to assist their teenage children in dealing with the difficulties of daily life. Schools exist at great expense to society in order to facilitate learning about everything from the English language to physical health. And friends can be a useful source of support whatever one's problem might be. The culture provides numerous agents to help make sense out of this complex world.

However, when all is said and done, only teenagers can help themselves. Opportunities are important, but they make no difference unless the adolescent uses them. Beauty, wealth, talent, intelligence—all of these gifts easily become traps that retard growth instead of fostering it. Handsome young men and beautiful young women all too often become so absorbed with their looks, with their power to attract others, that they never learn to focus their attention on anything else. Affluent teenagers frequently learn to assume that their goals can be reached with money, and thus fail to develop their skills; by the time they realize that it is not what they own, but what they do that makes life rich, it may be too late. Likewise, an adolescent's talent easily becomes an obsession that stamps out every other goal, leaving a narrow and unhappy young genius behind.

Illness, poverty, and discrimination, on the other hand—all considered to be major impediments to development—sometimes spark a response from an adolescent that will start progressive growth toward a competent, directed existence. Every teenager has the power to ignore the precious knowledge and skills of adulthood. Yet every teenager also has the power—as Lincoln and Malcolm X demonstrated—to search out knowledge and inner strengths no matter how difficult they may be to find.

But if none of the help we try to give children is sure to make any difference, what can an adult do for an adolescent? Perhaps the best thing we can offer is examples—examples of how to choose among goals, how to persevere, how to have patience, how to recognize the challenges of life and enjoy meeting them. We can help adolescents by letting them share our own hard-won habits of skill and discipline. We can help by letting them see that achieving control over experience can bring serenity and enjoyment in its wake.

At least some of the teenagers in this study were demonstrating that they understood the requirements of growth. They had found out that it is impossible to avoid constraint and frustration in life. They had grasped that it does little good to deny disorder, or to attempt to escape complexity through refuge in the pleasant and familiar. They had learned to face obstacles squarely and see them as challenges that provide opportunities for their skills. To the extent that each comprehends these basic lessons of experience, he or she will find enjoyment while growing into an increasingly complex person, able to create order within, and in the complex, surrounding world.

Appendices

A. Research Procedures   287
    1. Sample Selection Procedures   287
    2. Membership of the Final Sample   288

B. Coding External Dimensions of Experience   289
    1. Locations   290
    2. Activities   290
    3. Companions   291

C. Measures of Internal States   293
    1. Intercorrelations among the Internal Dimensions of
       Experience   294
    2. The Affect and Activation Scales   293

D. Additional Tables and Figures   295
    1. Shifts in Activities and Companions   295
       Activities across the Weekday   295
       Activities across the Weekend   296
       Companions across Weekend Days   296
    2. The Interrelation of Location, Activity, and
       Companion   297
    3. Comparison of Adolescents' and Adults' Average
       States   298
    4. Average Experiential States   299
       By Locations   299
       By Activities   300
       By Companions   301

5. Experiential States with Different
   Companions   302
     When Studying   302
     During Chores, Errands, and Other Practical
     Activities   302
     When Socializing   302
6. The Variability of Moods for Adolescents
   and Adults   303
7. Frequency of Changes for Adolescents and
   Adults   303
8. How Quality of Experience with the Family Varies,
   Depending on Activity Pursued   304
9. Correlates of Amount of Time Spent with
   Family   305
10. Comparison of the Experience of Teenagers from
    Intact and from One-Parent Families   305
11. Differences in Affect with Same-Sex and
    Opposite-Sex Friends   306
12. Systemic Properties of Interactions with Family and
    Friends   306
13. Dynamics of Friendship Interactions   307
14. Correlations between Sense of Control and Moods
    when with Friends   307
15. Correlates of Amount of Time Spent with
    Friends   308
16. Quality of Experience by Classroom Subject
    Matter   308
17. Quality of Experience by Type of Classroom
    Activity   309
18. Changes in the Quality of Experience As Students
    Alternate from Classes to Friends, and Vice
    Versa   310
19. Stability of States across School Transitions   311
20. Intercorrelations of Students' Ranking of Flow in
    Classes, with Their Mean Moods, Motivation, and
    Grades   312
21. Consistency of Experiences across a Two-Year Period
    in Adolescence   313

Appendix A

Research Procedures

A.1/Sample Selection Procedures

We began with the objective of working with a representative sample of eighty students from the Belmont High School population. To control for possible attrition, a three-dimensional stratification design was developed. It called for equal numbers of boys and girls, equal numbers of students from all four high-school grades, and equal numbers from two contrasting residential zones, a lower-middle-class sector of the community and an upper-middle-class sector. This design specified five students in each of sixteen cells of a three-dimensional matrix. The fit of the final sample to this design is shown in Appendix A2.

Because everyone in the school was required to take history or social science each year, these classes provided an ideal context for introducing the study and selecting students in an informal manner. Arrangements were made to meet with classes from all three ability tracks (Advanced, Regular, and Basic) to discuss the research and to invite students to participate. For each class, we obtained a student list from the teacher and randomly selected in advance four to six students who fit into cells of the sample design matrix that were not yet filled. Patrick Mayers introduced the research to the classes as a study of adolescent experience. It was explained that: "Adults have a limited sense of what it is like to be a teenager. We want to get *your* story of what you go through in a typical week." Invited students were given a couple of days to think about the study and get permission forms signed by their parents and teachers.

The study was conducted in the spring of 1977. Over the months of April and May, five to fifteen students were participating at all times, carrying pagers and taking part in supplementary interviews. Students from different cells of the sample design were spread evenly over this period. The researchers were in the school every day, to be available. As expected, there were problems for different students: lost pagers, lost books, difficulties scheduling around the students' vacations, sporting events, and periods when school pressures were too intense. One student was using the pager to disrupt class and had to be withdrawn from the study. Only students who had filled out self-reports for at least 40 percent of the signals were included in the final sample. In all, 76 percent of those students who began the study completed it within the necessary criteria.

As summer vacation approached, it became clear that we would not obtain students for all sixteen cells of the design, so we opted to include data from a group of eleven seniors from the autumn pilot study (see Larson 1979). With this addition, we came very close to meeting the design goal (Appendix A.2). Data for ten students who began the study but did not complete it showed no significant differences in intelligence, creativity, or ego development as compared with the final seventy-five. However, one might infer from past research that attrition was higher among reclusive, rebellious, and socially maladjusted individuals (Rosenthal and Rosnow, 1969).

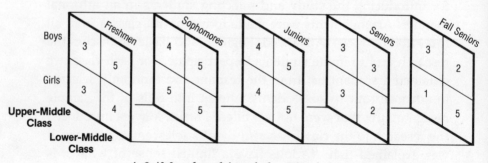

A.2/Membership of the Final Sample

Appendix B

Coding External Dimensions of Experience

This table shows the categories used to code the students' reports as to where they were, what they were doing, and whom they were with.

APPENDIX B

B.1/Locations

School	Public
1. Classroom—Includes shops, labs, art and music rooms	16. Walking—in transit, on foot
2. Gym and Locker room	17. In an Automobile
3. Library	18. On a Bus or Train
4. Cafeteria	19. At Friend's Home
5. Halls and Bathrooms	20. At Work
6. Student Center	21. Store, Cafe, Restaurant
7. School Grounds	22. A Park
8. Other	23. Indoor Recreational Facility
	24. Street or Corner
Home	25. A Church or Temple
	26. Other Places in Public
9. Kitchen	
10. Bedroom	
11. Dining Room	
12. Living Room or Family Room	
13. Bathroom	
14. Basement or Laundry Room	
15. Yard or Garage	

B.2/Activities

PRODUCTIVE

1. Classwork—All classroom activities except individual work (Includes gym class, labs, and shop classes)

2. Studying—Homework and individual study in school

3. Job and Other Productive Activities—Working at a job, also participating in an organization or club

MAINTENANCE

4. Eating—Includes eating, drinking, and snacking

5. Personal Care—Grooming, dressing, bathing, combing, using bathroom, etc.

6. Transportation—Driving and riding in a car, walking from one place to another place in public (includes joyriding)

7. Chores, Errands, and Other Practical Activities—Housework, food preparation, shopping, child care, walking around house or school

8. Rest and Napping

LEISURE

9. Socializing—All conversation, partying, goofing around, sexual activity, and talking on the phone

10. Sports and Games—Informal and formal sports and games outside of class

11. Watching TV

12. Listening to Music

13. Art and Hobbies—Doing art, music, dance, and hobby activities outside of class

14. Reading—Reading newspapers, magazines, and books not assigned for school

15. Thinking—Mental reflection, daydreaming

16. Other Leisure—Doing nothing, sitting, playing with a pet, being a spectator, attending a movie

B.3/Companions

FAMILY

1. Siblings—With one or more sibling, parents not present

2. Parents—With one or more parent or guardian, siblings not present

3. Parents and Siblings—With one or more parent and one or more sibling

4. Extended Relatives—With uncles, aunts, or grandparents, parents not present

FRIENDS

5. Same-Sex Friend—With one peer, of the same sex as the respondent

6. Same-Sex Group—With two or more peers of the same sex

7. Opposite-Sex Friend—With one peer of the other sex

8. Opposite-Sex Group—With a group of peers that includes at least one person of the other sex

9. Friends and Parents—With one or more friends and one or more parent

Appendix B

Alone

10. Alone—The respondent is with no one (Includes being with pets; times talking on the phone alone are included in the "friends" categories)

11. Strangers—The respondent is in a public place in the presence of strangers

Classmates

12. Classmates, Teachers, Other School Personnel

Other

13. Other Companions—Includes boss, co-workers not considered friends, children being babysat

Appendix C

Measures of
Internal States

C.2/The Affect and Activation Scales

Appendix C.1 shows the presence of two clusters within the mood items. These were identified by our colleague Pat Mayers (1978). The first cluster includes items dealing with emotional feelings; these four items have been added together to create a scale of Affect. An alpha value of .85 indicates that the four items are strongly intercorrelated with each other. The second and somewhat weaker cluster includes items dealing with potency, activity, and manifest energy; these four items have been added together to create a scale of Activation (alpha = .78). As can be seen in Appendix C.1, both these clusters show some correlation with the motivation and cognitive efficiency items.

A mood scale (alpha = .83) based on eight of the items used in all ESM studies has also been developed (Larson, Csikszentmihalyi, and Graef 1980), and is used when an overall measure of mood is needed. It includes the items happy-sad, cheerful-irritable, sociable-lonely, excited-bored, alert-drowsy, strong-weak, active-passive, and free-constrained.

C.1

Intercorrelations among the Internal Dimensions of Experience

This table shows the degree of association between the different items. Entries are Pearson's correlations among z-scores, adjusted for each individual's mean and standard deviation (N = 2,734). Higher values indicate stronger empirical associations.

Items	1	2	3	4	5	6	7	8	9	10	11	12	13	14	15	16
Affect																
1. Happy	—															
2. Cheerful	.69	—														
3. Sociable	.52	.52	—													
4. Friendly	.52	.58	.45	—												
Activation																
5. Alert	.38	.35	.33	.23	—											
6. Active	.36	.32	.37	.23	.51	—										
7. Strong	.38	.36	.35	.28	.48	.46	—									
8. Excited	.52	.51	.48	.35	.43	.43	.37	—								
Cognitive Efficiency																
9. Concentration	.15	.15	.14	.09	.41	.26	.23	.24	—							
10. Ease of Concentration	.11	.14	.08	.10	.12	.07	.09	.14	.06	—						
11. Unselfconscious	-.09	-.07	-.15	-.04	-.20	-.22	-.12	-.11	-.22	.13	—					
12. Clear	.36	.38	.31	.37	.24	.25	.30	.35	.10	.18	.06	—				
Motivation																
13. Wish Doing Activity	.26	.27	.19	.20	.13	.08	.08	.37	.04	.23	.06		—			
14. Control of Actions	.07	.06	.05	.06	.07	.00	.07	.03	.05	.00	-.02	.05	-.03	—		
15. Free	.45	.44	.36	.31	.23	.26	.30	.47	.09	.13	-.02	.30	.26	.10	—	
16. Involved	.37	.37	.44	.38	.38	.40	.32	.42	.28	.05	-.13	.34	.17	.08	.25	—
	1	2	3	4	5	6	7	8	9	10	11	12	13	14	15	16

Appendix D

Additional Tables and Figures

D.1/Shifts in Activities and Companions

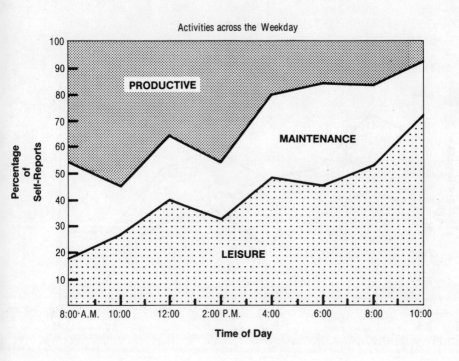

Activities across the Weekday

APPENDIX D

Activities across the Weekend

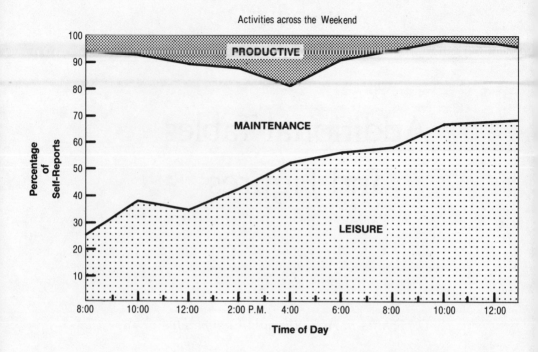

Companions across Weekend Days

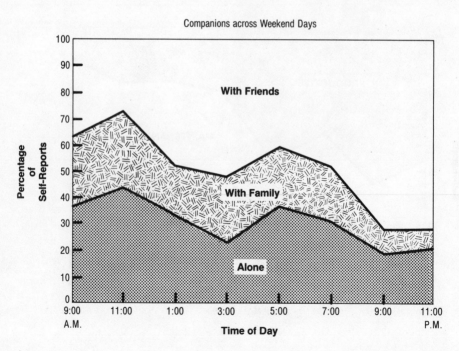

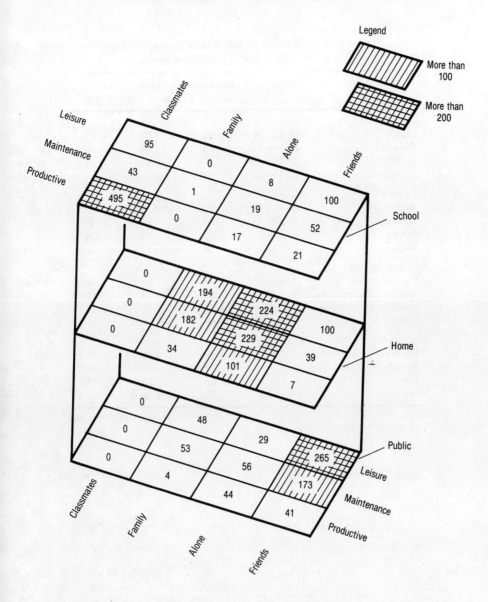

D.2/The Interrelation of Location, Activity, and Companion

Diagram shows the number of self-reports in each cell.
60 self-reports when the companion was "other" have not
been included.

APPENDIX D

D.3
Comparison of Adolescents' and Adults' Average States
This table shows mean means of raw scores.

Items		Adolescents (N = 75)	Adults (N = 107)	Difference
Affect				
Happy	(−3 to 3)	1.04	1.05	.01
Cheerful	(−3 to 3)	.80	.85	.05
Sociable	(−3 to 3)	.97	.86	−.11
Friendly	(−3 to 3)	.92	not used	—
Activation				
Alert	(−3 to 3)	.92	1.29	.37***
Active	(−3 to 3)	.39	.79	.40***
Strong	(−3 to 3)	.53	.79	.26*
Excited	(−3 to 3)	.23	.37	.14
Cognitive Efficiency				
Concentration	(0 to 9)	4.70	5.30	.60**
Ease of Concentration	(0 to 9)	7.80	8.53	.73**
Unself-consciousness	(0 to 9)	6.82	6.67	−.15
Clear	(−3 to 3)	.60	not used	—
Motivation				
Wish Doing Activity	(0 to 9)	4.98	5.83	.85***
Control of Actions	(0 to 9)	6.50	7.26	.76**
Free	(−3 to 3)	.62	.70	.08
Involved	(−3 to 3)	.75	not used	—

Significance tests: * $p < 0.05$; ** $p < 0.01$; *** $p < 0.001$. (All significance tests used in this book are two-tailed.)

Additional Tables and Figures

D.4
Average Experiential States
By Locations
(N = 2,734)

	N	Affect (z-score)	Activation (z-score)	Concentration (z-score)	Wish to Be Doing (z-score)
School					
Classroom	541	−.09	−.16***	.15***	−.44***
Gym	52	.18	.68***	.14	−.02
Library	33	−.01	−.13	.31	−.25
Cafeteria	60	.30**	.30**	−.11	.21*
Halls	55	.04	.08	−.35**	−.31*
Student Center	36	.41**	.37*	.08	.32*
School Grounds	22	.14	.16	−.27	−.01
Other	63	.29**	.27*	.22	.32***
	862	.02	.00	.10**	−.26
Home					
Kitchen	220	−.06	.06	−.11	.10
Bedroom	351	−.40**	−.55***	−.08	.06
Dining Room	90	.10	.00	−.06	.11
Living Room	242	−.10	−.19**	−.11	.06
Bathroom	44	−.32*	−.28*	−.34*	.07
Basement	60	.01	.10	.34*	.31*
Yard or Garage	112	.04	.23*	.11	.16
	1095	−.16***	−.17***	−.05	.10***
Public					
Walking	41	−.09	.04	−.20	.00
Automobile	104	−.39	.22	−.02	.15*
Bus or Train	11	.09	−.25	.01	.26
Friend's Home	147	.48***	.30***	−.18*	.38***
At Work	144	−.29***	.02	.02	−.49***
Store or Cafe	77	.51***	.32**	−.09	.32***
Park	47	.47**	.53***	.24	.64**
Indoor Recreation	22	.04	.62**	.37	.23
Street Corner	55	.18	.24*	−.28*	.15
Church	22	.21	.09	.02	−.08
Other Public	81	.17	.38***	.04	.43***
	751	.21***	.24***	−.03	.14***

Significance of difference from zero: * p <0.05; ** p <0.01; *** p <0.001.

D.4 (*continued*)
By Activities

	N	Affect (z-score)	Activation (z-score)	Concentration (z-score)	Wish to Be Doing (z-score)
Productive					
Classwork	328	−.07	− .08	.24***	−.34***
Studying	346	−.27***	− .13**	.49***	−.44***
Job	118	−.22**	.13*	.15	−.40***
	792	−.18***	− .07*	.34***	−.40***
Maintenance					
Eating	153	.30***	.06	−.29***	.45***
Personal Care	82	−.21*	− .25*	−.25*	.16
Transportation	134	.26**	.22*	−.06	.07
Chores and Errands	393	−.09*	.10*	−.07	−.18***
Rest and Napping	87	−.59***	−1.37***	−.94***	.57***
	849	−.02	− .07*	−.21***	.09**
Leisure					
Socializing	436	.36***	.26***	−.16***	.26***
Sports and Games	93	.22**	.80***	.36***	.48***
Watching TV	197	−.09	− .37***	−.17**	.08
Listening to Music	38	.12	.03	−.09	.54***
Art and Hobbies	41	−.01	.77***	.61***	.65***
Reading (nonschool)	96	−.25**	− .36***	−.11	.16
Thinking	66	−.27***	− .36**	.06	−.46***
Other Leisure	126	.24**	.11	−.12	.19*
	1093	.14***	.11***	−.06*	.21***

Additional Tables and Figures

D.4 (continued)
By Companions

	N	Affect (z-score)	Activation (z-score)	Concentration (z-score)	Wish to Be Doing (z-score)
Family					
Siblings	153	−.12	−.02	−.17	−.01
Parents	131	.00	.06	−.11	.04
Parents and Siblings	216	.12	−.01	−.18	.19**
Extended Relatives	16	.69***	.63**	.28	.38
	516	.04	.03	−.14***	.10*
Friends					
Same-Sex Friend	265	.29***	.26**	−.11	.31***
Same-Sex Group	167	.48***	.36**	−.15	.27*
Opposite-Sex Friend	85	.71***	.50***	.16	.52***
Opposite-Sex Group	224	.46***	.44***	−.12	.48***
Friends and Parents	57	.45***	.28*	.01	.51***
	798	.43***	.35***	−.08	.39***
Alone					
Alone	691	−.38***	−.34***	.01	−.03
Strangers	36	−.41*	.22	.34	−.44**
	727	−.38***	−.31***	.02	−.05
Classmates					
Classmates, Teachers	633	−.07	−.09*	.16***	−.39***
	633	−.07	−.09*	.16***	−.39***
Other					
Other Companions	60	−.06	.26*	.15	−.06
	60	−.06	.26*	.15	−.06

Appendix D

D.5
Experiential States with Different Companions
(Analysis of Variance [ANOVA] of
Average z-scores by type of companion)

When Studying

	In Class	Alone	With Family	With Friends	p (ANOVA)
N	164	117	33	28	
Wish Doing Activity	−.55	−.42	−.44	−.05	.06
Affect	−.25	−.43	−.22	.21	.01
Activation	−.14	−.29	.17	.29	.002

During Chores, Errands, and Other Practical Activities

	In Class	Alone	With Family	With Friends	p (ANOVA)
N	29	129	114	107	
Wish Doing Activity	−.40	−.27	−.23	.13	.005
Affect	−.14	−.32	−.11	.27	.0001
Activation	−.08	−.06	.20	.25	.06

When Socializing

	With Parents	With Friends†	"t" Value	p
N	68	255		
Wish Doing Activity	.24	.37	−1.09	.28
Affect	.19	.45	−1.78	.08
Activation	.17	.34	−1.38	.17

† Excludes occasions with parents and friends together.

Additional Tables and Figures

D.6
The Variability of Moods for Adolescents and Adults

Mood Items	Standard Deviations (mean values)		
	Adolescents (N = 75)	Adults (N = 107)	Difference
Affect			
Happy	1.18	1.07	−0.16**
Cheerful	1.35	1.19	−0.11
Sociable	1.30	1.09	−0.21***
Activation			
Alert	1.62	1.35	−0.27***
Active	1.49	1.24	−0.25***
Strong	1.24	0.96	−0.28***
Excited	1.47	0.97	−0.50***

Significance tests: * $p < 0.05$; ** $p < 0.01$; *** $p < 0.001$.
From: Larson, Csikszentmihalyi, and Graef 1980.

D.7
Frequency of Changes for Adolescents and Adults

The table shows the percentage of time the adolescents and adults changed context (e.g., from one place to another, from one activity to another) over the span of time between two reports. Only instances when the span is less than or equal to two hours have been included and only occasions when the adolescents were not at school and the adults were not at work.

	Adolescents (N = 698)	Adults (N = 1231)	Difference (t test)
Change of Location	30.8	26.2	4.6
Change of Activity	77.5	70.0	7.5***
Change of Companion	51.4	43.3	8.1***

Significance tests: *** $p < 0.001$.

D.8

How Quality of Experience with the Family Varies Depending on Activity Pursued

Activities[1]	N Observations	Quality of Experience (Mean z-score)			
		Affect	Activation	Concentration	Wish to Be Doing
Productive					
Studying	31	−.22	.17	.39	−.44
Maintenance					
Eating	78	.28	.01	−.32	.51
Personal care	12	−.57	−.51	−.07	.15
Transportation	15	.35	.01	−.35	−.23
Chores and errands	108	−.11	.20	.05	−.23
Leisure					
Socializing	79	.18	.14	−.26	.24
Sports and games	21	.41	.97	.30	.37
Watching television	85	.03	−.26	−.17	.22
Reading (nonschool)	10	−.19	−.39	−.51	.31
ANOVA F		1.99	4.53	3.11	5.96
Probability		.02	.0001	.0001	.0001

[1] Only those activities are listed that had at least ten reports with the family.

Additional Tables and Figures

D.9
Correlates of Amount of Time Spent with Family
(N = 75)

The table shows the degree of association between the amount of time a teenager spends with his family and the various indicators of his school participation and psychosocial adjustment. High positive values indicate strong associations.

	Pearson Correlation Coefficient (r)
School Participation	
Number of Absences	$-.29^{**}$
Academic Performance	
(school grade point average, controlled for ability)	$.38^{**}$
Intellectual Involvement in Class	
(teachers' ratings)	$.21$
Social Involvement in Class	
(teachers' ratings)	$-.27^{*}$
Psychosocial Adjustment	
Alienation from Others	$-.02$
Ego Development	$-.06$
Mean Affect Score	$.10$
Variability of Affect	$-.22^{*}$
Multiple R (Adjusted)	$.46^{**}$

Table shows partial correlations of percentage of time with family, controlling for respondent's age. (From: Larson 1983).
Significance tests: $*p < 0.05$; $** p < 0.01$.

D.10
Comparison of the Experience of Teenagers from Intact
and from One-Parent Families

Overall self-ratings on which the two groups differ at a significant level	Teenagers from two-parent families (N = 50)	Teenagers from one-parent families (N = 13)	t	p
Strong	4.39	4.82	-2.30	.03
Free	4.47	4.94	-2.35	.03
Clear	4.45	5.16	-4.15	.001
Skills	5.06	6.26	-2.13	.05
Goals Congruent	2.57	3.29	-2.13	.05

Appendix D

D.11
Differences in Affect with Same-Sex and Opposite-Sex Friends

	Average Affect Level (z-score)	
	Same-Sex Friends (N = 432)	Opposite-Sex Friends (N = 309)
Freshmen	.47	.18
Sophomores	.41	.61
Juniors	.09	.51
Seniors	.25	.54

Multivariate Analysis of Variance: Sex of Friends $F = 3.03$, $p = 0.08$; Grade (linear) $F = 0.06$, not significant; Interaction $F = 4.61$, $p = 0.03$.

D.12
Systemic Properties of Interactions with Family and Friends

The table shows the students' average self-ratings on the six system items when they were with their families and their friends.

Items	Mean z-Score with Family (N = 74)	Mean z-Score with Friends (N = 75)	Family versus Friends t
Feedback Positive	−.16	.25	−3.96***
Goals Same	−.25	.16	−3.78***
Talking, Joking	−.25	.26	−5.87***
Open	−.04	.36	−4.38***
Free	.03	.34	−4.06***
Clear	.04	.17	−1.83*

Significance tests: * $p < 0.05$; *** $p < 0.001$.

D.13
Dynamics of Friendship Interactions

This table shows how perceived positive properties of the interaction system correlate with mood for the times students were with friends.

(N = 798)

	Correlates With:	
Items	Affect	Activation
Feedback Positive	.37***	.19***
Goals Same	.13**	.17***
Talking, Joking	.27***	.07
Open	.45***	.39***
Clear	.44***	.41***
Free	.51***	.37***

Significance tests: ** $p < 0.01$; *** $p < 0.001$.

D.14
Correlations between Sense of Control and Moods when with Friends

	Control of Actions When with Friends	
Items	A. Moment-to-Moment Relationship (N = 798 self-reports)	B. Person-to-Person Relationship (N = 75 persons)
Affect		
Happy	.07	−.24*
Cheerful	.09**	−.12
Sociable	.06	.08
Friendly	.10*	−.35**
Activation		
Alert	.24***	.19
Active	.13***	−.15
Strong	.18***	−.15
Excited	−.03	−.31**
Cognitive Efficiency		
Concentration	.25***	.26*
Ease of Concentration	.28***	.02
Unselfconsciousness	−.02	.26*
Clear	.22***	−.09
Motivation		
Wish Doing Activity	.05	−.13
Control of Actions	—	—
Free	.01	−.40***
Involved	.04	−.19

Significance tests: * $p < 0.05$; ** $p < 0.01$; *** $p < 0.001$.

APPENDIX D

D.15
Correlates of Amount of Time Spent with Friends
(N = 75)

	Pearson Correlation Coefficient (r)
School Participation	
Number of Absences	.26*
Academic Performance	
(school grade point average, controlled for ability)	−.38**
Intellectual Involvement in Class	
(teachers' ratings)	−.44***
Social Involvement in Class	
(teachers' ratings)	.02
Psychosocial Adjustment	
Alienation from Others	−.26*
Ego Development	−.02
Overall Affect	.20
Variability of Affect	.27*
Multiple *R* (adjusted)	.49**

Significance tests: * $p < 0.05$; ** $p < 0.01$; *** $p < 0.001$.
From: Larson 1983.

D.16
Quality of Experience by Classroom Subject Matter
(Figures represent mean z-score)

	N	Affect	Activation	Concentration	Wish Doing Activity
English	251	−.11	−.21	.18	−.54
Foreign Language	156	−.03	−.27	−.05	−.54
History and Social Science	283	−.04	−.14	.09	−.40
Mathematics	154	−.18	−.27	.34	−.56
Science	158	−.09	.02	.30	−.41
Business	67	−.51	−.17	.59	−.57
Speech	46	.07	.05	−.11	.34
Art	23	−.20	−.26	.03	−.28
Music	86	.05	.21	.39	.01
Home Economics	52	−.04	−.33	.10	−.32
Shop	31	−.12	−.11	.07	−.23
Physical Education	136	.19	.60	.14	−.07

Additional Tables and Figures

D.17
Quality of Experience by Type of Classroom Activity
(Figures represent mean z-scores)

	N	Affect	Activation	Concentration	Wish Doing Activity
Listening to Teacher	286	−.07	−.35	.07	−.44
Listening to Student	52	−.07	−.17	−.15	−.50
Test	115	−.44	.21	.99	−.62
Correcting Test	30	−.24	−.20	.06	−.34
Individual Work	404	−.21	−.12	.39	−.49
Group Work	85	.08	.21	.23	−.20
Discussion	81	−.01	−.06	.23	−.32
Individual Talk with Teacher	21	.17	.26	.28	−.25
Homework	153	−.26	−.02	.60	−.21
Nonwork in Class	485	.09	−.19	−.23	−.37
Athletics	47	.24	1.01	.48	−.31
	1,718				

D.18
Changes in the Quality of Experience As Students Alternate from Classes to Friends, and Vice Versa
(Figures refer to mean z-scores)

Only pairs of self-reports occurring within 60 minutes of each other are included.

Items	Changes from Class to Friends (N = 155)			Changes from Friends to Class (N = 134)		
	In Class†	With Friends†	Change	With Friends†	In Class†	Change
Affect						
Happy	−.10	.17*	.27**	.23**	−.24***	−.47***
Cheerful	−.13*	.15	.28**	.23**	−.19*	−.44***
Sociable	−.10	.47***	.57***	.38***	−.01	−.40***
Friendly	.04	.35***	.33**	.36***	−.10	−.46***
Activation						
Alert	.04	.28***	.24***	.12	.01	−.11
Active	−.10	.13	.23*	.07	−.19**	−.28**
Strong	.04	.26***	.22*	.21**	−.05	−.26**
Excited	−.25**	.24***	.50***	.11	−.37***	−.48***
Cognitive Efficiency						
Concentration	.20*	−.07	−.28*	−.21**	.12	.33**
Ease of Concentration	−.26**	.23***	.50***	.01	−.40***	−.41***
Unselfconsciousness	.22**	.19**	−.03	.13*	.16*	.03
Clear	−.04	.12	.16	.25**	−.12	−.38***
Motivation						
Wish to Do Activity	−.47***	.15*	.61***	.21**	−.55***	−.77***
Control of Actions	−.09	.09	.18*	.04	−.14	−.18*
Free	−.43***	.26***	.69***	.26***	−.52***	−.78***
Involved	.07	.22**	.14	.24***	.13	−.11

† Significance tests evaluate difference of mean from grand mean of 0.0. * $p < 0.05$; ** $p < 0.01$; *** $p < 0.0001$.

D.19

Stability of States across School Transitions

(Correlations between self-reports occurring within one hour of each other.)

Items	Friends → Friends (N = 35)	Friends → Class (N = 134)	Class → Class (N = 578)	Class → Friends (N = 155)
Affect				
Happy	.30	.14	.13**	.09
Cheerful	.47**	.08	.18***	−.01
Sociable	.64***	.04	.10	.04
Friendly	.31	.13	.13**	.07
Activation				
Alert	.59***	.12	.22***	.13*
Active	.17	.01	.23***	.13
Strong	.52***	.18*	.25***	.19*
Excited	.21	.16*	.13**	.08
Cognitive Efficiency				
Concentration	.22	−.11	.11**	−.10
Ease of Concentration	.10	−.05	.09*	.10
Unselfconsciousness	.32	−.05	.29***	.13
Clear	.31	.15	.14**	.17*
Motivation				
Wish to Do Activity	.15	−.01	.12	.04
Control of Actions	.48**	.03	.23***	.16*
Free	.50**	.05	.20***	−.08
Involved	.41	.02	.16***	.07

Significance tests: * $p < 0.05$; ** $p < 0.01$; *** $p < 0.001$.

D.20

Intercorrelations of Students' Ranking of Flow in Classes, with Their Mean Moods, Motivation, and Grades
(N = 401 classes for 75 students)

	Ranking of Classes on Flow Scales	Intrinsic Motivation (Wish to Be in Class)	Average Affect in Class	Average Activation in Class
Intrinsic Motivation	0.53***	1.00		
Affect (happy, cheerful, sociable)	0.18***	0.14**	1.00	
Activation (strong, active, alert)	0.30***	0.36***	0.62***	1.00
Semester Grades in the Same Classes	0.35***	0.26***	0.02	0.04

Adapted from Mayers 1978. Significance tests: * $p < 0.05$; ** $p < 0.01$; *** $p < 0.001$.

Additional Tables and Figures

D.21
Consistency of Experience Across a Two-Year Period in Adolescence

[Pearson correlations between mean individual responses at time
1 (freshman and sophomore years) and time 2 (junior and senior years).]
(N = 27)

	With the Family	With Friends	Alone	In School	Overall
Affect	.23	.42*	.07	.48*	.77***
Activation	.47**	.41*	.39*	.36*	.62***

Significance tests: * $p < 0.05$; ** $p < 0.01$; *** $p < 0.001$. (From: Freeman 1982)

References

Aderman, D., and Berkowitz, L. 1970. Observation set, empathy, and helping. *Journal of Personality and Social Psychology* 14: 141–148.

Altmann, J. 1980. *The ecology of motherhood and infancy in the savannah baboon.* Cambridge: Harvard University Press.

Arendt, H. 1958. *The human condition.* Chicago: The University of Chicago Press.

Ariès, P. 1962. *Centuries of childhood.* New York: Vintage.

Augustine. *Confessions* Ca. A.D. 400. In Howie, G., ed., *Saint Augustine: on education.* Chicago: Regnery, 1969.

Bachman, J. 1970 *Youth in transition.* 2d ed. Ann Arbor, Mich.: Institute for Social Research.

Bagley, W. 1905. *The educative process.* New York: Macmillan.

Baltes, P. B., ed. 1978. *Life-span development and behavior,* vol. 1. New York: Academic Press.

Barker, R. G. 1968. *Ecological psychology: concepts and methods for studying the environment of human behavior.* Stanford, Calif.: Stanford University Press.

Barker, R. G., and Gump, P. 1964. *Big school, small school.* Stanford, Calif.: Stanford University Press.

Bateson, G. 1972. *Steps to an ecology of mind.* New York: Ballantine.

Beattie Emory, O., and Csikszentmihalyi, M. 1981. The socialization effects of cultural role models in ontogenetic development and upward mobility. *Child Psychiatry and Human Development* 11: 3–18.

Bell, D. 1976. *The cultural contradictions of capitalism.* New York: Basic Books.

Bell, R. Q. 1968. A reinterpretation of the direction of effects in studies of socialization. *Psychological Review* 75: 81–95.

Bell, R. Q., and Harper, L. V. 1977. *Child effects on adults.* New York: Wiley.

Benedict, R. 1938. Continuities and discontinuities in cultural conditioning. *Psychiatry* 1: 161–67.

Berger, P. L. 1963. *Invitation to sociology.* Garden City, N.Y.: Doubleday.

Berger, P. L., and Luckmann, T. 1967. *The Social construction of reality.* Garden City, N.Y.: Doubleday Anchor.

Berndt, T. 1979. Developmental changes in conformity to peers and parents. *Developmental psychology* 15: 608–16.

Blos, P. 1962. *On adolescence: a psychoanalytic interpretation.* New York: Free Press.

Blumer, H. 1939. Collective behavior. In Park, R. ed., *Outlines of the principles of sociology.* New York: Barnes and Noble.

Bossard, J. H. S., and Bell, E. S. 1955. Marital unhappiness in the life cycle. *Marriage and Family Living* 17: 10–14.

314

References

Botkin J., Elmandjra, M., and Malitza, M. 1979. *No limits to learning: bridging the human gap.* (A report to the Club of Rome). New York: Pergamon Press.

Bowen, E. S. (pseud. of Laura Bohannan). 1954. *Return to laughter.* New York: Harper & Bros.

Bowerman, C., and Kinch, J. 1959. Changes in family and peer orientation of children between the fourth and tenth grades. *Social Forces* 37: 206–11.

Bowles, S., and Gintis, H. 1976. *Schooling in capitalist America.* New York: Basic Books.

Bradburn, N. M. 1969. *The structure of psychological well-being.* Chicago: Aldine.

Brandwein, R. A. 1977. After divorce: a focus on single parent families. *Urban and Social Change Review* 10: 21–25.

Braungart, R. 1980. Youth movements. In Adelson, J., ed., *Handbook of adolescent psychology.* New York: Wiley.

Brim, O. G., Jr., and Kagan, J. 1980. Constancy and change: a view of the issues. In Brim, O. G., Jr., and Kagan, J., eds., *Constancy and change in human development.* Cambridge, Mass.: Harvard University Press.

Brittain, C. 1963. Adolescent choices and parent-peer cross-pressures. *American Sociological Review* 28: 385–91.

Bronfenbrenner, U. 1967. Makarenko and the collective family. In: A.S. Makarenko, *The collective family: A handbook for Russian parents.* Garden City, NY: Anchor Doubleday.

———. 1972. The roots of alienation. In Bronfenbrenner, U., ed., *Influences on human development*, pp. 658–77. Hinsdale, Ill.: Cryden Press.

———. 1979. *The ecology of human development.* Cambridge, Mass.: Harvard University Press.

Brooks, H. 1980. Technology, evaluation, and purpose. *Daedalus* 109: 65–82.

Buckley, W. 1967. *Sociology and modern systems theory.* Englewood Cliffs, N.J.: Prentice-Hall.

Bühler, C. 1933. *Der menschliche Lebenslauf als psychologishes Problem.* Leipzig: Hirzel.

Camus, A. 1960. *Resistance, rebellion, and death.* Translated by J. O'Brien (1961). New York: Knopf.

Carver, C. S., and Scheier, M. F. 1981. *Attention and self-regulation.* New York: Springer-Verlag.

Chalip, L., Csikszentmihalyi, M., Kleiber, D., and Larson, R. 1984. Variations of experience in formal and informal sport. *Research Quarterly for Exercise and Sport.*

Coleman, J. S. 1961. *The adolescent society.* New York: Free Press.

Coleman, J. S., et al. 1974. *Youth: transition to adulthood.* Chicago: University of Chicago Press.

Coleman, J. S., Hoffer, T., and Kilgore, S. 1982. *High school achievement: public, catholic and private schools compared.* New York: Basic Books.

Conant, J. 1959. *The American high school today.* New York: McGraw-Hill.

Conger, J. J. 1977. *Adolescence and youth.* New York: Harper & Row.

Cooper, D. 1970. *The death of the family.* New York: Pantheon.

Coser, L. A. 1951. The case of the Soviet family. *American Journal of Sociology* 56: 424–54.

Costanzo, P. 1970. Conformity development as a function of self-blame. *Journal of Personality and Social Psychology* 14: 366–74.

Csikszentmihalyi, M. 1975. *Beyond boredom and anxiety.* San Francisco: Jossey-Bass.

———. 1976. What play says about behavior. *Ontario Psychologist* 8: 5–11.

———. 1978a. Attention and the wholistic approach to behavior. In Pope, K. S., and Singer, J. L., eds., *The stream of consciousness*, pp. 335–58. New York: Plenum.

———. 1978b. Intrinsic rewards and emergent motivation. In Lepper, M. R., and Greene, D., eds., *The hidden costs of reward*, pp. 205–16. New York: L. Erlbaum.

———. 1980. Love and the dynamics of personal growth. In Pope, K. S., ed., *On love and loving*, pp. 306–26. San Francisco: Jossey-Bass.

———. 1981. Leisure and socialization. *Social Forces* 60: 332–40.

———. 1982a. Toward a psychology of optimal experience. In Wheeler, L., ed., *Review of personality and social psychology*, vol. 2. Beverly Hills, Calif.: Sage.

315

References

————. 1982b. Education and life-long learning. In Gross, R., ed., *Invitation to life-long learning*, pp. 166–89. New York: Fowlett.

————. 1982c. Intrinsic motivation and effective teaching: a flow analysis. In Bess, J., ed., *Motivating professors to teach effectively*, pp. 15–26. San Francisco: Jossey-Bass.

Csikszentmihalyi, M., and Beattie, O. 1979. Life themes: a theoretical and empirical exploration of their origins and effects. *Journal of Humanistic Psychology* 19: 45–63; 677–93.

Csikszentmihalyi, M., and Figurski, T. 1982. The experience of self-awareness in everyday life. *Journal of Personality* 50: 14–26.

Csikszentmihalyi, M., and Graef, R. 1980. The experience of freedom in daily life. *American Journal of Community Psychology* 8: 401–14.

Csikszentmihalyi, M., Graef, R., and Larson, R. 1979. *Age differences in the quality of subjective experience*. Paper presented at the 87th Convention of the American Psychological Association, New York City.

Csikszentmihalyi, M., and Kubey, R. 1981. Television and the rest of life. *Public Opinion Quarterly* 45: 317–28.

Csikszentmihalyi, M., and Larson, R. 1978. Intrinsic rewards in school crime. *Crime and Delinquency* 24: 322–35.

Csikszentmihalyi, M., Larson, R., and Prescott, S. 1977. The ecology of adolescent activity and experience. *Journal of Youth and Adolescence* 6: 281–94.

Csikszentmihalyi, M., and Rochberg-Halton, E. 1981. *The meaning of things: domestic symbols and the self*. New York: Cambridge University Press.

Cusick, P. A. 1973. *Inside high school*. New York: Holt, Rinehart and Winston.

Davis, K. 1940. The sociology of parent-youth conflict. *American Sociological Review* 5: 523–35.

Day, H. I., Berlyne, D. E., and Hunt, D. E., eds. 1971. *Intrinsic motivation: a new direction in education*. New York: Holt.

De Charms, R. 1968. *Personal causation*. New York: Academic Press.

————. 1976. *Enhancing motivation: change in classrooms*. New York: Irvington.

————, and Muir, M. S. 1978. Motivation: social approaches. *Annual Review of Psychology* 29.

Deci, E. L. 1975. *Intrinsic motivation*. New York: Plenum.

Dipboye, R. 1977. Alternative approaches to deindividualization. *Psychological Bulletin* 84: 1057–75.

Donner, E., Nash, K., Csikszentmihalyi, M., Chalip, L., and Freeman, M. 1981. Subjective experience in marital interaction. Paper presented at the Experimental Social Psychology meetings, Nashville, Tenn.

Douglas, W. O. 1974. *Go east, young man*. New York: Random House.

Douvan, E., and Adelson, J. 1966. *The adolescent experience*. New York: Wiley.

Dumazedier, J. 1974. *Sociology of leisure*. New York: Elsevier.

Dunphey, D. 1963. The social structure of urban adolescent peer groups. *Sociometry* 26: 230–46.

Durkheim, E. 1912. *The elementary forms of the religious life*. Reprint. New York: Free Press, 1965.

Elder, G. H. 1963. Parental power legitimation and its effects on the adolescent. *Sociometry* 26: 50–65.

Elkind, D. 1967. Egocentrism in adolescence. *Child Development* 38. 1025–34.

Ellinwood, C. 1969. Age development of verbal expression of feeling in psychotherapy interviews with TAT protocols. Ph.D. dissertation, University of Chicago.

Erikson, E. H. 1950. *Childhood and Society*. New York: Norton.

————. 1968. *Identity: youth and crisis*. New York: Norton.

Ferguson, M. 1980. *The aquarian conspiracy*. Boston: Houghton Mifflin.

Firth, R. 1929. *Primitive economics of the New Zealand Maon*. New York: Dutton.

Fortune, R. F. 1932. *Sorcerers of Dobu*. New York: Dutton, 1963.

Fox, V. 1977. Is adolescence a phenomenon of modern times? *Journal of Psychohistory* 1: 271–90.

Freeman, M. 1982. The dialectic of immediate experience and reflection in adolescence. Unpublished manuscript, University of Chicago.

REFERENCES

Freud, A. 1958. Adolescence. *Psychoanalytic Study of the Child* 13: 255–78.

Freud, S. 1921. *Group psychology and the analysis of the ego.* Translated by J. Strachey (1949). Reprint. New York: Bantam.

Friedenberg, E. Z. 1966. The dignity of youth and other atavisms. Boston: Beacon.

Frith, S. 1981. *Sound effects: youth, leisure, and the politics of rock 'n' roll.* New York: Pantheon.

Gianinno, S. M., Graef, R., and Csikszentmihalyi, M. 1979. Well-being and the perceived balance between opportunities and capabilities. Paper presented at the 87th American Psychological Association meetings, New York City.

Giele, J. Z. 1980. Adulthood as transcendence of age and sex. In Smelser, N., and Erikson, E., eds., *Themes of love and work in adulthood.* Cambridge, Mass.: Harvard University Press.

Glick, P. G. 1979. Children of divorced parents in demographic perspective. *Journal of Social Issues* 35: 170–82.

Gold, M. 1970. *Delinquent behavior in an American city.* Belmont, Calif.: Brooks/Cole.

Goodman, P. 1964. *Compulsory mis-education.* New York: Horizon.

Graef, R. 1979. Behavioral consistency: an analysis of the person by situation interaction through repeated measures. Ph.D. dissertation, University of Chicago.

Graef, R., Csikszentmihalyi, M., and Gianinno, S. M. 1983. Measuring intrinsic motivation in everyday life. *Leisure Studies.*

Graef, R., Csikszentmihalyi, M., and Giffin, P. 1978. Flow and work satisfaction. Unpublished manuscript, University of Chicago.

Greenberger, E., and Steinberg, L. D. 1981. The workplace as a context for the socialization of youth. *Journal of Youth and Adolescence* 10: 185–210.

Greenberger, E. et al. 1980. Adolescents who work: effects of part-time employment on family and peer relations. *Journal of Youth and Adolescence* 9: 189–202.

Gunter, B. G., and Gunter, N. C. 1980. Leisure styles: a conceptual framework for modern leisure. *Sociology Quarterly* 21: 361–74.

Hamilton, J. A. 1981. Attention, personality, and the self-regulation of mood: absorbing interest and boredom. In Maher, B. A., ed., *Progress in Experimental Personality Research* 10: 282–315.

Hannay, N. B., and McGuinn, R. 1980. The anatomy of modern technology: prolegomenon to an improved public policy for the social management of technology. *Daedelus* 109: 25–54.

Harris, L. et al. 1975. *A survey on aging: experience of older Americans vs. public expectation of old age.* National Council on Aging.

Havighurst, R. J. 1948. *Developmental tasks and education.* Reprint. New York: McKay, 1972.

———. 1953. *Human development and education.* New York: McKay.

———. 1976. A cross-cultural view. In Adams, J. F., ed., *Understanding adolescence.* Boston: Allyn and Bacon.

Havighurst, R. J. et al. 1962. *Growing up in River City.* New York: Wiley.

Hebdige, D. 1979. *Subculture: the meaning of style.* London: Methuen.

Heidegger, M. 1927. *Being and time,* trans. J. Macquarrie and E. Robinson. New York: Harper & Row, 1962.

Henry, J. 1965. *Culture against man.* New York: Vintage.

Hersey, R. 1932. *Workers' emotions in shop and home.* Philadelphia: University of Pennsylvania Press.

Hess, R., and Goldblatt, I. 1957. The status of adolescents in American society: a problem in social identity. *Child Development* 28: 459–68.

Hetherington, E. M. 1972. Effects of father absence on personality development in adolescent daughters. *Developmental Psychology* 7: 313–26.

———. 1979. Divorce: a child's perspective. *American Psychologist* 34: 851–58.

Hilgard, E. 1980. The trilogy of mind: cognition, affectation, and conation. *Journal of the History of the Behavioral Sciences* 16: 107–17.

Hill, J. 1980. The family. In Johnson, M., ed. *Toward adolescence: the middle school years.* Chicago: University of Chicago Press.

Hobson, R. 1974. Loneliness. *Journal of Analytic Psychology* 19: 71–89.

317

REFERENCES

Hollinger, P. 1978. Adolescent suicide: an epidemiological study of recent trends. *American Journal of Psychiatry* 135: 754–56.

Hollingshead, A. B. 1949. *Elmstown's youth.* New York: Wiley.

Holt, J. 1967. *How children fail.* New York: Pitman.

Illich, I. 1971. *De-schooling society.* New York: Harper & Row.

Izard, C. 1977. *Human emotions.* New York: Plenum.

Jacob, F. 1977. Evolution and thinking. *Science* 196: 1161–66.

James, W. 1890. *Principles of psychology.* Reprint. New York: Dover, 1950.

Japanese Finance Ministry. 1980. White paper on adolescence, pp. 10–91. Tokyo: Printing Office.

Jessop, D. 1981. Family relationships as viewed by parents and adolescents: a specification. *Journal of Marriage and the Family* 43: 95–106.

Johnson, C., and Larson, R. 1982. Bulimia: an analysis of moods and behavior. *Psychosomatic Medicine* 44: 341–51. Erratum published in 45: 185.

Johnston, L., Bachman, J., and O'Malley, P. 1981. *Student drug use in America.* U.S. Department of Health and Human Services. National Institute of Drug Abuse.

Jourard, S. 1966. Some psychological aspects of privacy. *Law and Contemporary Problems* 31: 307–18.

Kahneman, D. 1973. *Attention and effort.* Englewood Cliffs, N.J.: Prentice-Hall.

Kandel, D. B. 1973. Adolescent marijuana use: role of parents and peers. *Science* 181: 1067–70.

———. 1978. Homophily, selection and socialization in adolescent friendships. *American Journal of Sociology* 84: 427–36.

Kandel, D. B., and Lessor, G. 1969. Parental and peer influences on educational plans of adolescents. *American Sociological Review* 34: 213–23.

Kandel, D. B. et al. 1978. Antecedents of adolescent initiation into stages of drug use: a developmental analysis. *Journal of Youth and Adolescence* 1: 13–40.

Katz, M., and Davey, I. 1978. Youth and early industrialization in a Canadian city. In Demos, J., and Brocock, S., eds., *Turning points: historical and sociological essays on the family.* Chicago: University of Chicago Press.

Kelly, J. G., ed. 1979. *Adolescent boys in high school: a psychological study of coping and adaptation.* Hillsdale, N.J.: Lawrence Erlbaum.

Kenyatta, J. 1962. *Facing Mount Kenya.* New York: Random House.

Kiell, N. 1969. *The universal experience of adolescence.* London: University of London Press.

Kitwood, T. 1980. *Disclosures to a stranger: adolescent values in an advanced industrial society.* London: Routledge & Kegan Paul.

Kobasa, S. C., and Maddi, S. R. 1977. Existential personality theory. In Corsini, R., ed., *Current personality theories.* Itasca, Ill.: Peacock.

Kotsch, W., Gerbing, D., and Schwartz, L. 1982. The construct validation of the differential emotions scale as adapted for children and adolescents. In Izard, C., ed., *Measuring emotions in infants and children.* New York: Cambridge University Press.

Kramer, M., Roehrs, T., and Roth, T. 1976. Mood change and the physiology of sleep. *Comprehensive Psychiatry* 17: 161–65.

Krug, E. 1964. *The shaping of the American high school, 1880–1920.* Madison, Wis.: University of Wisconsin Press.

Lange, C. G. 1922. The emotions. In Lange, C., and James, W., *The emotions,* vol. 1. Baltimore: Williams & Wilkins.

Larkin, R. W. 1979. *Suburban youth in cultural crisis.* New York: Oxford University Press.

Larson, R. 1979. The significance of solitude in adolescents' lives. *Ph.D. dissertation.* Chicago: University of Chicago.

———. 1983. Adolescents' daily experience with family and friends: contrasting opportunity systems. *Journal of Marriage and the Family.* 45(4): 739–750.

Larson R., and Csikszentmihalyi, M. 1978. Experiential correlates of time alone in adolescence. *Journal of Personality* 46: 677–93.

Larson, R., and Csikszentmihalyi, M. 1980. The significance of time alone in adolescents' development. *The International Journal of Adolescent Medicine* 2: 33–40.

References

Larson, R., and Csikszentmihalyi, M. 1983. The experience sampling method, in Reis, H., ed., *New directions for naturalistic methods in the behavioral sciences.* San Francisco: Jossey-Bass.

Larson, R., Csikszentmihalyi, M., and Freeman, M. 1984. Alcohol and marijuana use in adolescents' daily lives. *International Journal of the Addictions* 19.

Larson, R., Csikszentmihalyi, M., and Graef, R. 1980. Mood variability and the psychosocial adjustment of adolescents. *Journal of Youth and Adolescence* 9: 469–90.

Larson, R., Csikszentmihalyi, M., and Graef, R. 1982. Time alone in daily experience: loneliness or renewal? In Peplau, L. A., and Perlman, D., eds., *Loneliness: a sourcebook of research and theory.* New York: Wiley Interscience.

Larson, R., and Kubey, R. 1983. Television and music: contrasting media in adolescent life. *Youth and Society* 15: 13–31.

Larson, R., Mayers, P., and Csikszentmihalyi, M. 1977. Experiential sampling of adolescents' socialization: the contexts of family, friends, and being alone. Paper presented at the Conference on Research Perspectives in the Ecology of Human Development, Cornell University, Ithaca, New York. August, 1977.

Lasch, C. 1977. *Haven in a heartless world.* New York: Basic Books.

———. 1979. *The culture of narcissism.* New York: Norton.

Lazarus, R. S. 1966. *Psychological stress and the coping process.* New York: McGraw-Hill.

Lazarus, R. S., Averill, J. R., and Opton, E. M. 1974. The psychology of coping: issues of research and assessment. In Coelho, G. V., et al., eds., *Coping and adaptation.* New York: Basic Books.

Le Play, F. 1879. *Les Ouvriers européens.* Paris: Alfred Mame et Fils.

Lepper, M. R., and Greene, D., eds. 1978. *The hidden costs of reward.* Hillsdale, N.J.: Lawrence Erlbaum.

Lerner, R. M. 1982. Children and adolescents as producers of their own development. *Developmental Review* 2: 342–70.

Levy, R. 1973. *Tahitians: mind and experience in the society islands.* Chicago: University of Chicago Press.

Lewin, K. 1936. *Principles of topological psychology.* New York: McGraw-Hill.

———. 1938. Field theory and experiment in social psychology: concepts and methods. *American Journal of Sociology* 44: 868–96.

Lidz, T. 1969. The adolescent and his family. In Caplan, G., and Lebovici, S., eds., *Adolescence: psychosocial perspectives.* New York: Basic Books.

Lieberman, J. 1981. *The litigious society.* New York: Basic Books.

Loeb, R., Horst, L., and Horton, P. 1980. Family interaction patterns associated with self-esteem in preadolescent girls and boys. *Merrill-Palmer Quarterly* 26: 205–17.

Looft, W. R. Egocentrism and social interaction in adolescence. *Adolescence* 6: 489–94.

Malik, S. 1981. Psychological modernity: a comparative study of some African and American graduate students. *Ph.D. dissertation,* University of Chicago.

Mann, H. 1891. *The life and works of Horace Mann,* vol. 5. Boston: Lee and Shepard.

Marx, K. 1844. Economic and philosophic manuscripts of 1844. In Tucker, R. C., ed., *The Marx-Engels Reader.* New York: Norton, 1972.

Mayers, P. 1978. Flow in adolescence and its relation to school experience. *Ph.D. dissertation,* University of Chicago.

McCormack, J. 1984. Formative life experiences and the channeling of adolescent goals. *Ph.D. dissertation,* University of Chicago.

Mead, G. H. 1934. *Mind, self and society from the standpoint of a social behaviorist.* Chicago: University of Chicago Press.

Mead, M. 1928. *Coming of age in Samoa.* New York: Morrow.

Meichenbaum, D. H. 1977. *Cognitive behavior modification.* New York: Plenum.

Micksch, J. *Jugend und Freizeit in der DDR.* Opeoden: Westdeutscher Verlag, 1972.

Mischel, W. 1981. A cognitive-social learning approach to assessment. In Merluzzi, T., Glass, C., and Genest, M., eds., *Cognitive assessment.* New York: Guilford Press.

Moos, R. 1979. *Evaluating educational environments.* San Francisco: Jossey-Bass.

Murray, H. A. 1938. *Explorations in personality.* New York: Oxford University Press.

Musgrove, F. 1963. Intergenerational attitudes. *British Journal Soc. Clin. Psychol.* 2: 209–23.

References

National Commission on Excellence In Education. 1983. *A nation at risk: the imperative for educational reform.* Washington, D.C.: Government Printing Office.

Neihardt, J. *Black Elk speaks.* 1932. New York: Washington Square Press.

Neugarten, B. L. 1969. Continuities and discontinuities of psychological issues into adult life. *Human Development* 12: 121–30.

Noelle-Neumann, E. 1984. *The spiral of silence.* Chicago: University of Chicago Press.

Novaco, R. W. 1975. *Anger control: the development and evaluation of an experimental treatment.* Lexington, Mass: Lexington Books.

Offer, D. 1969. *The psychological world of the teenager.* New York: Basic Books.

Offer, D., Ostrov, E., and Howard, K. 1981. *The adolescent: a psychological self-portrait.* New York: Basic Books.

Offer, D., Ostrov, E., and Howard, K. 1982. Family perceptions of adolescent self-image. *Journal of Youth and Adolescence* 11: 281–92.

Offer, D., and Sabshin, M. 1967. Research alliance versus therapeutic alliance: a comparison. *American Journal of Psychiatry* 123: 1519–26.

Osgood, C. E., Suci, G. J., and Tannenbaum, P. H. 1957. *The measurement of meaning.* Urbana, Ill.: University of Illinois Press.

Parsons, T. 1942. Age and sex in the social structure of the United States. *American Sociological Review* 7: 604–16.

Payot, J. 1904. *The education of the will.* Translated by Smith Jelliffe, 1910. New York: Funk and Wagnalls.

Petersen, A. C., and Taylor, B. C. 1980. The biological approaches to adolescence: biological change and psychological adaptation. In Adelson, J., ed., *Handbook of adolescent psychology.* New York: Wiley.

Piaget, J. 1965. *The moral judgment of the child.* Translated by M. Gabain. New York: Free Press.

———. 1981. *Intelligence and affectivity.* Translated by T. A. Brown and C. E. Kaegi. Palo Alto, Calif.: *Annual Reviews.*

Plihal, J. 1982. Intrinsic rewards in teaching. *Ph.D. dissertation,* University of Chicago.

Polansky, N., Lippitt, R., and Redl, F. 1950. An investigation of behavioral contagion in groups. *Human Relations* 3: 319–48.

Prigogine, I. 1976. Order through fluctuations. Self-organization and social systems. In Jantsch, E., and Waddington, L. H., eds., *Evolution and consciousness.* Reading, Penn.: Addison-Wesley.

———. 1980. *From being to becoming: time and complexity in the physical sciences.* San Francisco: W. H. Freeman.

Radin, P. 1920. *The autobiography of a Winnebago Indian.* New York: Dover.

Redfield, R. 1953. *The primitive world and its transformations.* Ithaca, N.Y.: Cornell University Press.

Riegel, K. 1976. The dialectics of human development. *American Psychologist* 31: 689–700.

Rosenberg, M. 1965. *Society and the adolescent self-image.* Princeton: Princeton University Press.

Rosenthal, R., and Rosnow, R. 1969. The volunteer subject. In Rosenthal, R., and Rosnow, R., eds., *Artifact in behavioral research.* New York: Academic Press.

Ross, E. 1901. *Social control.* New York: Macmillan.

Rubinstein, B., Csikszentmihalyi, M., and Graef, R. 1980. Attention and alienation in daily experience. Paper presented at the 88th annual convention of the American Psychological Association, Montreal.

Rutter, M. et al. 1979. *Fifteen thousand hours: secondary schools and their effects on children.* Cambridge, Mass.: Harvard University Press.

Rychlak, J., ed. 1976. *Dialectic: humanistic rationale for behavior and development.* Basel: S. Karger.

Ryle, G. 1949. *The concept of mind.* New York: Barnes and Noble.

Sahlins, M. 1972. *Stone age economics.* Chicago: Aldine Press.

Sanders, S. H. 1979. Behavioral assessment and treatment of clinical pain: appraisal of current status. In Hersen, M., et al., eds., *Progress in behavior modification,* vol. 8. New York: Academic Press.

320

REFERENCES

Savin-Williams, R. C. 1976. An ethological study of dominance formation and maintenance in a group of human adolescents. *Child Development* 47: 972–79.

Savin-Williams, R. C., and Janquish, A. 1981. The assessment of adolescent self-esteem: a comparison of methods. *Journal of Personality* 49: 324–36.

Schachtel, E. G. 1959. *Metamorphosis: on the development of affect, perception, attention, and memory.* New York: Basic Books.

Schachter, S. 1959. *The psychology of affiliation.* Stanford, Calif.: Stanford University Press.

Schachter, S., and Singer, J. 1962. Cognitive, social, and physiological determinants of emotional state. *Psychological Review* 69: 379–99.

Seligman, M. 1975. *Helplessness: on depression, development, and death.* San Francisco, Calif.: W. H. Freeman.

Shaver, P., and Rubenstein, K. 1980. Childhood attachment experience and adult loneliness. In Wheeler, L., ed., *Review of personality and social psychology,* vol. 1, pp. 42–73. Beverly Hills, Calif.: Sage.

Sherif, M., and Sherif, C. W. 1964. *Reference groups.* Chicago: Regnery.

Shore, M. 1972. Youth and jobs: educational, vocational and mental health aspects. *Journal of Youth and Adolescence* 1: 315–23.

Simmons, R., Rosenberg, F., and Rosenberg, M. 1973. Disturbance in the self-image of adolescents. *American Sociological Review* 38: 553–68.

Singer, J. L. 1975. *The inner world of daydreaming.* New York: Harper & Row.

Smith, M. B. 1968. Competence and socialization. In Clausen, J., ed., *Socialization and society,* pp. 270–320. Boston: Little, Brown.

Steinberg, L. 1981. Transformations in family relations at puberty. *Developmental Psychology* 17: 833–40.

———. 1982. Jumping off the work experience bandwagon. *Journal of Youth and Adolescence* 11: 183–206.

Stigler, J. W., Lee, S., Lucker, G. W. and Stevenson, H. W. 1982. Curriculum and achievement in mathematics: A study of elementary school children in Japan, Taiwan, and the U.S., *Journal of Educational Psychology* 74: 315–22.

Suedfeld, P., Grissom, R., and Vernon, J. 1964. The effects of sensory deprivation and social isolation on the performance of an unstructured cognitive task. *American Journal of Psychology* 77: 111–15.

Sullivan, H. S. 1953. *The interpersonal theory of psychiatry.* New York: Norton.

Suomi, S., and Harlow, H. 1976. The facts and functions of fear. In Zuckerman, M., and Spielberger, C., eds., *Emotions and anxiety.* New York: Wiley.

Sutherland, R., and Cressey, D. 1974. *Criminology.* Philadelphia: Lippincott.

Taschdjian, E. 1979. On volition. *Revue Européenne des Sciences Sociales* 17: 103–14.

Tessman, J. 1978. *Children of parting parents.* New York: Aronson.

Thompson, E. P. 1963. *The making of the English working class.* New York: Vintage.

Tucker, R. C. 1978. *The Marx-Engels reader.* New York: Norton.

Turner, R., and Killian, L. 1957. *Collective behavior.* Englewood Cliffs, N.J.: Prentice-Hall.

Turner, V. 1969. *The ritual process: structure and anti-structure.* Ithaca, N.Y.: Cornell University Press.

Ugurolglu, M., and Walberg, H. 1979. Motivation and achievement: a quantitative synthesis. *American Educational Research Journal* 16: 375–89.

U.S. Department of Commerce. 1981. *Social Indicators,* vol. 3, Washington, D.C.

United Way of Chicago, Community Analysis Project: Suburban Cook County Analysis. 1978. Report No. 1.

Wallace, A. F. C. 1978. *Rockdale.* New York: Knopf.

Weber, M. 1924. *On charisma and institution building.* Translated by S. N. Eisenstadt, 1968. Chicago: University of Chicago Press.

Weiss, R. S. 1973. *Loneliness.* Cambridge, Mass.: Massachusetts Institute of Technology Press.

———. 1979. Growing up a little faster: the experience of growing up in a single parent household. *Journal of Social Issues* 35: 97–111.

Weitzman, M. S. 1978. Finally the family. *Annals of the AAPSS* 435: 60–82.

REFERENCES

Wessman, A., and Ricks, D. 1966. *Mood and personality.* New York: Holt, Rinehart and Winston.

White, L., and Brinkerhoff, D. 1981. Children's work in the family: its significance and meaning. *Journal of Marriage and the Family* 43: 789 98.

White, R. W. 1959. Motivation reconsidered: the concept of competence. *Psychological Review* 66: 297–333.

Whiting, B. B., and Whiting, J. W. M. 1975. *Children of six cultures.* Cambridge, Mass.: Harvard University Press.

Wolman, R., Lewis, W., and King, M. 1971. The development of the language of emotions: conditions of emotional arousal. *Child Development* 42: 1288–93.

Wright, P., and Keple, T. 1981. Friends and parents of a sample of high school juniors: an exploratory study of relationship intensity and interpersonal rewards. *Journal of Marriage and the Family* 43: 559–70.

Wynne, E. A. 1978. Behind the discipline problem: youth suicide as a measure of alienation. *Phi Delta Kappan* 59: 307–15.

———. 1980. *Looking at schools: good, bad, and indifferent.* San Diego: Lexington Books.

Yankelovich, D. 1981. *New rules: searching for self-fulfillment in a world turned upside down.* New York: Random House.

Young, L. 1966. *Life among the giants.* New York: McGraw-Hill.

Youniss, J. 1980. *Parents and peers in social development.* Chicago: University of Chicago Press.

Zuzanek, J. 1980. *Work and leisure in the Soviet Union: a time-budget analysis.* New York: Praeger.

Name Index

Adelson, J., 79, 131, 148, 152, 174, 276, 316
Aderman, D., 47, 314
Averill, J. R., 277, 319
Altmann, J., 178, 314
Arendt, H., 177, 314
Ariès, P., 200, 314
Augustine, 51, 314

Bachman, J., 15, 318
Bagley, W., 216, 314
Baltes, P. B., 4, 314
Barker, R. G., 40, 89, 314
Bateson, G., 168, 314
Beattie, Emory, O., 279, 280, 314, 316
Bell, E. S., 131, 314
Bell, R. Q., 140, 314
Benedict, R., 124, 314
Berger, P. L., 129, 143, 314
Berkowitz, L., 47, 314
Berndt, T., 276, 314
Blos, P., 130, 156, 314
Blumer, H., 170, 314
Bossard, J. H. S., 131, 314
Botkin, J., 226, 315
Bowen, E. S., 177, 315
Bowerman, C., 155, 315
Bowles, S., 199, 315

Brandwein, R. A., 133, 315
Brim, O. G., Jr., 4, 315
Brinkerhoff, D., 65, 322
Brittain, C., 31, 315
Bronfenbrenner, U., 74, 134, 315
Brooks, H., 225, 315
Buckely, W., 168, 315
Bühler, C., 4, 315

Camus, A., 194, 315
Carver, C. S., 48, 315
Chalip, L., 167, 315
Coleman, J. S., et al., 31, 39, 92, 156, 174, 199, 260, 275, 315
Conant, J., 202, 315
Conger, J. J., 131, 276, 315
Cooper, D., 133, 315
Coser, L. A., 134, 315
Costanzo, P., 276, 315
Cressey, D., 156, 321
Csikszentmihalyi, M., 14, 23, 25, 33, 35, 49, 66, 72, 76, 87, 91, 94, 106, 122, 123, 138, 141, 153, 160, 167, 184, 185, 186, 187, 192, 193, 194, 195, 215, 232, 250, 252, 255, 258, 266, 279, 293, 303, 314, 315, 316, 317, 319, 320
Cusick, P. A., 31, 42, 316

323

Name Index

Davey, I., 173, 318
Davis, K., 131, 316
De Charms, R., 49, 316
Deci, E. L., 49, 316
Dipboye, R., 171, 246, 316
Donner, E., 161, 316
Douvan, E., 79, 131, 148, 152, 174, 276, 316
Dumazedier, J., 76, 256, 316
Dunphey, D., 79, 160, 316
Durkheim, E., 246, 316

Elder, G. H., 147, 316
Elkind, D., 34, 316
Ellinwood, C., 47, 316
Elmandjra, M., 226, 315
Erickson, E. H., 4, 8, 156, 316

Figurski, R., 35, 316
Firth, R., 256, 316
Fortune, R. F., 177, 316
Fox, V., 16, 316
Freeman, M., 35, 50, 106, 273, 313, 316, 319
Freud, A., 123, 130, 316
Freud, S., 170, 317
Friedenberg, E. Z., 198, 199, 317
Frith, S., 246, 317

Gintis, H., 199, 315
Gerbing, D., 47, 318
Giannino, S. M., 49, 266, 317
Glick, P. G., 133, 317
Gold, M., 31, 317
Goldblatt, I., 123, 317
Goodman, P., 199, 317
Graef, R., 35, 49, 66, 87, 91, 122, 123, 141, 185, 192, 232, 255, 266, 293, 303, 316, 317, 319, 320
Greenberger, E., 64, 93, 317
Greene, D., 49, 319
Grissom, R., 182, 321

Gump, P., 40, 314
Gunter, B. G., 256, 317
Gunter, N. C., 256, 317

Hamilton, J. A., 13, 317
Hannay, N. B., 225, 317
Harlow, H., 22, 321
Harper, L. V., 140, 314
Havighurst, R. J., 4, 80, 130, 199, 317
Hebdige, D., 237, 317
Heidegger, M., 120, 317
Henry, J., 31, 133, 156, 174, 199, 317
Hersey, R., 47, 317
Hess, R., 123, 317
Hetherington, E. M., 31, 149, 317
Hilgard, E., 46, 48, 317
Hill, J., 130, 317
Hobson, R., 182, 317
Hollingshead, A. B., 80, 199, 318
Holt, J., 199, 318
Horst, L., 147, 319
Horton, P., 147, 319
Howard, K., 15, 31, 86, 147, 320

Illich, I., 199, 318
Izard, C., 47, 318

Jacob, F., 25, 318
James, W., 13, 318
Japanese Finance Ministry, 63, 64, 66, 67, 72, 80, 318
Jessop, D., 140, 318
Johnson, C., 75, 190, 318
Johnston, L., 15, 318
Jourard, S., 183, 318

Kagan, J., 4, 315
Kahneman, D., 13, 318
Kandel, D. B., et al., 31, 72, 156, 318
Katz, M., 173, 318

Name Index

Kelly, J. G., 213, 318
Kenyatta, J., 178, 318
Keple, T., 143, 322
Kiell, N., 16, 318
Killian, L., 170, 321
Kinch, J., 155, 315
King, M., 47, 322
Kitwood, T., 157, 318
Kleiber, D., 167, 315
Kobasa, S. C., 276, 277, 318
Kotsch, W., 47, 318
Kramer, M., 47, 318
Krug, E., 201, 216, 318
Kubey, R., 35, 69, 94, 95, 316, 319

Lange, C. G., 23, 318
Larkin, R. W., 42, 174, 199, 318
Larson, R., 25, 33, 39, 43, 45, 50, 69,
  72, 75, 87, 91, 94, 95, 106, 122,
  123, 136, 138, 141, 147, 160, 165,
  167, 168, 182, 184, 185, 186, 187,
  190, 192, 193, 194, 195, 232, 288,
  293, 303, 305, 315, 316, 318, 319
Lasch, C., 114, 133, 319
Lazarus, R. S., 51, 277, 319
Lee, S., 63, 321
Le Play, R., 270, 319
Lepper, M. R., 49, 319
Lerner, R. M., 4, 319
Lessor, G., 31, 318
Levy, R., 173, 319
Lewin, K., 89, 123, 124, 319
Lewis, W., 47, 322
Lidz, T., 144, 319
Lieberman, J., 225, 319
Lippitt, R., 170, 320
Loeb, R., 147, 319
Looft, W. R., 276, 319
Lucker, G. W., 63, 321
Luckmann, T., 129, 143, 314

Maddi, S. R., 276, 277, 318
Malik, S., 74, 319
Malitza, M., 226, 315

Mann, H., 201, 319
Marx, K., 132, 319
Mayers, P., 39, 43, 62, 138, 148, 160,
  184, 253, 266, 293, 312, 319
McCormack, J., 194, 216, 319
McGuinn, R., 225, 317
Mead, G. H., 70, 319
Mead, M., 82, 319
Meichenbaum, D. H., 277, 319
Micksch, J., 67, 80, 319
Mischel, W., 51, 319
Moos, R., 89, 205, 319
Muir, M. S., 49, 316
Murray, H. A., 182, 319
Musgrove, F., 123, 319

National Commission on Excellence
  in Education, 225, 320
Neihardt, J., 174, 320
Neugarten, B. L., 4, 320
Noelle-Neumann, E., 180, 320
Novaco, R. W., 277, 320

Offer, D., 15, 30, 42, 86, 131, 147,
  320
O'Malley, P., 15, 318
Opton, E. M., 277, 319
Ostrov, E., 15, 30, 31, 86, 147, 320

Parsons, T., 70, 124, 320
Payot, J., 156, 320
Petersen, A. C., 124, 320
Piaget, J., 46, 157, 320
Plihal, J., 215, 320
Polansky, N., 170, 320
Prescott, S., 72, 94, 316
Prigogine, I., 240, 320

Radin, P., 70, 173, 320
Redfield, R., 11, 320

Name Index

Redl, F., 170, 320
Ricks, D., 47, 322
Riegel, K., 125, 276, 320
Rochberg-Halton, E., 153, 186, 316
Roehrs, T., 47, 318
Rosenberg, F., 31, 321
Rosenberg, M., 31, 147, 320, 321
Rosenthal, R., 288, 320
Rosnow, R., 288, 320
Ross, E., 201, 320
Roth, T., 47, 318
Rubenstein, K., 180, 321
Rubinstein, B., 49, 255, 320
Rutter, M., 260, 320
Rychlak, J., 276, 320

Sabshin, M., 42, 320
Sahlins, M., 256, 320
Sanders, S. H., 277, 320
Savin-Williams, R. C., 31, 321
Schachter, S., 182, 321
Scheier, M. F., 48, 315
Schwartz, L., 47, 318
Seligman, M., 22, 321
Shaver, P., 180, 321
Sherif, C. W., 31, 321
Sherif, M., 31, 321
Shore, M., 92, 321
Simmons, R., 31, 321
Singer, J. L., 197, 321
Steinberg, L. D., 64, 93, 143, 317, 321
Stevenson, H. W., 63, 321
Stigler, J. W., 63, 321
Suedfeld, P., 182, 321
Sullivan, H. S., 157, 182, 321
Suomi, S., 22, 321
Sutherland, R., 156, 321

Taylor, B. C., 124, 320
Tessman, J., 150, 321
Thompson, E. P., 256, 270, 321
Tucker, R. C., 132, 321
Turner, R., 170, 321
Turner, V., 171, 321

Ugurolglu, M., 205, 321
U. S., Department of Commerce, 15, 321
United Way of Chicago, 39, 321

Vernon, J., 182, 321

Walberg, H., 205, 321
Wallace, A. F. C., 270, 321
Weber, M., 181, 321
Weiss, R. S., 149, 182, 321
Weitzman, M. S., 133, 321
Wessman, A., 47, 322
White, L., 65, 322
Whiting, B. B., 74, 182, 322
Whiting, J. W. M., 74, 182, 322
Wolman, R., 47, 322
Wright, P., 143, 322
Wynne, E. A., 16, 199, 322

Yankelovich, D., 16, 322
Young, L., 183, 322
Youniss, J., 72, 157, 322

Zuzanek, J., 63, 66, 67, 72, 322

Subject Index

Academic performance, 199; and enjoyment, 258–60; and family, 147, 148, 305; and friends, 172, 308; and solitude, 193, 194

Activation: difference between adolescents and adults, 86–87; in different activities, 96–99; with different companions, 99–103; measurement of, 47, 293–94; *see also* Experience, Moods

Activities, 44, 45, 290; across the week, 76–87, 296; effects of, 61–70; enjoyable activities, 241–43; and experience, 91–96, 98–99, 104–6, 300, 302; with family, 99–103, 135–36; with friends, 158; in school, 203; in solitude, 184; variability in, 122–23, 303

Adolescence: comparisons with adults, 86–88, 120–23, 184, 185, 192, 298, 303; conflicts in consciousness, 19–23, 234–37; conflicts with society, 13–18; direction of growth, 29, 264–84; measuring experiences of, 46–51; most enjoyable activities, 241–43; obstacles to growth, 22, 233–37; in other cultures, 16, 41, 62–70, 72–74, 80, 82, 124, 171, 173, 174, 177–82, 246, 256; sample of adolescence in study described, 41–44, 287–88; turmoil, *see* Variability

Adulthood, 26, 27, 28, 29, 59, 65, 70, 73, 78, 149, 161, 217, 237–38, 278–84; solitude in, 184, 185, 192; variability in, 120–23; *see also* Growth

Affect: difference between adolescents and adults, 86–87; in different activities, 96–99; with different companions, 99–103; measurement of, 46, 47, 293–94; negative, 20, positive, 24, 165; *see also* Experience, Moods

Age differences, 78–81, 87, 130, 138, 160, 193, 271–78

Alcohol, *see* Drugs

Alone, time spent, *see* Solitude

Anger, 52–53, 139–42, 162, 273–74; *see also* Affect, Conflict, Psychic entropy

Anxiety, 22, 47, 190, 227, 234, 267–69; defined, 251–52, 265; *see also* Psychic entropy

Athletics, *see* Sports

Attention, 13, 18, 26, 27, 29, 75, 133, 141, 143, 153; effective use of, 236–37, 269; and enjoyment, 250–51; and moods, 106–7; patterns of, 181, 256; as psychic energy, 14; in school, 210, 214; in solitude, 187, 195; *see also* Cognition, Concentration, Consciousness, Psychic energy

Autonomy, *see* Goals, Individuality

327

Subject Index

Boredom, 21, 22, 83, 114, 235, 267–69; defined, 252, 265; in school, 211, 212; *see also* Activation, Psychic entropy

Cars, 61, 65
Challenges, 50, 206, 234–36, 250–52, 259–60, 279, 282; and skills, 265–70
Charisma, 181
Chores and errands, 63, 65–66, 80, 92, 93, 97, 101–2, 136; *see also* Activities
Classmates, 71, 72, 100–101, 206–14, *see also* Companionship, Schools
Classroom, 61; moods in, 204–6, 211–14, 299, 302, 308–11; types of, 208–11; *see also* Locations, Schools
Classwork, 63–65, 92, 97–99, 203, 206–7, 216–17, 300; enjoyment of, 253–60, 266; *see also* Activities, Schools
Cognition, 46, 47; cognitiive efficiency, 101, 159, 189, 256; cognitive reinterpretation, 277; *see also* Concentration
Community: maintenance of, 180, 199; of study described, 35–41; *see also* Social system
Companionship, 70–76; across the week, 76–78, 296; defined, 45, 291–92; experience with different companions, 99–103, 104–6, 301, 302; *see also* Classmates, Family, Friends, Solitude
Complexity, 252, 260; defined, 266, 267; and flow, 264–70; and growth, 267, 279, 282–84
Concentration, 21, 23, 83, 105–7, 118, 170, 248, 249; difference between adolescents and adults, 86–87; measurement of, 48; in school, 205–7, 214, 215; in solitude, 187; *see also* Cognition
Conflict: between adolescents and society, 13–18, 25, 28, 65, 66, 167; in

consciousness, 19–23, 233–36; with families, 131–33, 139–44, 222–24; and growth, 26, 125, 237; with peers, 157, 171–73; with school, 224–26, 227–29; in solitude, 226–27; *see also* Psychic entropy
Consciousness, 13, 16, 18, 46, 51, 188; disorder in, 20–23, 187; and locations, 57; order in, 23–26, 107, 157, 247, 271–78, 281; quality of, 44, 49, 206; transformation of, 141–42
Control, 49; with friends, 167–71, 307; in solitude, 197
Correlation coefficient, *see* Statistical terms

Denial, 277, 284
Development, *see* Adulthood, Growth
Dialectic psychology, 276
Dissipative structures (psychic), 240, 241, 244, 246, 260, 262, 268, 271, 276; *see also* Flow, Life themes, Meaning
Disorder, *see* Psychic entropy
Divorce, 27, 150; *see also* Single-parent families
Drugs, 14, 15, 39, 41, 59, 112–14, 156, 164, 169, 197, 237

Eating, 63, 65–66, 92, 93, 97, 146; eating disorders, 75, 190, 197; *see also* Activities
Education, 25, 28, 62, 106, 213; effects of, 199–202; and enjoyment, 256–60; social goals of, 216, 217, 225–26; *see also* Classroom, Classwork, Schools
Ego identity, *see* Identity
Emotion, 50, 165, 170, 195, 246, 277; *see also* Affect, Experience, Mood
Enjoyment, 23, 25, 26, 159, 167; characteristics of enjoyable experi-

ences, 248–52; in different activities, 241–48; in everyday life, 255–60; and growth, 260, 264–70; *see also* Flow, Psychic negentropy

Entropy, *see* Psychic entropy, Social entropy

Environments, *see* Locations

Existential psychology, 276

Experience, 8, 73, 82; definition of, 31–32; with family, 134–39; flow experience, 248–60; with friends, 157–61; interpretation of, 273–78; measurement of, 46–51; sampling method (ESM) described, 32–35, 41–51; in school, 198, 204, 213; in solitude, 184–87; stability and change, 272, 313; variability in, 108–26

Family, 45, 58, 71, 73–76, 304–5; activities with, 99–103, 135–36, 304; in different cultures, 133–34, 151; experience with, 99–103, 134–38, 304; growth in, 151–54, 273–74; history of, 129–34; negentropic patterns, 144–47, 152, 153; separation from 78–79; socializing with, 73–75, 102–3; sources of conflict, 131–33, 139–44, 222–24

Feedback, 50, 72, 75, 98, 109, 118, 146, 186, 189, 236, 244, 249, 268–69; from family, 146, 224; from friends, 165, 169–72, 229, 245–47; runaway feedback, 169–72, 229, 264, 275; in school, 198, 207, 214; in solitude, 195, 197

Feelings, *see* Affect, Experiences, Moods

Flow, 23, 261–63; characteristics of, 248–52; in different activities, 253–55; in education, 256–57, 312; growth and flow, 259–60, 264–70; measurement of, 253–55; *see also* Dissipative structures, Enjoyment

Freedom, 49, 70, 77, 81–83, 159, 165, 173, 183, 227, 275

Friends and friendship, 45, 60, 71–74, 79, 155–75; activities with, 99–103, 158, 308; age differences in friendship, 79; enjoyment with, 241–43, 245–47; experience with, 99–103, 157–67, 306; friendships with adults, 74; and growth, 172–75, 275–76; as interactive system, 165–67, 228–29, 307; opposite-sex friends, 71, 100, 160, 161, 277–78, 306; same-sex friends, 71, 100, 160, 306–8; socializing with, 43, 67, 72–73, 102, 158

Goals, 19, 58, 75, 140, 275; conflict between individual and social, 17, 25, 28, 125, 152, 178, 198, 207, 211, 224, 234; identification with, 24, 28, 118, 165, 167; long-range, 109, 115, 189, 263, 264, 278–82; organize psychic energy, 14, 42, 46, 80, 146, 227, 250, 270, 279; sexual, 15, 194; short-range, 229; social systemic, 27, 59, 109, 133, 180, 201, 256

Grades, *see* Academic performance

Growth, 22, 28, 29, 81, 125, 157, 174, 236–37, 261–63, 271–78, 282–84; in family, 151–54, 273–74; and friends, 172–75, 275–76; optimal conditions for, 107, 252, 259–60, 264–70; in solitude, 176, 274–75; *see also* Adulthood

Habits, 17, 18, 26, 29, 57, 62, 65, 171, 256, 284

Happiness, *see* Affect, Mood

Helplessness, *see* Psychic entropy

Home, 58, 90; *see also* Family, Location

Homeostasis, 26, 168–71, 229, 264; *see also* Dissipative structures, Feedback

Homework, *see* Studying

Subject Index

Identity, 8, 156, 173, 223, 273; *see also* Life themes, Self

Individuality, 178, 181, 183, 187, 201, 223–24

Instincts, 17–19

Job, *see* Work

Joking, 50, 103, 158, 165, 212, 247

Leisure, 63, 67–70, 74, 80, 82–83, 92, 94–96, 98–99, 136, 255–56; across the weekday, 76–78, 296; and enjoyment, 241–43, 255–56; with friends, 158, in solitude, 187; transitional leisure activities, 95–96, 98–99, 103; *see also* Activities

Life-span development, 4, 22, 70, 189, 200; *see also* Adulthood, Growth

Life theme, development of, 263, 278–82; *see also* Dissipative structures

Locations: defined, 44, 290; effects of, 58–61; and experience, 299; and intrinsic motivation, 88–91

Loneliness, 180, 182, 184, 187, 196, 197; *see also* Solitude

Meaning, creation of, 262, 263, 271–78, 280, 282; *see also* Dissipative structures

Models, cultural, 280, 281, 284; *see also* Socialization

Mood, 20, 23, 43, 50, 101, 116, 120, 298, 299; in classrooms, 204–14; with family, 137; with friends, 99–103, 157–67, 247; measurement of, 293–94; in solitude, 184–87, 191, 192; variability in, 108–26, 162–64, 229–33, 303

Motivation, 21, 24, 25, 27, 46, 68, 85, 106; difference between adolescents and adults, 86–87; in different activities, 91–96, 97–104; with different companions, 99–104; in different locations, 88–91; in learning, 259; measurement of, 48, 49; in teaching, 216

Music: listening to, 63, 69, 92, 95–96, 97–99, 245–46; playing, 115–18, 188–89, 267–69; *see also* Activities

Negentropy, *see* Psychic negentropy

Norms, 14, 15, 27, 157, 179; of peer group, 171, 174, 228–29

Observational methods, 31

Order, *see* Psychic negentropy

p-value, *see* Statistical terms

Parents, *see* Family

Peers, *see* Classmates, Friends

Pleasure, its difference from enjoyment, 251, 252, 260, 264, 265

Psychic energy, 14, 20, 26, 28, 46, 57, 62, 63, 65, 80, 115, 130, 151, 162, 206; conflicts over, 142, 223–24; efficient use of, 48, 146, 247, 275, 277, 279, 281; waste of, 15, 235, 236, 261, 277; *see also* Attention, Consciousness

Psychic entropy, 26, 84, 85, 118; in classes, 205–11, 213, 224–26, 255, 257; in daily life, 221–37, 261, 263; defined, 19–23; in the family, 132, 139–44, 152, 222–24, 273; with friends, 156, 171–73, 228–29; measurement of, 46–51; shaping growth, 279; in solitude, 179, 182, 190, 226–28

Psychic negentropy, 75, 85, 240; defined, 23–26; in different activities,

Subject Index

241–48; with family, 137, 144–47, 152; as flow experience, 248–60, 264–70; with friends, 156, 164, 167, 170, 246, 247; as life theme, 278–82; measurement of, 46–51; as ordering of experience, 271–78; in solitude, 196

Public opinion, 180, 181

r, see Statistical terms

School, 58, 60, 63, 65, 89, 90, 198–217, 297; activities in, 202–3; experiences in, 204, 255, 299, 300, 302, 308–11; history of schools, 200–202; performance in, 147, 148, 258–60, 312; sources of conflict in, 224–26; in the study described, 39–41, 74; *see also* Education

Self, 14, 24, 28, 70, 72, 81, 109, 140, 146, 152, 198; emergence of, 8, 26, 129, 157, 222, 263; in the flow experience, 250, 251, 260; growth of, 276–84; maintenance of, 180, 186, 187, 190, 196, 228

Self-consciousness, 43, 171, 194, 249; measurement of, 48

Sex differences, 79–81, 87, 138, 150, 159, 193

Sexuality, 14, 17, 18, 41, 44, 131, 132, 161, 173, 216, 243, 264

Siblings, 71, 100, 138; *see also* Family

Single-parent families, 133, 135, 148–51, 305

Skills, 50, 114, 115, 175, 211, 251–52, 259, 279, 281, 284; and challenges, 265–70; and solitude, 189, 194, 196, 227

Social class, 42, 80, 87, 159, 193, 194, 287, 288

Social entropy, 27, 28, 132, 183

Social system, 19, 58, 133, 224; conditions for its existence, 27, 28, 151,

225, 226, 270; friendship as, 165–67, negentropic qualities of, 144–47, 164–67, 246, 247, 273–78, 281; prerequisites, 15; and solitude, 178, 179

Socialization, 12, 15, 21, 26, 28, 58, 62, 66, 69, 70, 71, 75, 179, 182; by adults, 80, 81, 88, 146, 152, 167, 280, 281; and enjoyment, 25; by peers, 60, 167, 172; in schools, 201; and transformation of consciousness, 14, 99, 140, 142

Socializing, *see* Friends

Solitude, 17, 59, 61, 71, 74, 75, 99–103; activities in, 184; advantages of, 180–83; dangers of, 177–80, 226–28; experience in, 183–87; and growth, 176, 274–75; individual differences in, 193; long-term effects of, 191–97; thoughts in 188–91; *see also* Companionship

Sports, 40, 62, 68, 69, 79, 92, 95–96, 160; adults vs. peer organized, 167; as most enjoyable activities, 241, 242, 244; *see also* Activities

Statistical terms: correlation coefficient, 106; *p*-value, 106, 107; *r*, 106; *z*-score, 90

Storm-and-stress, *see* Variability

Stress, 276, 282; *see also* Psychic entropy

Studying, 62, 64, 74, 92, 97, 99, 101, 189, 193; *see also* Activities

Suicide, 15, 237

Talking, *see* Family, socializing with; Friends, socializing with

Teachers, 60, 62, 73, 74, 207, 260; role of, 214–16

Teaching, 39, 259–60; styles of, 214–16; *see also* Education

Television, 41, 45, 67–68, 73, 74, 79, 92, 94, 97, 99, 102, 146, 186, 187, 230, 242, 243; *see also* Activities

Thoughts, 43, 63, 69, 92, 94–95, 97;

in classes, 208–11, 257; with family, 139, 140; measurement of, 50; in solitude, 188–91, 193; *see also* Activities

Values, 17–19, 26, 61, 75, 140, 179; and peers, 157, 174; *see also* Goals
Variability: and academic performance, 148; in activities, 122–23, 303, 304; adolescents and adults compared, 120–23, 303, 313; and biological changes, 124; in classes, 208–14, 310, 311; in moods, 108–126, 162–164, 172; and pathology, 123

Violence, 14, 15, 39, 72, 191, 244

Weekdays: the schoolday, 211–14; use of time on, 76–78, 296
Weekend, use of time on, 76–78, 112, 169, 174, 296
Work, 63–65, 79, 91–93, 97–99; across the week, 76; and enjoyment, 243, 251, 255–58, 270, 278–84; *see also* Activities

z-score, *see* Statistical Terms